"With great clarity and cultural insight, Smith sets out an Augustinian-Reformed antidote to the highly polarized forms of politics we see around us today, in which churches—whether on the left or the right—are too often raucous and rancorous participants. In doing so, he joins a growing chorus of those arguing for a constructive theological account of the politics of a common life."

—**Luke Bretherton**, Kenan Institute for Ethics, Duke Divinity School

"*Awaiting the King* presents Smith's mature public theology—a carefully nuanced plea for 'calculated ambivalence' and 'cultivated circumspection' toward culture. It is a vision of resident aliens invested in the world around them. Lucid and persuasive as always, Smith challenges the ways in which contemporary Christians—including his own Neocalvinist tradition—run the risk of naturalizing shalom. Smith's account unabashedly advocates making life's final, heavenly end the starting point for the way we structure our social life together. This final, crowning volume of the Cultural Liturgies project has the potential to profoundly redirect contemporary public theology and practice."

—**Hans Boersma**, Regent College

"Smith's *Awaiting the King* is a thoughtful, wise, and provocative book. In it, we are challenged to recognize certain truths that run counter to the Western tradition: that the state is deeply religious, being as it is an incubator of love-shaping practices; that the church is profoundly political, being as it is a place of public ritual centered on and led by a King; and that the church's public theology must therefore resituate the political in light of creation and reframe it in light of eternity. *Awaiting the King* is not only smart but also well written and relevant to a broad range of interests, including public theology, political science, philosophy, and social ethics."

—**Bruce Riley Ashford**, Southeastern Baptist Theological Seminary

Awaiting the King

REFORMING PUBLIC THEOLOGY

Volume 3 of Cultural Liturgies

James K. A. Smith

Baker Academic

a division of Baker Publishing Group
Grand Rapids, Michigan

© 2017 by James K. A. Smith

Published by Baker Academic
a division of Baker Publishing Group
PO Box 6287, Grand Rapids, MI 49516-6287
www.bakeracademic.com

Printed in the United States of America

Library of Congress Cataloging-in-Publication Data
Names: Smith, James K. A., 1970– author.
Title: Awaiting the King : reforming public theology / James K. A. Smith.
Description: Grand Rapids : Baker Academic, 2017. | Series: Cultural liturgies ; Volume 3 | Includes index.
Identifiers: LCCN 2017028470 | ISBN 9780801035791 (pbk. : alk. paper)
Subjects: LCSH: Christianity and politics. | Public theology. | Political theology.
Classification: LCC BR115.P7 S565 2017 | DDC 261.7—dc23
LC record available at https://lccn.loc.gov/2017028470

17 18 19 20 21 22 23   7 6 5 4 3 2 1

For our friends at Cardus
and the team at *Comment*,
in partnership for the renewal of
North American social architecture

Joseph of Arimathea, a prominent member of the Council, who was himself waiting for the kingdom of God, went boldly to Pilate and asked for Jesus' body.

Mark 15:43

Theology must be political if it is to be evangelical. Rule out the political questions and you cut short the proclamation of God's saving power; you leave people enslaved where they ought to be set free from sin—their own sin and others'.

Oliver O'Donovan, *The Desire of the Nations*

So long as the Church preaches the gospel and functions as a properly "political" reality, a polity of her own, the kings of the earth have a problem on their hands. . . . As soon as the church appears, it becomes clear to any alert politician that worldly politics is no longer the only game in town. The introduction of the church into *any* city means that the city has a challenger within its walls.

Peter Leithart, *Against Christianity*

[Political theology] has, in the first place, pastoral importance: to give guidance to those who, believing the Christian faith or capable of suspending their unbelief, have to exercise political responsibilities. Nothing very specialized need be envisaged here; we need not confine political ethics to the mirror-for-princes mold, as a professional science of politicians or civil servants. The responsibilities are those which we all face, regardless of our views on political institutions and the propriety of taking a leading role in them. . . . Hermit and politician both have to make up their minds as to whether they can acknowledge the institutions that claim to serve them.

Oliver O'Donovan, *The Ways of Judgment*

Fear is not a Christian habit of mind.

Marilynne Robinson, *The Givenness of Things*

Contents

Sidebars

Preface

If this book has taken much longer than I ever would have anticipated, that's because it's a very different book from the one I envisioned when *Desiring the Kingdom* was published in 2009. At that time, I imagined the projected third volume of the Cultural Liturgies project as something like "Hauerwas for Kuyperians," a come-to-Yoder altar call for all those who were so enthusiastic about "transforming" culture and affirming common grace. My primary concern was to revivify what in the Reformed tradition we call the "antithetical" side of the tradition—the critical, prophetic impetus that says "No!" to cultural assimilation and political injustice (a voice one can hear most clearly in Richard Mouw's books from the early 1970s). In my experience, the affirmative "common grace" side of the tradition had been enlisted to say "Yes!" to culture in ways that simply baptized the status quo. Under the banner of "transforming" culture, we marched straight into our own assimilation.

However, as my questions continued to percolate, some of my assumptions and analyses began to shift underfoot. I can particularly recall a conversation with my friend Hans Boersma that lodged a question I couldn't quite shake. That question, in turn, propelled me toward two concurrent immersions over the past five years: an ongoing engagement with Augustine's *City of God* and serious interaction with the corpus of Oliver O'Donovan. Both occasioned serious rethinking that took me back to the core convictions behind *Desiring the Kingdom* but then helped me to plot a different path to volume 3. As a result, one of my new hopes for this book is diaconal: I have tried to come alongside the seminal work of Augustine and O'Donovan as a translator and teacher, hoping to tease out the implications of their theology for a wider audience of practitioners.

So in the decade that I've been at work on the Cultural Liturgies project, the arc of my thinking has taken me from common grace to antithesis and back to an emphasis on our common life, but with what Paul Ricoeur would call a "second naïveté": attentive to the deformative power of our political participation but not willing to give up on the call to love our neighbor by building healthy, just, shared institutions conducive to flourishing. The result, I think, is a "reformed" Reformed public theology that is more catholic. But I also hope it is now a work that is more constructively helpful to those engaged in the beautiful mess that is our common life, and a resource for those who shepherd such practitioners.

That said, this makes no claims to being a handbook for princes or a manual for congressional staffers. Nor is this anything close to the last word. I can already see a more fine-grained book I want to write on an implicit theology of public policy. But my hope is that this book provides a new frame for political theology and public engagement that moves us beyond the postfundamentalist need for permission ("the good of politics") as well as the (understandable) suspicion of liberalism and the state (the so-called Benedict Option). Refusing both activism and quietism, we face the task of learning how to actively wait in the meantime of the *saeculum*.

Every political theology is exorcising demons—the question is which demons. At the beginning of the Cultural Liturgies project, I was wrangling with the effects of Kuyperian triumphalism—or at least a particular evangelical rendition of such; today it's the surprise of Trumpism and a newly energized (white) nationalism. Tomorrow? Who knows what rough beast will come slouching our way. But this generational context perhaps explains why, for many political theologians of my generation, the work of Stanley Hauerwas has been both a launching pad and a foil. Reading *Resident Aliens* is a kind of Rorschach test: the way a mainline Methodist reads it will be different from the way someone like me—an evangelical (of sorts) in the Reformed tradition—does. An heir of a certain version of Abraham Kuyper encouraged to "transform culture," I learned from Hauerwas and Willimon how often, under the banner of cultural transformation, we end up with cultural assimilation.

It wasn't until I read *Resident Aliens* that I realized I lacked a functional ecclesiology. Hauerwas and Willimon woke me up to a sense that the church has its own cultural center of gravity. We didn't have to figure out how to hook up "Christ" with "culture," because the body of Christ is a culture, and specifically a formative culture. For those of us breaking out of fundamentalism, the Reformed tradition offered a "common grace" license that enabled us to say yes to culture. But in our new enthusiasm for affirmation, we tended to lose the other side of Kuyper's philosophy—an emphasis on antithesis.

And as North American evangelicals, we tended to be deaf to Kuyper's own, thicker ecclesiology. So *Resident Aliens* was apocalyptic for me in the sense of unveiling the deformative power of those other spheres of life we were so eager to affirm and transform.

Many of my generation, I think, received this antithesis as a dichotomy: church *instead of* state. We would devote ourselves to setting up an "alternative *polis*," the liberal democratic state be damned. I don't think this was the authors' intention, but their rhetoric didn't do much to curb that conclusion.

But a funny thing happened on the way to the church-as-*polis*: rereading Augustine's *City of God* alongside the work of Oliver O'Donovan and Peter Leithart, I can now imagine being a resident alien *and* invested in the state, in all of its glorious failing. The antithesis is always ad hoc. And the Spirit can bend political orders. You might say that, ironically, *Resident Aliens* brought me to a new, highly qualified appreciation of Christendom—not in the sense of a diminished "civil religion," but in O'Donovan's robust sense of a society that bears the "crater marks" of the gospel's impact. Charles Marsh's account of the civil rights movement in *The Beloved Community* was a catalyst in this respect. He described a "resident alien" community that hoped its specifically Christian witness would make a dent on the laws of the land. Marsh's tale also narrates what happened when the civil rights movement lost its ecclesial center of gravity. Faithful witness is a precarious dance. Thus I've come back to my Reformed inheritance with new lenses, honed by this Augustinian encounter, in hopes of *reforming* Reformed public theology rather than rejecting it or razing it to the ground. Therefore, just as I envisioned *Desiring the Kingdom* as a corrective supplement to the "worldview" approach of the Reformed tradition, I hope *Awaiting the King* comes alongside to nuance the earlier work of my confreres in the Reformed tradition, like Abraham Kuyper and Herman Bavinck, and especially those more recently who have been mentors and models, like Nicholas Wolterstorff and Richard Mouw. While it sometimes comes with the bite of critique, the Cultural Liturgies project—including this volume—has always been offered in the spirit of an "assist" (something I learned by playing from the blue line as a defenseman for fifteen years of my life).

The citizen of the city of God, Augustine emphasizes, will always find herself thrown into a situation of being a resident alien in some outpost of the earthly city. Citizens of the heavenly city, Augustine tells us, lead "what we may call a life of captivity in this earthly city as in a foreign land, although it has already received the promise of redemption, and the gift of the Spirit as a kind of pledge of it."[1] This demands neither a stance that is positive or sanguine vis-à-vis the earthly city nor a posture that is fundamentally dismissive with respect to political society. Rather, the first political impetus is one of calculated ambivalence and circumspection tempered by ad hoc evaluations about selective collaborations for the common good. The heavenly city on this pilgrimage, Augustine continues, "does not hesitate to obey the laws of the earthly city by which those things which are designed for the support of this mortal life are regulated; and the purpose of this obedience is that, since this mortal condition is shared by both cities, a harmony may be preserved between them in things that are relevant to this condition."[2] It's not just a question of *whether* to be "resident aliens," but how.

I offer *Awaiting the King* as a foray into thinking about the *how*. As such, this book is most concerned with the cultivation of a posture, not the recommendation of specific policies. While the church has spent a generation wrangling about what views we hold and what positions we should advance, we have lost our footing, slouching toward relevance or digging in our heels in defense. In the meantime, we've ceded our imaginations to the earthly city and forgotten the posture that should characterize citizens of the heavenly city. To worship Christ the King is to be a people with a kingdom-oriented stance, which will sometimes look aloof and will at other times pitch us into the fray. The posture of heavenly citizenship is a posture of uplift, tethered by hope to a coming King. As Paul reminds us, it is those whose citizenship is in heaven (Phil. 3:20) who are called to shine like stars in the sky (2:15). *Awaiting the King* is an exercise in posture correction: part diagnosis and part prescription, it is, I hope, a way of reframing the liturgical heritage of the church as a resource for the Spirit to shape a peculiar people for the common good.

1. Augustine, *City of God*, trans. Henry Bettenson (London: Penguin, 1984), 19.17.
2. Ibid.

Acknowledgments

This book has been so long in the making I can't possibly hope to remember all of my debts. Let me name just a few of the most obvious.

In many ways, this book is the culmination of a trajectory that started with gentle pushback from my friend Hans Boersma at a critical juncture. I'm grateful to him for his work and charitable challenge; he has been a valued dialogue partner over the years. I have also been challenged and influenced by the work of Peter Leithart in ways that my footnotes don't do justice to.

Some of these ideas were field-tested in graduate seminars on Augustine, political theology, and Oliver O'Donovan's corpus at Trinity College of the University of Toronto and Calvin Theological Seminary. I'm grateful to Dean David Neelands for my appointment at Trinity and his flexibility in allowing me to offer experimental courses. I'm grateful to students in these seminars for their serious engagement with texts and ideas, and for the questions they posed that helped me hone my own thinking. No doubt I could have learned still more from them.

Pieces of this have been presented in a number of different contexts, but several opportunities deserve special mention. The invitation to be scholar-in-residence at Union University in 2015 provided a venue to articulate the core ideas here over the course of four public lectures. I'm grateful to Scott Huelin for the invitation and to the Union community for their kind hospitality during my week in Jackson, Tennessee. Thanks, also, to the small cadre of students who met for thoughtful, intense discussion after each lecture. The Payton Lectures at Fuller Theological Seminary provided another chance to field-test my analysis and argument in a very different context. My thanks to President Mark Labberton and (then) Dean Joel Green for the opportunity. I'm also grateful to those who participated in a seminar called "Cultivating

Faithful Citizens" at Calvin College in the summer of 2016, especially my codirector, Kevin DenDulk, and our guest scholars, Jonathan Chaplin, John Inazu, and Kristen Deede Johnson. That week of conversation helped crystallize a number of ideas below. Finally, chapter 4 was originally delivered as the annual Bavinck Lecture at the Theologische Universiteit Kampen in the Netherlands, where Deanna and I enjoyed both lovely hospitality and lively conversation with faculty and graduate students. Kampen has clearly emerged as one of the most dynamic places for Neocalvinist reflection today.

In the final stage of my work on the book, several friends and colleagues took time out of their busy schedules to read a complete draft of the book and offer their candid, incisive, and helpful comments. A special thank-you to Brian Dijkema, Matthew Kaemingk, Micah Watson, and Bruce Ashford for helping me in this way and being patient with my stubbornness where I didn't take their advice.

There are important reasons why Calvin College continues to be my intellectual home. I owe thanks to those families who made it possible for me to hold the Gary & Henrietta Byker Chair in Applied Reformed Theology and Worldview, which has afforded me the time for sustained writing and reflection. Thanks, also, to my colleagues in the philosophy department for giving me a long leash.

My friends at Baker Publishing Group were invested in this project from the beginning, open to dreaming with me as I took an idea for one book and turned it into a trilogy. The Cultural Liturgies project has taken up a decade of my life from conception to realization, and with the publication of this final volume I am both humbled and grateful. The folks at Baker Academic have been unfailing champions and supporters, and I feel like we've also grown together through this experience. A special thanks to my friend and editor Bob Hosack, but thanks as well to the entire team of editors, designers, and marketers who do such good work for the sake of Christian intellectual witness. I look forward to many more years together, Lord willing.

I've dedicated this volume to my friends and colleagues at Cardus, a think tank in Hamilton, Ontario, of which I am a senior fellow and for which I edit *Comment* magazine. Cardus devotes itself to "the renewal of North American social architecture," drawing on the resources of "two thousand years of Christian social thought." That, I hope, is also a succinct description of what this book hopes to do. My association with Cardus has been energizing and lifegiving. I am especially grateful for the way they have also received Deanna as part of the community. I have found there a circle of comrades and a fellowship of Christians alongside whom I'm happy to labor for kingdom come.

As always, my family continues to be an incalculable means of grace, a tiny little outpost of the kingdom where I am constantly reminded of the reality of mercy, grace, forgiveness, and love.

This book carries some of the wonderful aroma of beans roasting at Ferris Coffee & Nut, whose hospitable staff inducted me into the delights of pour-over coffee and made room for countless afternoons of writing. I'm grateful to have a "third place" like this. The soundtrack I listened to while writing there is eclectic to say the least: Radiohead's *Kid A*, Sandra McCracken's *Psalms*, Jason Isbell's stellar album *Something More Than Free*, Coltrane's *Love Supreme*, and way more Bonobo and Explosions in the Sky than you might have guessed.

Some of the material in this book previously appeared, in different form, in *Comment* magazine, *Books & Culture*, and *Calvin Theological Journal*. It also draws from my contributions to two books: *Augustine and Postmodern Thought: A New Alliance against Modernity?*, edited by Lieven Boeve, Mathijs Lamberigts, and Martin Wisse (Peeters, 2009), and *Becoming a Pastor Theologian: New Possibilities for Church Leadership*, edited by Todd Wilson and Gerald Hiestand (InterVarsity, 2016). I'm grateful to the editors and publishers for permission to use that work here.

Introduction

Liturgical Politics: Reforming Public Theology

Picturing Political Liturgies: Opening Exercises

In her nineteenth year, Shonda would finally participate in a much-anticipated rite of passage at Trinity Reformed Church: her first election. Shonda would enter the church—which had long served as a polling place for this urban neighborhood—on a crisp Tuesday evening in early November to exercise her sacred duty as a citizen. She would be given the opportunity to vote, and this year was particularly intense. She would be asked to cast a vote for leaders at almost every level of government: in the city, in her state, in federal congress, and even for president. Her parents accompanied her with encouragement and excitement. As longtime activists in the city, serving on school boards and community foundations, knocking on doors for candidates and hosting neighborhood block parties, Shonda's parents had modeled for her a life of public service and engagement. In some sense, her whole life was a preparation to realize this responsibility—an opportunity that subjects of tyrants around the world could only dream of.

Of course, like most rites of passage, this was more an event than a ritual—a sporadic, though momentous, episode rather than a habitual rhythm. And yet all sorts of rituals had prepared Shonda for this moment. The opening exercises of her schooling had been a litany aimed toward this act, a daily rite in which she pledged allegiance to a flag and a republic. Hundreds of football games and soccer matches had commenced with a hymn to the same republic, rehearsing in song a story, a veritable mythology, about the founding of a nation wrapped up in the iconic symbol of a flag

1

whose colors and stars were a ubiquitous presence in her life. The story about this
nation had been a consistent frame for the emergence of her own story, and this act,
tonight, was in some sense the realization of her identity: a citizen.

But there was surely an irony here, since this was hardly the first time Shonda had visited Trinity Church. Indeed, she had haunted these halls since she was a child, accompanied through the door by her parents. Eighteen years ago, after she was born, they would
have walked through these same doors, as they'd done almost every Sunday since. But
on Sundays, instead of heading to the basement, they would proceed to the sanctuary.
And on that day so many years ago, they had brought a tiny Shonda wrapped in a shining white baptismal gown, adorned like a princess. Her parents had been asked another
question about allegiance: "Who is your Lord and Savior?" "Jesus Christ is my Lord and
Savior," they had replied—a confession that has made every emperor anxious since Caesar pretended to be lord (*kyrios*). Presenting her to be baptized in the name of the Father,
Son, and Holy Spirit, the minister had spoken a powerful truth over squirming Shonda.

> Shonda,
> for you Jesus came into the world;
> for you he died and conquered death;
> all this he did for you, little one,
> though you know nothing of it as yet.
> We love because God first loved us.

And with Shonda's staccato whimpers waiting to burst into a cry, the pastor then
declared:

> In the name of the Lord Jesus Christ,
> the only King and Head of the Church,
> these sisters and brothers are now
> received into the visible membership of the holy catholic Church,
> engaged to confess Christ and
> to be God's faithful servants until life's end.

Perhaps somehow the words had slid over without the force of their political echo
being felt ("the only King"). But on this November night, as Shonda was in the nonde-
script fellowship hall charged with political significance, she heard anew the words
that had been spoken over her and the congregation almost every Sunday at the beginning of the service—a benediction she had heard so many times she could recite it
from memory, another declaration that had seeped into her unconscious and was now
bubbling up from an unexpected angle:

> Grace and peace to you from him who is, and who was, and who is to come, and
> from the seven spirits before his throne, and from Jesus Christ, who is the faith-

> ful witness, the firstborn from the dead, and the ruler of the kings of the earth.
> (Rev. 1:4–5)

And in that moment before passing through the curtain of the polling booth, Shonda realized that every Sunday had been a political assembly, every worship service a civic rite. And while she enthusiastically pulled the lever to exercise the privilege of national citizenship, she did so now with a kind of sanctified ambivalence, realizing that every president was ruled by a King she'd known—and been known by—her entire life.

⸎

A Parable for Public Life: *The Postman*

There is something political at stake in our worship and something religious at stake in our politics. And yet we are made for life in common; we are, as Aristotle said, "political animals." So there is something creaturely—and *good*—about political life, our life in common. But that might also be why politics is prone to be something more. A visual parable of this dynamic might help motivate our inquiry.

You won't remember the film; it's a forgettable movie—something Kevin Costner did in the doldrums of his *Waterworld* phase (Gene Siskel called it *Dances with Myself*). It is schmaltzy, sentimental, and indulgent. It even features rocker Tom Petty in a performance that pretty much confirms why you never saw him in another movie. But embedded in all of that is a sort of parable that invites us to ask some important questions about our common life, our shared institutions, even our craving for government.

There's something about apocalyptic scenarios that crystallizes what matters. The catastrophe winnows us down to the state of nature, strips us of our civilizational accoutrements. We don't know what we miss until all is lost.[1] In *The Postman*, some sort of vaguely atomic disaster has eviscerated the accomplishments of centuries. Cars sit derelict while people travel on horseback; humans once again become hunter-gatherers whose days are consumed simply with the tasks of survival. It is a steampunk world. Significantly, most of the institutions that constituted both the government and the market have dissolved, leaving an anarchic vacuum filled by the fascism (and racism) of the Holnists, a marauding clan led by the Napoleonic General Bethlehem.

---

1. This is surely what is so focusing about the scenario in Cormac McCarthy's novel *The Road*, a world in which humanity is reduced to bare life, where even the scaffolding of civilization has toppled and all that's left are the resources of prior formation (or lack thereof). We will return to *The Road* in chap. 2.

Through this world wanders our protagonist, a nameless drifter who is a thespian-errant, staging snippets of Shakespeare in exchange for soup and shelter.[2] But while he is happy to play the part of a soldier, dueling with his mule Bill, our drifter is no revolutionary. That would require him to care for someone or something other than himself! When the Holnist army descends on a village and extorts tribute, they see the drifter trying to slink away and accost him. "I'm not with these people," he pleads. "I'm just passing through." He is not interested in solidarity; he prefers his solitary independence.

This all changes, despite his preferences. One night, on the run as a fugitive from Bethlehem's clan, the drifter seeks shelter in an abandoned vehicle. Soaked to the bone, he shivers beside the skeletal remains of its driver and is delighted to find a lighter and a flask—both sources of warmth—and then looks longingly at the dry clothing the skeleton possesses. The drifting fugitive greedily claims them for himself and then realizes: the vehicle is a mail truck; the clothing is a postal uniform. By the light of a small fire, he begins to entertain himself with the undelivered letters in the cab and is overwhelmed by nostalgia: these banalities are a testament to an entire social system that has been lost. He recalls a civilizational institution that is the very embodiment of trust and hope—in which little Jimmy could write a note to his grandpa, tell him about his lost tooth, seal it in an envelope, and trust the news would reach a grandpa he couldn't see. He is holding the relics of a communicative institution that made possible a kind of extended communion.

Our drifter has clothed himself in the postal uniform as a matter of mere expediency and self-interest: he needs dry clothes. But, ever the thespian, he's not above leveraging its symbolism and power to score a warm bath, a soft bed, and a meal or two. So when he wanders up to the gates of Pineview, Oregon, he improvises a new character: he is there as a representative of the (fictional) "restored United States government." Carrying his leather satchel filled with letters (and even the junk mail we thought no one would miss), his new character dangerously plies the hopes of a hungry people. "We're delivering old stockpiles," he says, "but I'll deliver all new correspondence." Before he leaves Pineview, he is inundated with new mail. Even the skeptical sheriff can't resist the hope.

What the drifter doesn't realize is that, while he thought he could just put on a costume and pretend, he has actually clothed himself in the vestments of a civilization. The remainder of the film is the story of how he learns to live into that stolen uniform. The vestments come with a significance he can't

2. While it is Shakespeare who is constantly evoked in the movie, Don Quixote's shadow looms across this whole story.

control. He is now the Postman. He will henceforth embody the memory and vision of a *nation*, a mode of community and solidarity that these former citizens crave. The postal service represents a network of communication that both assumes and creates a community that exceeds the self, is wider than family, and outstrips the tribe and the village—a kind of community that requires solidarity beyond blood and familiarity. Indeed, there is something altruistic in the endeavor—a concern that transcends self-regard. And people are immediately willing to sign up for this project of self-transcendence.[3] This is foreshadowed in a scene (that is, granted, just a bit too obvious) where a young man, Ford Lincoln Mercury, after being sworn in as a carrier, confesses: "I'd die to get a letter through."[4]

Which is why this cinematic parable also illustrates the dark, perverted underbelly of this deep human craving for solidarity. It's not long before we see the specter of nationalism and the shadow side of the political, the ways in which the political is often not content to be penultimate but rather slides toward its own kind of civil religion. Why does being "willing to die" for an ideal so quickly devolve into being willing to *kill* for it?[5] Soon the postal service is militarized and the resistance fighters devolve into their own reign of terror, fighting back with Holnist weapons of massacre, terror, and intimidation. In a final battle of machismo, the Postman makes his confession: "I believe in the United States of America!" This is supposed to be an accomplishment—the self-interested drifter now *believes* in something bigger than himself. But be careful what you believe in; not all credos are created equal. Because the real question is, what do you *love*?

The Postman is a parable precisely because it pushes us to ask some fundamental questions about who we are, what we want, and what we hope for.

3. The Postman himself takes a while to embrace this self-transcendence. His habits of self-regard are well developed. When he is injured during another flight from the Holnists and he and Abby, a romantic companion, take up residence in a secluded cabin, he is content to remain in bed, hide from the world, and be served—until Abby falls in the river and he dashes to save her. Concern for Abby pulls him out of himself again: love draws him out. But he still seems quite content to remain in the secluded retreat of the cabin—which is why, come spring, Abby has to burn down the cabin to propel him back toward civilization. Upon his return, he finds that the postal service is now bigger than the Postman: the system has a life of its own.

4. While at times a bit ham-fisted, a persistent critique of racism develops in the film: the ugliness of the Holnists' ethnic ideology is contrasted with the black leadership of the restored postal service. The (still fictional) "restored United States of America" is realizing promises the original never kept.

5. An irony noted in U2's "Peace on Earth": "You become the monster so the monster will not break you." Cf. William Cavanaugh's critical discussion in "Killing for the Telephone Company: Why the Nation-State Is Not the Keeper of the Common Good," *Modern Theology* 20 (2004): 243–74.

Indeed, it presses us to ask a question before these questions: What is this "we"?[6] What are the boundaries and limits and lineaments of any sense of "us"? Do we belong to more than one "we"? How do we forge a "we" that doesn't dissolve "me"? And where do we find the will to build up an "us" that counters our predilections for self-preservation? (Would we have the will to *start* what we take for granted today?) A Christian political theology must articulate one more crucial question: In what ways—and to what extent—can the "peculiar people" that is the church live *in common* with citizens of the earthly city? In short, the film implicitly raises questions I want to consider in this book—questions about the common good, the role of government, the gift of solidarity, and the tensions inherent in the good work of statecraft.

Questions about the possibility and limits of human solidarity—which I'm suggesting are the fundamental questions of a political theology—lead us back to the animating core of the Cultural Liturgies project: philosophical anthropology. Or, conversely, a philosophical anthropology has to generate an account of solidarity and sociality. Even if solidarity is called for by our very nature as creatures, its realization is always a kind of accomplishment.

Every political theory assumes an anthropology, and every anthropology underwrites some political trajectory. If we are merely thinking things, or consuming animals, then our autonomy and independence are prior to any "we," in which case the social will be a kind of grand fiction and noble lie, a derivative, secondary, "unnatural" invention.[7] Instead of laboring in solidarity, moving in common toward a shared *telos*, we relate only as competitors. In a prescient article that argues for a theology of "commonness" rooted in the incarnation, Willie James Jennings notes that the postmodern dissolution of the subject throws us back into a kind of state of nature. In the name of the "emancipation" of the subject, we are all unhooked from any common humanity. Instead we get varying cautionary cries of "Don't tread on me!" Jennings cites Jean-François Lyotard: "Contemporary society no longer speaks of fraternity at all, whether Christian or republican. It only speaks of the sharing of the wealth and benefits of 'development.' Anything is permissible, within the limits of *what is defined* as distributive justice. We owe nothing other than services, and only among ourselves. We are socioeconomic partners in a very large business, that of development."[8] A just and rightly ordered desire to be emancipated from oppression becomes an

6. For a powerful, dystopian consideration of collectivist identity, see Yevgeny Zamyatin, *We*, trans. Natasha Randall (1921; repr., New York: Modern Library, 2006).

7. See John Milbank, *Theology and Social Theory* (Oxford: Blackwell, 1990), chap. 1.

8. Lyotard, *Political Writings*, trans. Bill Readings and Kevin Paul German (Minneapolis: University of Minnesota Press, 1993), 161, quoted in Willie James Jennings, "'He Became

overwrought penchant to be liberated from every other, from the obligations of human community, from anything that impinges on the project of what David Brooks calls "The Big Me."[9]

In contrast, Jennings points to the anthropology implicit in the doctrine of the incarnation as a nuanced picture of human solidarity, a forge for commonness.[10] Instead of appealing to some generic, abstract "humanity," Jennings—following in the wake of Irenaeus and Athanasius[11]—points to the concrete body of the Jewish Jesus as liberator. "From Irenaeus," Jennings remarks, "we learn that whenever the desire for emancipation is separated from the reality of the incarnation, Jesus' body becomes merely a fleeting liberating *form* while the desire for freedom becomes primary and eternal."[12] When we contrast Athanasius with Arius, we see that their difference has to do with either "a humanity saved and liberated by the actual hands of God and thus joined together in the body of Jesus or a humanity that is yet to be liberated by the work of its own hands and is thus joined together only by the *needed work* of liberation itself."[13] Jennings looks to the resurrection of Jesus to underwrite solidarity that refuses "the false universal of a common humanity as well as the abstract longing for human liberation."[14] This is found, he counsels, "in an incarnational view of emancipation that proceeds from baptism and moves toward a kind of intellectual revival," for "neither the supporters of the humanism(s)

Truly Human': Incarnation, Emancipation, and Authentic Humanity," *Modern Theology* 12 (1996): 243.

9. David Brooks, *The Road to Character* (New York: Random House, 2015), chap. 10.

10. Jennings notes that Christian discourse can become captive to this disordered desire for emancipation too: "For many of us, Christian identity no longer gives us sight of our humanity. Instead, Christian identity is pressed into the service of so many important causes for emancipation—emancipation, that is, 'being freed' now understood as *the* defining point of our humanity. And there is much to be celebrated in this current state of affairs, not the least of which is recognizing that Christian faith *is* life-affirming and liberating. However, Christian faith ordered by the desire for freedom often becomes misguided faith, because such faith cannot really discern the humanity it wishes to free. Having moved away from the abstract idea of humanity of earlier generations, we find ourselves caught by belief in abstract freedom" ("'He Became Truly Human,'" 244). I will return in chap. 6 below to Jennings's more developed discussion of these matters in *The Christian Imagination: Theology and the Origins of Race* (New Haven: Yale University Press, 2010).

11. See J. Kameron Carter's discussion of Irenaeus in *Race: A Theological Account* (New York: Oxford University Press, 2008), 11–36.

12. Jennings, "'He Became Truly Human,'" 246.

13. Ibid., 247. He continues a little later: "Those who look to Jesus as only a radical model for emancipation conceal a perverted triumphalism: while they want real social and political change, their plans for such change will continue no matter what becomes of Jesus. . . . There is something terribly tragic about theologians, Christian philosophers, and like-minded intellectuals who have simply joined their voices to the prevailing emancipatory critiques" (251–52).

14. Ibid., 253.

nor the post-modern emancipationists have been sufficiently haunted by that strange call to death signified by the biblical practice of baptism."[15] Solidarity points to liturgy. And insofar as solidarity is at once the ground and goal of the political, the political requires us to consider the liturgical.

Public Theology in a Liturgical Mode

My goal in this book is twofold. I want to work out the implications of a "liturgical" theology of culture for how we imagine and envision political engagement. But in doing so, I also hope to offer an alternative paradigm that moves us beyond contemporary debates in political theology—or at least reframes the questions in view *of*, and with a view *to*, practice. It's in this sense that I hope to "reform" Reformed public theology, offering something of an "assist" to the tradition in order to articulate what I hope, in the end, is a catholic proposal.[16]

As I see it, our current paradigms have at least two problems. First, we tend to think of Christianity and politics in largely "spatialized" terms. So the questions are focused on how to relate the "spheres" of church and state, for example; or how to move between the jurisdictions of two kingdoms; or how to create an "alternative" *polis* that eludes the clutches of liberalism. Across different theological streams that counsel quite different modes of Christian engagement with (or distance from) politics, we can nonetheless discern a common assumption that "the political" is a kind of realm, a turf, a territory. In this sense we spatialize political theology and reduce it to boundary management and border patrols.

Second, we tend to assume that citizens (i.e., political agents) are "rational actors" of the sort economists like to dream of—decision-making machines whose actions are the outcome of conscious deliberation rooted in beliefs and ideas.[17] We picture citizens striding into the proverbial public square as

---

15. Ibid., 251–52.

16. I must note up front that my proposal and argument in this book largely assume—and build on—a Reformed model of public theology articulated in the work of Abraham Kuyper, Herman Bavinck, Herman Dooyeweerd, and their heirs in our own time (especially Nicholas Wolterstorff, Richard Mouw, and Jonathan Chaplin). This book, therefore, depends on—or at least assumes—fundamental arguments and articulations I have made elsewhere, especially in my chapter "The Reformed (Transformationist) View," in *Five Views on the Church and Politics*, ed. Amy E. Black (Grand Rapids: Zondervan, 2015), 139–62. While my proposals for *reforming* Reformed public theology will involve critique, those criticisms are offered in the spirit of reform, with the goal of faithfully extending and revising this tradition. They in no way constitute a dismissal. I hope readers will keep this proviso in mind all the way to the end.

17. Cf. discussions of philosophy of action in James K. A. Smith, *Imagining the Kingdom: How Worship Works*, Cultural Liturgies 2 (Grand Rapids: Baker Academic, 2013), 31–41. It is precisely this reductionistic picture of humans as "Econs" that is criticized by the behavioral

thinking things who vote—both on the basis of their "beliefs" and as a way to *express* those beliefs (don't ask me how a *res cogitans* pulls those levers in the polling booth). The political is thus pictured as an arena in which we express our beliefs, legislate what we know, and codify laws to be disseminated. In this way we *rationalize* politics.[18]

As a result, many of our debates—and our culture wars—tend toward a kind of proceduralism or formalism about who or what can be admitted to "the political," which we in turn conceive of as a space for the expression of beliefs and ideas. So, for example, against those who would police admission to political discourse, we fight for the right to bring "our" beliefs and ideas into the public square. "The political" is thereby reduced to the rules and procedures that govern a "space" where we swap ideas and beliefs.

But our "political" lives are not sequestered to a particular sphere. The political is not a square with discernible gates.[19] While we often speak of the public "square," the metaphor is antiquated and unhelpful. There's no square there. And it certainly isn't the case that "the political" is restricted to our capitols, legislatures, and polling booths. The political is not synonymous with, or reducible to, the realm of "government," even if there is significant overlap.

The political is less a space and more a way of life; the political is less a realm and more of a *project*. When we reduce the political through this twofold spatialization and rationalization, what is lost and forgotten is an appreciation for the way the *polis* is a *formative* community of solidarity and the fact that political participation requires and assumes just such formation—a citizenry with habits and practices for living in common and toward a certain end, oriented toward a *telos*. Even if this Aristotelian (and Augustinian) intuition has been buried by the rationalistic proceduralism of modern liberalism, that doesn't mean it isn't true.[20] Political animals are *made*, not born.[21]

---

economist Richard Thaler. For a summary account, see Thaler, *Misbehaving: The Making of Behavioural Economics* (New York: Penguin, 2016).

18. For a deconstruction of this kind of "rational actor" picture of politics, see Jonathan Haidt, *The Righteous Mind: Why Good People Are Divided by Politics and Religion* (New York: Vintage, 2012).

19. Nor is it a stage that we can be either "on" or "off" (like when I've spoken in places where the microphone becomes hot as soon as I step on stage and is muted as soon as I step off). Politics bleeds across our neat and tidy boundaries.

20. "Liberalism" in this argument refers to a particular sort of political theory and not the policy leanings of particular parties. On this more technical use of the term, for example, both the Republican and Democratic parties in the United States fall quite obviously within the legacy of "liberalism."

21. And even if we (rightly) want to argue that human beings are "by nature" political animals, that is still a claim about a capacity that requires cultivation and training—and which can be misformed.

This is why our political theologies need to worry less about policing boundaries and securing a platform for expressing our beliefs and instead carefully consider the ways that political life is bound up with the formation of habits and desires that make us who we are. What if we aren't fundamentally "thinking things" who enter the "space" of politics with ideas to get off our chests? What if we are creatures of craving, defined by our desires, who make our way in the world governed by what we long for? And what if the political is not just some procedural gambit to manage our mundane affairs but an expression of a creational desire and need, a structural feature of creaturely life that signals something about the sociality of human nature? What if politics, as John von Heyking puts it (commenting on Augustine), is really about "longing in the world"?[22]

Politics, then, both requires formation and forms us. The political is more like a repertoire of rites than a "space" for expressing ideas. Laws, then, are not just boundary markers; they are social nudges that make us a certain kind of people. Institutions are not just abstract placeholders for various functions; they are incubators of habituation that make us a certain kind of people—indeed, they forge the very notion of an "us." If politics is habit forming, it is also *love* shaping, which means that we are on the terrain of liturgy.[23]

When we recover an appreciation of politics as a repertoire of formative rites—as a nexus of habit-forming practices that not only govern us but also form us—then we will remember that politics is bound up with matters of virtue.[24] And truly appreciating the dynamics of virtue requires recovering a sense of teleology, a purview on the political that takes into account the *ends* we are pursuing, the vision of the good that animates our collaboration and common life.[25] What unites a "people," an "us," is a project, something we're

---

22. John von Heyking, *Augustine and Politics as Longing in the World* (Columbia: University of Missouri Press, 2001).

23. Recall that in *Desiring the Kingdom: Worship, Worldview, and Cultural Formation*, Cultural Liturgies 1 (Grand Rapids: Baker Academic, 2009), we defined liturgies as "rituals of ultimate concern" that "are formative for identity, that inculcate particular visions of the good life, and do so in a way that means to trump other ritual formations" (86). Since our identity is rooted in desire/love, liturgies are love-shaping practices "that function as pedagogies of ultimate desire" (87).

24. This should not be confused with saying, of course, that *only* politics is bound up with virtue. Indeed, much of my argument that follows will relativize the significance of what we might call "electoral politics" when we grapple with the challenges of the *polis*. In this sense, I am in sympathy with James Davison Hunter's critique of a narrow politico-centrism that has too often dominated evangelical Protestant concepts of cultural influence. See Hunter, *To Change the World: The Irony, Tragedy, and Possibility of Christianity in the Late Modern World* (New York: Oxford University Press, 2010), esp. 101–49.

25. Such a teleology, we'll discuss below, is precisely what is precluded by the modern liberal view of the self as autonomous. See Charles Taylor, *Modern Social Imaginaries* (Durham, NC: Duke University Press, 2004).

after together. We collaborate in a common life insofar as we find goods to pursue in common; and we establish institutions, systems, and rhythms that reinforce the pursuit of those goods. Thus a liturgical account of the political not only analyzes the formative power of our public rites; it also (finally) requires that we zoom in and get more specific about the different visions of the good that animate the many *poleis* we inhabit.

For Christian thought, zooming out to take account of teleology is intimately bound up with an eschatology. Our teleology *is* an eschatology: a hope for kingdom come that arrives by the grace of providence and doesn't arrive without the return of the risen King. And this changes everything. A teleology that is at once an eschatology will be countercultural to every political pretension that assumes either a Whiggish confidence in human ingenuity and progress or alarmist counsels of despair. But precisely because Christian eschatology is a teleology of *hope*, it will also run counter to cynical political ideologies of despair that reduce our common life to machinations of power and domination. Furthermore, a Christian political theology attuned to eschatology will run counter to a kind of postmillennial progressivism to which the so-called justice generation sometimes seems prone (the "Arian" option described by Jennings above).

But if Christian hope reframes the political in light of eternity, we might say that Christian faith resituates the political in light of creation. If eschatology "relativizes" the political from above and beyond, a biblical theology of creation and culture relativizes the political from below, so to speak. This is why my quarry is not just a *political* theology but more broadly what I'd call a *public* theology. I want to encourage us to overcome a narrow fixation on certain modes of electoral politics and realize that much of what constitutes the life of the *polis* is modes of "life in common" that fall outside the narrow interests of state and government—and certainly well beyond the purview of the cable news fixation on presidential politics.[26] So a Christian account of our shared social-economic-political life might be described more properly as a "public" theology—an account of how to live in common with neighbors who don't believe what we believe, don't love what we love, don't hope for what we await. The institutions of government are a part of that life in

26. Drawing on Gene Healy's phrase, Ross Douthat names this "cult of the presidency" as a persistent political temptation. "To disciples of this cult, the president *is* the government: 'He is a soul nourisher,' Healy writes, 'a hope giver, a living American talisman against hurricanes, terrorism, economic downturns, and spiritual malaise'" (Douthat, *Bad Religion: How We Became a Nation of Heretics* [New York: Free Press, 2012], 269, citing Healy, "The Cult of the Presidency," *Reason* [June 2008]). I hope one takeaway from this book will be an appreciation for the many layers and expressions of "the political" that are both beyond our fixation on federal electoral politics and not infected by partisanship.

common, but only a slice of a much wider web of institutions and practices that govern our common life. We might say that it is not only government that governs, or conversely, that the state is not the only—or even the most primordial—mode of solidarity.

Bernd Wannenwetsch makes a similar point in his important work *Political Worship*. While in some contexts and epochs political theology might have to address totalizing political regimes, in the late modern era of liberalism it is "society" that pretends to be "total." Society is now a "super-system" that at once absorbs and marginalizes the state and private life, "not least because of the triumphal march of the mass media" and "an impersonal dictatorship of 'the crowd.'"[27] Thus "the Church would be wrong if it were to conclude from its experiences with the totalitarian state that the critical power of its own public should be always primarily directed to the public of the State" because, today, this critique "must be levelled (at least in the political community of the West) against the total claim of *society*, which has long since also claimed the public of the State."[28] If the church is a "public"[29] that stands, in some sense, *counter* to the pretensions of the earthly *polis*, we can't narrowly mistake this as a critique targeted only at the state because, in the current configuration of globalized capitalism, the state has in many ways been trumped by the forces of the market and society. Wannenwetsch points out that in Western societies—and globalized societies more and more—the economy functions as a "structure-building force" that shapes everything. The market now constitutes "the inner logic" of society itself: the dynamics of society are "moulded by the laws of the market: as a contest between participants competing for an increase of their shares."[30] This coupling of market forces and the crowd's demand for publicity means that everyone dreams of monetizing their Instagram feed. And *that* effectively becomes the ethos of a society. Thus a "political" theology is not narrowly an account

27. Bernd Wannenwetsch, *Political Worship: Ethics for Christian Citizens*, trans. Margaret Kohl (Oxford: Oxford University Press, 2004), 207–8.

28. Ibid., 238.

29. See Reinhard Hütter's important discussion of the "church as public" in *Bound to Be Free: Evangelical Catholic Engagements in Ecclesiology, Ethics, and Ecumenism* (Grand Rapids: Eerdmans, 2004), 19–42. Hütter points out that because of the pretensions of the earthly city in modernity, "a 'political theology' that attempts to 'politicize' the church can only and unavoidably deepen the church's irrelevance and undermine the church's public (political) nature by submitting and reconditioning the church according to the *saeculum*'s understanding of itself as the ultimate and normative public" (32). Instead of "politicizing" the church, we need to recover the sense in which it is a "public"—following Hannah Arendt—that is "defined by a particular telos, circumscribed by constitutive practices, and underwritten by normative convictions" (31). This *oikonomia* finds expression in the church's practices and disciplines (35–37).

30. Wannenwetsch, *Political Worship*, 241.

of the state or governmentality but rather a theological account of the *polis* that is "society." It is in this sense that I would describe our project here as a "public" theology, and it is because of this that our "political" theology will range into nongovernmental environs in order to do justice to the formative ethos of late modern society.

In this vein, I could nuance my earlier point about the unhelpful ways we have spatialized politics. Following John Milbank, we could say the problem is a *simple* spatialization rather than a rich, variegated, "gothic" account of our common life as a "*complex* space."[31] A Christian public theology, rooted in a creational theology and incarnational ontology, will appreciate the many layers and folds and features of a flourishing society—an affirmation of what we now describe as "civil" society, a network of institutions and communities beyond the state that are integral to its flourishing. Milbank likens the complexity of such a society to the richness of a gothic cathedral: "a building which can be endlessly added to, either extensively through new additions, or intensively through the filling in of detail. This condition embodies constant recognition of imperfection, of the fragmentary and therefore always-already 'ruined' character of the gothic structure, which, as John Ruskin argued, expresses the Christian imperative of straining for the ultimate at the risk of thereby more comprehensively exhibiting one's finite and fallen insufficiency."[32]

A Liturgical Lens on the Political

My task, then, is to look at the political (broadly construed) through the lens of liturgy. What difference will it make for our theological reflection on politics if we begin from the assumption that the same human beings who are by nature *zōon politikon* ("political animals") are also *homo adorans* ("liturgical animals")? What if citizens are not just thinkers or believers but *lovers*? How will our analysis of political institutions look different if we attend to them as incubators of love-shaping practices, not merely governing us but forming what we love? How will our political engagement change if we are not only looking for permission to express our "views" in the political sphere but actually hoping to shape the ethos of a nation, a state, a municipality to foster a way of life that bends toward shalom? How will our expectations of politics change if our imagination is disciplined by an eschatological vision?

31. See Milbank's dense but incisive essay "On Complex Space," in *The Word Made Strange: Theology, Language, Culture* (Oxford: Blackwell, 1997), 268–92.
32. Ibid., 276. We will return to these themes in a discussion of subsidiarity in chap. 3.

How might our enthusiastic activism be tempered if we begin to consider the assumptions carried in the practices of protest and rites of revolution?

My goal is to make things more complex, not more simple. These are knotty realities, and our theoretical and theological accounts should be sufficiently complex. So let me first note two implications of looking at the political through a liturgical lens.

Seeing the State as "Religious"

As I've tried to show in *Desiring the Kingdom* and elsewhere,[33] once we move away from a rationalist or intellectual paradigm that equates religion with beliefs and worldviews and instead identify the religious with rituals of ultimacy (i.e., liturgies), then cultural institutions and practices that we might have previously thought neutral or benign are recognized as having a kind of religious force about them precisely because they aim to shape our loves. What makes them religious is not just that they are informed by beliefs and worldviews but that they have formative pretensions that are nothing short of liturgical. It shouldn't be surprising when an institution that wants you to "pledge allegiance" is not happy with anything less than your heart.

In this case, a liturgical lens works like a cultural highlighter that draws our attention not just to the "laws of the land" or the decisions of supreme court justices but to the rites interwoven in our public life together—the rituals and liturgies that inculcate in us a national myth and habituate in us an unconscious allegiance to a particular vision of the good. When we undertake cultural analysis of the political through a liturgical lens, we will be attentive to the ways we are formed by the rites of democracy and the market, not just *in*formed by their institutions. Indeed, we will notice that the rites of democratic liberalism are not only—or perhaps even primarily—managed by the state; rather, we'll see an intricate web of liturgies, fostered by what Michael Hanby calls the "military-entertainment complex,"[34] that spill well beyond any delineated political "sphere."

This is why I think we postmoderns have so much to learn from an ancient but prescient voice like Augustine. Indeed, in some small way, my project is to reprise Augustine's liturgical analysis of the earthly city's "civic theologies" in the context of late modern liberalism. This will be the focus of chapter 1,

33. See James K. A. Smith, "Secular Liturgies and the Prospects for a 'Post-Secular' Sociology of Religion," in *The Post-Secular in Question*, ed. Philip Gorski, David Kyuman Kim, John Torpey, and Jonathan VanAntwerpen (New York: NYU Press, 2012), 159–84.
34. Michael Hanby, "Democracy and Its Demons," in *Augustine and Politics*, ed. John Doody, Kevin L. Hughes, and Kim Paffenroth (Lanham, MD: Lexington Books, 2005), 129.

To Think About: Renewing Social Architecture

Cardus, the Christian think tank of which I am a senior fellow, articulates its mission as "the renewal of North American social architecture," drawing on two thousand years of Christian social thought. The mission suggests a helpful metaphor: the *polis* is held together by an architecture, which also means that the *polis* is designed, is made, and needs to be sustained. As architecture critic Rowan Moore puts it, "Architecture starts with desire on the part of its makers, whether for security, or grandeur, or shelter, or rootedness. Built, it influences the emotions of those who experience and use it, whose desires continue to shape and change it."[a] The same is true of social architecture: we make the societies that make us.

But if we think of our common life together as the design and maintenance of a "social architecture," it should also help us to remember how deeply *collaborative* this endeavor is. It is no accident, for example, that the 2012 Venice Biennale of Architecture focused on the theme of "Common Ground." Architects have the luxury of being idealists only as long as their plans remain on the drafting table. As soon as they want to see something built, they are thrown into a web of obligations and partnerships that require creative compromise. As David Chipperfield notes in his introduction to the Biennale's portfolio, "Architecture requires collaboration, and most importantly it is susceptible to the quality of this collaboration. It is difficult to think of another peaceful activity that draws on so many diverse contributions and expectations. It involves commercial forces and social vision; it must deal with the wishes of institutions and corporations and the needs and desires of individuals. Whether we articulate it or not, every major construction is an amazing testament of our ability to join forces and make something on behalf of others."[b] The same is true of those who are called to contribute to the design, construction, and maintenance of our social architecture: by its very nature, such work requires solidarity, collaboration, and compromise even if, like Abraham, we are "looking forward to the city with foundations, whose architect and builder is God" (Heb. 11:10).

a. Rowan Moore, *Why We Build* (London: Picador, 2012), 18.
b. David Chipperfield, introduction to *Common Ground: A Critical Reader*, ed. David Chipperfield, Kieran Long, and Shumi Bose (Venice: Marsilio Editori, 2012), 14.

---

in which I'll show that the politics of the earthly city is not content to remain penultimate.

Seeing the Church as "Political"

If a liturgical lens highlights the religious (i.e., liturgical) aspects of "the state," it equally highlights the political nature of the church, that the body of Christ is a kind of republic of the imagination, a body politic composed of those whose citizenship is in heaven (Phil. 3:20). The practices of the body of Christ inculcate in us a social imaginary, orienting us to a *telos* that is nothing less than the kingdom of God. Worship is the "civics" of the city of God, habituating us as a people to desire the shalom that God desires for creation. The church is not a soul-rescue depot that leaves us to muddle through the regrettable earthly burden of "politics" in the meantime; the church is a body politic that invites us to imagine how politics could be otherwise. And we are sent from worship to be Christ's image-bearers to and for our neighbors, which includes the ongoing creaturely stewardship and responsibility to order the social world in ways that are conducive to flourishing but particularly attentive to the vulnerable—the widows, orphans, and strangers in our midst. The regenerating and sanctifying power of the Spirit also nourishes a *political* will that engenders solidarity.[35]

This is why we can't be satisfied with any kind of neat-and-tidy compartmentalization of the spiritual and the political, policing the jurisdictions between "the church" and "the state." In some significant sense, this distinction is not simply a division of labor; it is a contest and rivalry. As Peter Leithart observes, "So long as the Church preaches the gospel and functions as a properly 'political' reality, a polity of her own, the kings of the earth have a problem on their hands. . . . As soon as the church appears, it becomes clear to any alert politician that worldly politics is no longer the only game in town. The introduction of the church into *any* city means that the city has a challenger within its walls."[36] Even rumors of a rival king will send a Herod on a murderous rampage to quash the competition. There are always Hamans willing to rat out nonconformists who refuse to pledge allegiance to the emperor. And those like Joseph of Arimathea, "waiting for the kingdom of God," will have the boldness to confront their Pilates (Mark 15:43). Unpacking the lineaments of this ecclesial polity and teasing out the substantive vision of the good carried in the practices of Christian worship will be the focus of chapter 2.

However, these two observations—that the state is religious and the church is political—do *not* entail mutual exclusivity or total antithesis, though I do think they encourage a kind of holy ambivalence about our relationship to the political, a sort of engaged but healthy distance rooted in our specifically eschatological hope, running counter to progressivist hubris, triumphalistic culture wars, and despairing cynicism. Instead, the discipleship of our political lives requires discernment about how exactly to negotiate the collaboration and tensions between the heavenly and earthly cities. That monumental task

35. "The primary task of political ethics for the Christian churches today must be looked for not so much in political influence in particular cases or sectors, as in regaining the position and function of the congregation in worship, where they can develop their political form of life in accordance with the gospel" (Wannenwetsch, *Political Worship*, 163).

36. Peter Leithart, *Against Christianity* (Moscow, ID: Canon Press, 2002), 136.

is the focus of chapters 3–6 and the book's conclusion, from a number of different angles.

Holding both of these claims together without treating them as mutually exclusive—or concluding that we need to choose between the church and politics—invites us to add several layers of nuance and complexity that should inform our practice. I want to simply note these implications here and then explore them in more detail in subsequent chapters.

1. We need to recognize that "the political" is not synonymous with the earthly city's particular instantiation of politics. In other words, we must resist the temptation to see the current configurations of the political as equivalent to "the political" as such. The earthly city does not have the corner, or the last word, on politics—which is precisely why we can labor, hope, and pray that the terrain of the political can be bent toward the kingdom of God. *This* is what we mean by a "Christendom" project (contrary to almost everything you've ever heard about Christendom). Christendom is a *missional* endeavor that labors in the hope that our political institutions can be bent, if ever so slightly, toward the coming kingdom of love. If you want to see what Christendom looks like, read Charles Marsh's history of the civil rights movement, *The Beloved Community*.[37]

2. Not only should we hope and pray that our political institutions and practices might echo the coming kingdom; we should recognize that, in fact, it has already happened. This is why we can't simply dismiss even political liberalism: to the contrary, we need to appreciate the ways liberalism itself lives on borrowed capital and is only possible because of the dent of the gospel and the formative effects of Christian practices on Western societies (a story we'll rehearse with help from Charles Taylor and Oliver O'Donovan). Our stance toward liberal democracy is not only, or even fundamentally, antithetical.

3. Nonetheless, late-modern liberal democracy—as the default configuration of the earthly city today—is at the same time ultimately deficient and disordered, and often disorders our loves. So our political engagement requires not dismissal or permission or celebration but rather the hard, messy work of discernment in order to foster both ad hoc resistance to its ultimate pretensions and ad hoc opportunities to collaborate on penultimate ends.

37. Charles Marsh, *The Beloved Community: How Faith Shapes Social Justice, from the Civil Rights Movement to Today* (New York: Basic Books, 2005).

4. Finally, this liturgical lens on our political and public life should be an occasion for us to attend to our own assimilation, even provide resources to diagnose the source and cause of our capitulation to the earthly city. When we, armed with our "worldviews," confidently march in to transform culture with our ideas and arguments, we all too often underestimate the extent to which our own loves have been captivated by the rites of the earthly city—and so, in the name of transforming culture, what we get is the assimilation of the church. Focusing on the intellectual artifacts of the earthly *polis*, we miss the formative power of its rituals. *This* is the inconvenient truth that is pressed upon us by the new black theology of Willie Jennings, J. Kameron Carter, and Brian Bantum, for example.[38] The church's capitulation to ideologies of race will be a case study of our assimilation by earthly-city liturgies despite our best arguments and convictions.

Looming across this landscape is the giant shadow of St. Augustine, whose *City of God* is the animating source of my project, giving us the resources to diagnose our postmodern condition. He will help us name and distinguish the two aspects of our political cravings we see illustrated in *The Postman*: a good creaturely desire to build communities of cooperation beyond the comfort of kith and kin—to love our neighbors by building institutions for human flourishing—and also the fallen penchant to absolutize the penultimate, to confuse the political with the eternal. To be faithful citizens of the heavenly city is to learn how to actively wait, bearing witness to kingdom come.

38. Or as George Yancy puts it (in ways that intersect with the conceptual terrain of my *Imagining the Kingdom*), "Deep-seated racist emotive responses may form part of the white bodily repertoire, which has become calcified through quotidian modes of bodily transaction in a racial and racist world" (*Black Bodies, White Gazes: The Continuing Significance of Race* [Lanham, MD: Rowman & Littlefield, 2008], 5).

1

Rites Talk

The Worship of Democracy

Blurring the (Pen)Ultimate Distinction

Some of the confusion and muddle of our "folk" political theologies—the on-the-ground practice of Christians with respect to their civic engagement—stems, I am suggesting, from a tendency to "spatialize" political theology, carving out "church" and "state" as two realms or jurisdictions. Questions about Christian public theology are then framed as a matter of how to move between these different "spheres," or how to negotiate our "dual citizenship,"[1] or how to relate "church" and "culture."[2] The problem is that, in reality, many of these supposed borders are invisible. So it's often hard to know when you've crossed a frontier. There's no "city limit" sign to the earthly city precisely because the earthly city is less a *place* and more a *way of life*, a constellation of loves and longing and beliefs bundled up in communal rhythms, routines, and rituals. Theological wisdom about the political begins when we stop asking *where* and start asking *how*. This, I'm going to suggest, means overcoming the habit of spatializing the political.

1. As I will point out in a moment, this notion of dual citizenship (in the heavenly city and the earthly city) is *not* an Augustinian idea, despite many claims to the contrary.
2. A question itself further derailed by H. Richard Niebuhr's framing of the question as one of "Christ and culture." For a critical discussion see James K. A. Smith, "Thinking Biblically about Culture," review of *Christ and Culture Revisited*, by D. A. Carson, in *Discipleship in the Present Tense: Reflections on Faith and Culture* (Grand Rapids: Calvin College Press, 2013), 81–86.

It also means calling into question another distinction that is commonly invoked in political theology: between the "ultimate" and the "penultimate."[3] Both political liberalism and certain strains of Christian political theology like to confidently draw a line between the ultimate and the penultimate (sometimes taken as equivalent to the distinction between the "natural" and the "supernatural"). Political liberalism, for example, claims to be agnostic about "ultimate" matters and emphasizes that politics impinges on "penultimate" concerns. Some streams of Christian theology effectively agree, assuming that political life is merely about temporal, "penultimate" realities in contrast to ultimate, "spiritual" realities. Both share a picture of the cosmos as being made up of levels or steps that we can walk together *up to a certain point*, but then beyond this point we will venture into our ultimate disagreements. And we imagine "politics" happening on this lower tier. So, according to this common assumption, let's focus on what we can do together on the lower, penultimate levels.[4]

In this way, the (pen)ultimate distinction then licenses a division of labor between the temporal and the eternal, between transcendent expectations and this-worldly realities. Our ultimate beliefs and expectations have a kind of religious character about them (what political liberal John Rawls would have called "metaphysical conceptions of the good").[5] Even if you're a naturalistic atheist, you confess *some*thing as ultimate; you'll be committed to some macrovision of what's good and just and right. Now, your "ultimate" commitments might not be very grand; they might be very narrow, in fact. Your ultimate, sacrosanct commitments might be to your own self-preservation and

3. Note how this contrasts with the biblical distinctions, which are more *temporal* than spatial: the time of the *saeculum* versus the time of the eschaton (if "time" is even the right word for the eternal city). Michael Horton has often pressed this point that the biblical distinction is chronological rather than spatial, a matter of asking "What time is it?" rather than "Where are we?" For discussion, see Michael S. Horton, "Participation and Covenant," in *Radical Orthodoxy and the Reformed Tradition*, ed. James K. A. Smith and James H. Olthuis (Grand Rapids: Baker Academic, 2005), 107–32, and Horton, "The Time Between: Redefining the 'Secular' in Contemporary Debate," in *After Modernity? Secularity, Globalization, and the Re-enchantment of the World*, ed. James K. A. Smith (Waco: Baylor University Press, 2008), chap. 3.

4. See, for example, David VanDrunen, "The Importance of the Penultimate: Reformed Social Thought and the Contemporary Critiques of Liberal Society," *Journal of Markets and Morality* 9 (2006): 219–49.

5. In *A Theory of Justice* (Cambridge: Belknap Press of Harvard University Press, 1971), Rawls famously argued that in a liberal society, public deliberation about justice and fairness should be conducted as if everyone inhabited an "original position" that leveled our differences and hence displaced the influence of "interests." Most notably, he said that in the original position, political actors would have to set aside their ultimate beliefs about the good since these were a source of fundamental *difference*. We will return to this theme when we consider Jeffrey Stout's critique of Rawls (see "Democracy, Tradition, and Liturgy" below).

interests—an egoistic worldview. You might *believe* in Ayn Rand or Friedrich Nietzsche in a way that shapes your entire perception of the world and your calling within it. But if you're honest, you'll have to concede that not everyone believes what you believe (what Charles Taylor calls a "secular" situation, where no one's beliefs can be taken to be axiomatic, default for an entire society). Similarly, if you're a Christian, you have ultimate beliefs about God and transcendent expectations for the consummation of all things. But you also have to grant that not everyone believes that. And so we are in a situation where we are divided on the ultimate.[6]

But our ultimate disagreements, according to this logic, need not preclude our agreement on "penultimate," temporal matters like trash collection, traffic lights, public libraries, interstate systems, and the commercial exchange of goods and services. These are mundane, banal, "worldly" realities we all have to manage, whether or not you believe in God. Whether you think human beings are created in the image of God or are just sentient meat encased in skin, we can probably all agree that sewer systems are a good thing. We might not agree on the eternal destiny of the soul, or whether we *have* souls, but we might all be able to agree that laws requiring child car seats are a good idea. If we would only focus on mundane, *pen*ultimate issues, we need not be bothered by the ultimate beliefs that divide us. Save that stuff for weekends at home.

Liberalism prides itself on its politics of penultimacy; that is, liberalism likes to brag about its ultimate agnosticism and parade itself as the procedural system that only asks us to work together on the penultimate. "I don't have any specific vision of the good to purvey," Lady Liberalism purrs. "I'm not telling you what to believe. I don't really 'believe' anything. Let's just agree to some rules to help us arrive at some consensus about penultimate matters." It's when we fixate on the ultimate that people get hurt, according to this story; the penultimate never hurt anyone.

Except, of course, when it does. Recall the violence and destruction occasioned by the postal system in *The Postman*. How does the banal matter of transporting letters turn into a war? "Merely" political and social allegiances

6. Or on what's "fundamental," if you want to flip the picture to a more "ground motive" sort of orientation where what's ultimate, and what divides us, is our most fundamental, taken-for-granted starting points, the beliefs and commitments that are the bedrock of everything else. (This tends to be the formulation in the Neocalvinist tradition after Herman Dooyeweerd.) The claim remains the same: while our *fundamental* beliefs might divide us, we can come to pragmatic agreement on "mid-level principles." For a classic articulation of this from the field of bioethics, see Tom L. Beauchamp and James F. Childress, *Principles of Biomedical Ethics*, 7th ed. (New York: Oxford University Press, 2012). For a trenchant, somewhat MacIntyrean critique of this project, see H. Tristram Englehardt Jr., *Bioethics and Secular Humanism: The Search for a Common Morality* (Harrisburg, PA: Trinity Press International, 1991).

trump religious allegiances all the time, whether in presidential primaries, under the grotesque shadow of the lynching tree, or in horrifying cases like the Rwandan genocide.[7] The fact is, the ultimate/penultimate distinction is not the happy division of labor we imagine, mostly because the political is not content to remain penultimate.

Indeed, we are most prone to absolutize the temporal when our ultimate conviction is that there is no eternal. Joseph Bottum documents this absolutization of the penultimate in *An Anxious Age* (and a particularly incisive follow-up in *The Weekly Standard*).[8] Rehearsing the litanies of progressive outrage and the public excommunications of the left, Bottum confirms the prescience of G. K. Chesterton's observation that "the modern world is full of the old Christian virtues gone mad"—virtues "isolated from each other and wandering alone." A secularized culture is not devoid of religious fervor; it just finds new outlets. "As the post-Protestant generations gradually rose up to claim the high places formerly occupied by their mainline grandparents," Bottum argues, "what they carried with them was the mood and structure of once-coherent ideas of Christian theology, rather than the personal behaviors of Christian morality. What escaped the dying mainline denominations was not so much the old virtues as the old concepts, isolated from each other and wandering alone."[9] A secularized culture has its own renditions of original sin, its own version of sanctification (a sort of politically correct form of enlightenment), its own exercises in purification and excommunication (turns out the church of the penultimate, unlike the Christian church in America, actually exercises discipline). These are not the habits of an ethos that is agnostic about what's ultimate.[10]

---

7. See James H. Cone, *The Cross and the Lynching Tree* (Maryknoll, NY: Orbis, 2013), and Ephraim Radner, *A Brutal Unity: The Spiritual Politics of the Christian Church* (Waco: Baylor University Press, 2012).

8. Joseph Bottum, *An Anxious Age: The Post-Protestant Ethic and the Spirit of America* (New York: Image, 2014); Bottum, "The Spiritual Shape of Political Ideas," *Weekly Standard*, December 1, 2014, http://www.weeklystandard.com/the-spiritual-shape-of-political-ideas/article/819707.

9. Bottum, "Spiritual Shape."

10. What Tom Wilson describes as Irving Kristol's "great religious obsession" bears on just this point:

> [It is] the belief that secular liberalism breeds a valueless individualism that necessarily progresses toward moral disorder and even nihilism. Kristol feared that without religion, society would witness a growing discontent with what democratic capitalism can realistically provide. Stripped of any belief in the kind of higher consolation that makes sense of life's inevitable injustices and humdrum frustrations, the demands that people place on the political system "become as infinite as the infinity they have lost." Eventually the democratic regime is no longer able to justify or defend itself against the expectations of a citizenry that experiences no spiritual nourishment. Indeed, those expectations become unappeasable in the limitless material improvement that they insist government must

And you'd be hard-pressed to conclude the political is just temporal and penultimate when you visit the veritable temple mount that is the National Mall—which even the National Parks Service heralds as home to the "icons" of the nation's capital.[11] If we could teleport St. Paul from Mars Hill to the National Mall and lead him from the heraldry of the capitol, past the Washington Monument, and into the "temple"[12] that houses the eternal memory of Abraham Lincoln, I would imagine his observations would be similar: "I perceive that in every way you are very religious" (Acts 17:22 ESV). Democracy and freedom are not just good ideas for the "meantime" of our earthly sojourn; they are the ultimate goods for which we die (and kill). This is reinforced by the liturgies of the stadium and arena that stage spectacular displays of national mythology and military power akin to what Augustine described as the "fabulous" civil theologies of the Roman Empire, those public rituals that constituted nothing less than worship.[13] The political bleeds beyond the bounds of the penultimate; our public rituals have the force of rites.

Picturing "Fabulous" Theologies: Visiting the Stadium with David Foster Wallace

Let me take you to a scene that is quintessentially David Foster Wallace, from his widely acclaimed novel *Infinite Jest*. Surrounded by the vistas of the Arizona mesa, agent Steeply meets Rémy Marathe, a member of the Quebec separatist group the Wheelchair Assassins. Almost immediately, their conversation turns to matters of love. Initially this is the romantic love that launches ships and starts wars: Agamemnon and Helen, Dante and Beatrice, Kierkegaard and Regina. Not surprisingly, given their roles, this morphs into a conversation about the power of nationalism, which only encourages Marathe to return to a common trope. Here's the snippet of conversation that interests us:

provide and that capitalism promises. Without a religious culture, the slide into statism, if not authoritarianism, seems to become irresistible. (Wilson, "Irving Kristol's God," *First Things*, March 2015, https://www.firstthings.com/article/2015/03/irving-kristols-god)

Oliver O'Donovan offers analysis of a similar phenomenon in *The Ways of Judgment* (Grand Rapids: Eerdmans, 2005), 309–12. Modernity inherited Christian introspection but lost/rejected the God encountered in this interiority. Therefore new (transcendent) expectations are thrown on society/government, the result of which is despair (311), since modernity inherits the Christian burden to "judge for yourself" without the *good news* of God's judgment in Christ. Hence we spiral into self-conscious despair and cling ever more tenaciously to "secular" institutions—that is, institutions that are passing away and cannot save us.

11. "National Mall and Memorial Parks," National Park Service, accessed March 18, 2015, http://www.nps.gov/nama/index.htm.

12. As the inscription in the Lincoln Memorial explicitly reads.

13. Augustine, *City of God* 6.5–12.

"Your U.S.A. word for fanatic, 'fanatic,' do they teach you it comes from the Latin for 'temple'? It is meaning, literally, 'worshipper at the temple.'"

". . . here we go again," Steeply said.

"As, if you will give the permission, does this love you speak of, M. Tine's grand love. It means only the *attachment*. Tine is attached, fanatically. Our attachments are our temple, what we worship, no? What we give ourselves to, what we invest with faith."

Steeply made motions of weary familiarity. "Herrrrrre we go."

Marathe ignored this. "Are we not all of us fanatics? I say only what you of the U.S.A. only pretend you do not know. Attachments are of great seriousness. Choose your attachments carefully. Choose your temple of fanaticism with great care. . . ."

["After all," Marathe later pointed out,] "you are what you love."[14]

While this conversation unfolds between government agents and revolutionaries, taking place on a political terrain, in fact this scene that evokes the *religious* dynamics of fandom follows immediately on the heels of a more common scene in *Infinite Jest*: the rigors of the tennis novitiate at Enfield Tennis Academy. This cloistered, formative community is overseen by Gerhardt Schtitt. "Like most Europeans of his generation," the narrator observes, Schtitt has been "anchored from infancy to certain permanent values which—yes, OK, granted—maybe, admittedly, have a whiff of proto-fascist potential about them, but which do, nevertheless (the values), anchor nicely the soul and course of a life."[15] This is the inheritance of his education in a "pre-Unification *Gymnasium* under the rather Kanto-Hegelian idea that jr. athletics was basically just training for citizenship, that jr. athletics was about learning to sacrifice the hot narrow imperatives of the Self—the needs, the desires, the fears, the multiform cravings of the individual appetitive will—to the larger imperatives of a team (OK, the State) and a set of delimiting rules (OK, the Law)."[16] It shouldn't be entirely surprising, then, that the rituals of the tennis academy are also invested with the aura of the temple, the halo of devotion.[17]

But perhaps what's even more interesting is when Wallace invokes this intersection of athletics and religion in his *nonfiction*. While his writing on the phenom Roger Federer has garnered much attention, let me draw your attention to a provocative essay on the little-known US tennis pro Michael Joyce. In a dense footnote, Wallace homes in on Joyce's *identity*: "Tennis is what Michael Joyce loves and lives for and is. . . . It's the only thing he's devoted himself to, and he's given massive amounts of himself to it, and

14. David Foster Wallace, *Infinite Jest* (1996; repr., Boston: Back Bay Books, 2006), 107.
15. Ibid., 82.
16. Ibid., 82–83.
17. See, e.g., ibid., 117, 168–69.

as far as he understands it it's all he wants to do or be."[18] Then, evoking themes of free will and determinism that were, it turns out, the focus of Wallace's undergraduate thesis in philosophy,[19] Wallace raises an interesting question about *choice* and devotion:

> Because he started playing at age two and competing at age seven, . . . and had the first half-dozen years of his career directed rather shall we say *forcefully* and *enthusiastically* by his father . . . , it seemed reasonable to ask Joyce to what extent he "*chose*" to devote himself to tennis. Can you "*choose*" something when you are forcefully and enthusiastically immersed in it at an age when the resources and information necessary for choosing are not yet yours?[20]

Joyce's answer, Wallace comments, is "both unsatisfactory and marvelous": "It doesn't really matter much to him whether he originally '*chose*' serious tennis or not; all he knows is that he loves it."[21] You can see this love in Joyce's eyes, Wallace says, and you can feel a certain awe in Wallace's description, and maybe just a hint of jealousy. And then this parallel: "It's the sort of love you see in the eyes of really old people who've been happily married for an incredibly long time, or in religious people who are so religious they've devoted their lives to religious stuff: it's the sort of love whose measure is what it has cost, what one's given up for it. Whether there's '*choice*' involved is, at a certain point, of no interest . . . since it's the very surrender of choice and self that informs the love in the first place."[22]

Let's remember: we're talking about tennis here. But in doing so, we've already entered the temple, so to speak. The court and the field are terrains of devotion whose aspirations are described in religious tones, whose rituals draw temple-going "fanatics." Is it any wonder that Hubert Dreyfus and Sean Kelly, in their postmodern effort to retrieve paganism, look to sports for salvation? In a world of flattened immanence, where else could one look for a semblance of fanatic devotion? And so they conclude their book *All Things Shining* with a proposal that is at once remarkable and unbelievable, yet predictable. "Sports," they suggest, "may be the place in contemporary life where Americans find sacred community most easily. . . . There is no essential

18. David Foster Wallace, *A Supposedly Fun Thing I'll Never Do Again: Essays and Arguments* (Boston: Back Bay Books, 1997), 227–28n24.

19. Recently published as David Foster Wallace, *Fate, Time, and Language: An Essay on Free Will*, ed. Steven M. Cahn and Maureen Eckert (New York: Columbia University Press, 2011).

20. Wallace, *Supposedly Fun Thing*, 228n24. The scare quotes and italics every time Wallace talks about "*choice*" are, I take it, a kind of latent Augustinian intuition and are just right. Note also that for those Christians raised in catholic traditions that practice paedobaptism, the question Wallace poses here is a familiar *religious* question.

21. Ibid. This, by the way, turns out to be exactly the narrative arc of Andre Agassi's remarkable memoir, *Open* (New York: Knopf, 2009), which begins with him loathing a game that his father has "forced" him to play and closes with him wanting to stay on the court just a little while longer because he has come to love the game.

22. Wallace, *Supposedly Fun Thing*, 228n24.

difference, really, in how it feels to rise as one in joy to sing the praises of the Lord, or to rise as one in joy to sing the praises of the Hail Mary pass, the Immaculate Reception, the Angels, the Saints, the Friars, or the Demon Deacons."[23]

St. Augustine would both agree and beg to differ. He too would see the religious significance of sport's rituals, whether it's the liturgies of the Big 12 temple or the hushed, prayerful tranquility of Amen Corner at Augusta. But he would note a pretty "essential" difference between the rites of the arena and the sacramental rites of the body of Christ, since the point isn't just the "whoosh"[24] but *who* and *what* you love. Wallace was exactly right: "You are what you love." Which is why *what* you love constitutes an "essential difference."

In the spirit of Augustine, let's undertake a sort of liturgical analysis of the temples of sport, trying to discern what they teach us to love and how these rites shape and (de)form our devotion. Imagine we dropped a crew of proverbial Martian anthropologists in the midst of a NASCAR race, the Super Bowl, or any Texan high school on an autumn Friday night. Imagine these are alien anthropologists of religion, schooled in ritual studies. What would they notice? Wouldn't they be struck by the *rites* of sport and see these as a feature of our devotion, the stadiums as temples?

We don't need to engage in this sci-fi fantasy: we already have Augustine. In a way, Augustine gives us a kind of outside, "Martian" perspective on Rome's rituals because he had effectively emigrated to another city. The young man whose eyes were fixed on ascending to the imperial court found his home elsewhere; his heart carried the passport of the heavenly city, and thus he could inhabit his old haunts as an alien, a pilgrim, a stranger.

In this way, his *City of God* can be read as a theologically inflected anthropology that doesn't focus merely on the teachings or myths of Rome but homes in on the *rites* of the empire precisely because his account is ultimately about worship. Since true justice requires true worship, according to Augustine, Christian cultural criticism has to be a mode of *liturgical* analysis. Since, as he memorably puts it, "a people is the association of a multitude of rational

23. Hubert Dreyfus and Sean Dorrance Kelly, *All Things Shining: Reading the Western Classics to Find Meaning in a Secular Age* (New York: Free Press, 2011), 192–93.

24. Dreyfus and Kelly rather notoriously call this experience of transcendence a "whooshing up": "If we had to translate Homer's word *physis*, then whooshing is about as close as we can get. What there really is, for Homer, is whooshing up: the whooshing up of shining Achilles in the midst of the battle, or of an overwhelming eroticism in the presence of a radiant stranger like Paris. . . . And whooshing up is what happens in the context of the great moment in contemporary sport as well" (ibid., 200–201).

beings united by a common agreement on the objects of their love, then it follows that to observe the character of a particular people we must examine the objects of its love."[25] And if you want to see what a people *loves*, look at what they *worship*, what they devote themselves to. Hence a critical analysis of civic virtue is a liturgical analysis of the rituals that train a people's loves. The liturgies of a culture are the embodied scripts that form our loves and shape our devotion.

Rome is really just one outpost of the earthly city more generally—a city whose founding is coincident with the fall, not creation. The earthly city is defined by a disordered love that manifests itself as a *libido dominandi*, a lust for domination that is bound up with self-interest.[26] If, contra Dreyfus and Kelly, there is an "essential difference" between the liturgies of the heavenly and earthly cities, it is found by discerning their *telos*, their substantive—and substantively different—visions of the good.

Rome, of course, lustily embraces a *libido dominandi* in many ways, but it is just the latest dominant rendition of the earthly city. Furthermore, and of interest to us today, Augustine would note that the love-shaping rites of Rome are not all orchestrated by the emperor or "the state."[27] All kinds of sectors of civil society serve the same mythology, cultivating rituals that, while not "political" in the narrow sense, are nonetheless rites of the *polis* and its mythology of power, domination, and acquisition. Sectors of civil society don't need to be managed or owned by the state in order to serve the state.[28] The earthly city's liturgies are not narrowly "governmental."

A Christian cultural critique of Sports, Inc., has something to learn not only from Augustine's analysis of the gladiatorial games in book 3 of *Confessions* but also from book 6 of *City of God*, in which he analyzes what he calls the "fabulous theologies" of civic ritual.[29] His interlocutor, Varro, wants to distinguish between "mythical" (i.e., fabled, fabulous) theologies

25. Augustine, *City of God*, trans. Henry Bettenson (London: Penguin, 1984), 19.24.

26. Ibid., 1.preface, 14.1, 14.28.

27. Though I do think Augustine would have more than a passing interest in those widely circulated salary maps that show that the highest-paid public (i.e., government) employees across the United States are athletic coaches. See Reuben Fischer-Baum, "Infographic: Is Your State's Highest-Paid Employee a Coach? (Probably)," *Deadspin*, May 9, 2013, http://deadspin .com/infographic-is-your-states-highest-paid-employee-a-co-489635228.

28. Though payments from the state are obviously an enticement. See confirmed reports that the US Department of Defense paid millions of dollars to NFL teams for tributes to soldiers: Jared Dubin, "US Defense Department Paid 14 NFL Teams $5.4M to Honor Soldiers," May 11, 2015, CBSSports.com, http://www.cbssports.com/nfl/eye-on-football/25181085/nfl-teams -received-54-million-from-defense-department-in-last-4-years.

29. For a relevant discussion of *Confessions*, bk. 3, see Mark Hamilton, "An Augustinian Critique of Our Relationship to Sport," in *Theology, Ethics, and Transcendence*, ed. Jim Parry,

and the respectable "civil" theologies of the empire. The "fabulous" theologies are, well, mythical, fantastical, and even in Varro's day hard to believe; civil theology, on the other hand, is the respectable, necessary civil religion of the *polis*. But, Augustine says, let's look closely at these civil theologies—the acceptable gods "which should be worshipped officially and the rites and sacrifices which should be offered to each of them." When you do so, you'll find that the distinction becomes less tenable, that the fabulous and the civil bleed into one another: the gods of the republic demand sacrifices too.[30] They demand that we love rival gods.[31]

If you're looking for the liturgical rites of fabulous civil theologies today, is there anywhere more obvious than the stadium, the arena, the track? But the question to bring to these liturgical sites is *not* whether or not we idolize our teams or players. Granted, "sports" itself can perhaps become its own *telos*. Mark Hamilton is surely right when he points out that we "allow athletics to dictate to us what school districts we will live in, what jobs to hold, how to spend our leisure time, whom we marry, what activities we place our children in, how we will spend large sums of money, or with whom to socialize. It reaches into every nook and cranny of life. We give it a power over us."[32]

But I want to ask the question Augustine (and Wallace) brought to those fabulous, civil theologies: what do these "secular" cathedrals teach us to love? What are they enticing us to devote ourselves to? While there's good reason to consider the rabid, tribal devotion of team identity, that's less my interest here. I'm more interested in how the stadium is enfolded into our *civil* theologies and becomes a site of what Michael Hanby has described as the "military-entertainment complex," a powerful cultural machine that generates stories, images, and paeans to bravery, sacrifice, and devotion to the national cause, choreographed with bodily movements in contexts that are deeply affective.[33] This constitutes a liturgy because it is a material ritual of ultimate concern:

Mark Nesti, and Nick Watson (London: Routledge, 2011), 25–34. My thanks to my student Jason Zeigler for pointing me to this article.

30. Augustine, *City of God* 6.6–7.

31. It might be relevant to note that bk. 6 of *City of God* could be read as Augustine's demonology—that this is akin to Augustine's account of "principalities and powers."

32. Hamilton, "Augustinian Critique," 29. We might also consider the seemingly innocuous way the rhythms of youth sport take over the hum of households and families. For a relevant discussion, see James K. A. Smith, *You Are What You Love: The Spiritual Power of Habit* (Grand Rapids: Brazos, 2016), chap. 5.

33. Michael Hanby, "Democracy and Its Demons," in *Augustine and Politics*, ed. John Doody, Kevin L. Hughes, and Kim Paffenroth (Lanham, MD: Lexington Books, 2005), 129. For a fuller account and phenomenology of the rituals of the stadium, see James K. A. Smith, *Desiring the Kingdom: Worship, Worldview, and Cultural Formation*, Cultural Liturgies 1 (Grand Rapids: Baker Academic, 2009), 103–10.

through a multisensory display, the ritual both powerfully and subtly moves us, and in so doing implants within us a certain reverence and awe, a learned deference to an ideal that might someday call for *our* "sacrifice." This is not only true of professional sports; the rituals of national identity—and national*ism*—have been almost indelibly inscribed into the rituals of athletics from Little League to high school football.[34]

As I've already suggested, it's precisely when your ultimate conviction is that there is no eternal that you're most prone to absolutize the temporal. When the only gods left to you are the gods of the whoosh (or the swoosh, if you're the Oregon Ducks), then the stadium is the last sacred site, your team is the faithful remnant, game day is the last pilgrimage, and your donation to the alumni fund is as close as you'll get to almsgiving. We are on the terrain of the ultimate here. This is no longer just something you do; it does something *to* you. What are you learning to love here? What are we devoting ourselves to? To see the stadium in this light is to expand the scope of what we think counts as "political." It reminds us that the ethos of liberalism is shaped and primed by countless nongovernmental institutions.

In Adam Gopnik's remarkable book *The Table Comes First*—which looks like it's about food but is really a set of philosophical meditations[35]—he "goes meta," as the kids say, and writes *about* food writing. There are, he points out, "two schools of good writing about food: the mock-epic and the mystical microcosmic."[36] The mock-epic enlarges the significance of the gourmand by situating him or her in a story that is as big as the cosmos, making the eater a kind of hero: eating is about life and death, longing and desire, triumph and freedom! In the mock-epic, we zoom out from the table to the level of myth. In contrast, the mystical microcosmic is characterized by poetic compression, an attention to the fine-grained particularities of a recipe or a meal as a portal to a mystical insight. We zoom in only to pass through a portal that takes us to depths below the plate, below our consciousness, into mystery. Since both end up in places of charged existential significance, it can sometimes be hard to tell the two apart.[37]

In an aside, Gopnik suggests the same is true of sportswriting : "We go to it for either W. C. Heinz's tears or Jim Murray's jokes, Gary Smith's epics or

34. It might be interesting to consider how "extreme" sports are an exception to this rule. (Do they play the national anthem at the X Games? It would be tricky to have "Anarchy" scribbled all over your skateboard and then pause for the national anthem.) However, it seems to me that there is an individualism characteristic of extreme sports that is problematic in a different way.

35. He is a throwback for whom "gastronomy" is "an unexpected way to get at *everything*." See Adam Gopnik, *The Table Comes First: Family, France, and the Meaning of Food* (New York: Vintage, 2011), 6.

36. Ibid., 222.

37. Ibid., 223.

Roy Blount Jr.'s yarns, which suggests that, with the minor arts, our approach is classical."[38] This seems exactly right and gets at something about the nature of sport as a ritual feature of our social architecture. Our relationship to sport is ineluctably "nested" in layers and levels of significance that contextualize what it means to us and how it functions in society. This echoes Augustine's point: the mythical bleeds into the civil. The penultimate becomes charged with ultimate significance. To put it in Gopnik's terms, the epic bleeds into the micro. The amateur imitates the professional who is invested with mythic status and power. We can't make a neat-and-tidy distinction between the corporatized bastardization of "big time" sports and the supposed purity of the sandlot. We imitate what we see, and in an age of mutual display, where to be is to be *seen*, we all live as if the cameras are on us. The epic bleeds into the micro in every JV halfback who strikes the Heisman pose; the mythical bleeds into the professional when Russell Crowe's gladiator growls "I will win the crowd" at a Nashville Predators' hockey game. In an age of mutual display where the professionals are mythologized, our experience as spectators bleeds into our play. Indeed, we watch ourselves play, and we play as if we are being watched. (Think of players watching themselves run into the end zone on the jumbotron.) After *Friday Night Lights*, every high school football coach is living into the role of Coach Taylor.

The epic bleeds into the micro in the political sense as well: the anthem and color guard at high school football game are "nested" in the spectacular displays of college and professional football, crowned by the high holy day of the Super Bowl. In these repeated rites a story is lodged in our imagination.

Sport gives us scripts. So the games we watch become the games we play, the stories we enact. That means the games we play and watch *character*-ize us; they give us capital-S Stories to live into in a secular age, a place where we can look for Dreyfus and Kelly's *whoosh*. So we become characters in those stories. That means the scripts of sport—whether played or watched—seep into us and become part of the fabric of our character. Hence, Marathe's warning comes back to us: "Choose your temple of fanaticism with great care." What are the liturgies in these stadium-temples teaching us to love?

The Ultimate Bleeds into the Penultimate

So the neat-and-tidy distinction between the ultimate and the penultimate—which is taken to be roughly equivalent to the distinction between religion

38. Ibid.

and politics—turns out to be blurred because the political is not content to remain penultimate. However, the distinction is blurred from the other direction as well: our ultimate visions are not agnostic about the penultimate. The ultimacy of the biblical eschatological vision is not just a prescription for a distant eternity; it is also the norm for what good culture-making looks like now in a fallen-but-redeemed creation.[39] So the ultimate is not sequestered to kingdom come: it is the beacon for our cultural renewal in the penultimate present. That means our eschatology impinges on our politics.

This bleeding of the ultimate into the penultimate challenges some theological approaches in my own Reformed/Kuyperian tradition that tend to be more straightforwardly affirmative about political involvement. Trying to keep the peace between competing visions of the good, such Christian accounts of the political sometimes, it seems, encourage us to adopt a functionally agnostic stance about the ultimate in the way we organize our political and public life. Let me take up a specific proposal to get at my worry here.

In *Pluralisms and Horizons*, a remarkable little book that deserves much more attention than it has received, Richard Mouw and Sander Griffioen articulate an insightful, wise, and nuanced affirmation of what we might call "appropriate" pluralism as a Christian public philosophy.[40] In particular, they distinguish different kinds of "public pluralisms."

- *Directional* pluralism is a pluralism of worldviews, the deepest sort of "confessional" pluralism in a world where people have fundamentally different visions of the good. This includes, but is not reducible to, "religious" pluralism; it also includes what Charles Taylor would call "exclusive humanism" and the moral visions that fund political liberalism.[41] To live in a directionally pluralist society is to inhabit a world where we disagree about "the ultimate." Their point here is largely *descriptive*, recognizing the reality of confessional differences about "the ultimate."

- *Associational* pluralism is a pluralism of institutions and modes of human interaction. We inhabit a plurality of "spheres" that include families and schools, businesses and governments. The webs of association I'm plugged

39. And it is here that we will need to push back on certain Reformed accounts and affirmations of pluralism, which we'll do below in chap. 4.

40. Richard J. Mouw and Sander Griffioen, *Pluralisms and Horizons: An Essay in Christian Public Philosophy* (Grand Rapids: Eerdmans, 1993).

41. Charles Taylor coins the term "exclusive humanism" to describe a worldview or "social imaginary" (as he calls it) that imagines a life of meaning and significance without any reference to transcendence or the divine—a "self-sufficing humanism." Taylor discusses this in *A Secular Age* (Cambridge, MA: Harvard University Press, 2007), 19–21.

into as a citizen are different from the webs of association that characterize me as a father or a teacher. On this front, Mouw and Griffioen's point
is more *pre*scriptive, advocating for a robust plurality of institutions as
reflective of healthy civil society, pushing back on the tendency of either the
state or the market to swell and absorb every facet of human social life.[42]

• *Contextual* pluralism names the wide array of cultural differences that
  take root in regions and peoples, in languages and literatures. New York
  is not Jakarta; Peoria is not Seattle. Here Mouw and Griffioen's point is
  both *de-* and *pre-*scriptive: recognizing such cultural diversity as a gift
  and positively affirming it and enabling many cultural flowers to bloom
  as a plurality in which God delights.

With this taxonomy, Mouw and Griffioen offer a nuanced way for Christians to sift through the challenges associated with pluralism. As they show,
contrary to nostalgia for a WASPy consensus, a biblical vision affirms and
celebrates associational and contextual pluralism of all sorts. At the same time,
biblical Christianity will have to lament the reality of directional pluralism
even as it concedes that this is to be expected in the *saeculum.*

But even then we still have hard questions to ask, for how are we to live
in the meantime, between the cross and kingdom come? While we may not
celebrate directional pluralism, we also can't fail to recognize the reality. Then
the question is, what do we do with it? Can we imagine forging collaborative
relationships in the context of directional pluralism *for the sake of* contextual
pluralism and the common good? While we might disagree on what's ultimate,
could we partner on the penultimate, fostering healthy associational pluralism
in this time between times, this *saeculum* in which we wait?

I have reservations, however, about a specific aspect of Mouw and Griffioen's
proposal. As they rightly note, *how* we govern "associational" pluralism—the
diversity of institutions that compose society—will inevitably be informed by
some confessional "directional" perspective, some "ultimate" perspective. So
the question is, "Who will decide which directional perspective will provide the
appropriate integrating vision?" They suggest two possibilities: either some
specific group's vision will be "imposed" on society, *or* such a vision "will be
generated out of the give-and-take of public debate, without granting any
specific directional orientation a favored status in the discussion."[43] As you

42. This is a classic principle of Kuyperian social philosophy regarding the sovereignty of
each "sphere." For a succinct contemporary restatement, see Gideon Strauss, "Market Economy?
Yes! Market Society? No!," *Comment* 23, no. 1 (Fall 2005): 5–6.
43. Mouw and Griffioen, *Pluralisms and Horizons*, 118.

might guess, they prefer the latter option, and they articulate their rationale eschatologically: "We oppose the imposition of any specific directional vision on the public order prior to the eschaton," going so far as to describe this as "the more *just* arrangement."[44] But the result, it seems to me, is a kind of macroliberalism, a feigned neutrality at a group level that ends up with a kind of "live and let live" stance *that is itself a "directional" vision*. Though offered in the name of not "imposing" a substantive vision, what they describe as "just" is freighted with a particular—yea, ultimate—vision of justice that deserves Christian theological suspicion and critique.[45]

Mouw and Griffioen stipulate: "Wherever possible, people should be permitted to live out the implications of their chosen directional visions." Indeed, they go even further to make such a laissez-faire stance a matter of justice: "Justice requires that even people whose viewpoints we consider to be blatantly wrongheaded have a *prima facie* right to pursue their sincerely held convictions."[46] But *what* vision of justice "requires" this? And is this vision of justice "ultimately" neutral?[47]

Furthermore, one could legitimately worry about the effects of such agnosticism with respect to the ultimate, particularly for the poor and vulnerable. I think the recent work of social scientists like Charles Murray and Robert Putnam documents the disastrous social effects of basically "trying out" what Mouw and Griffioen advise here: for several generations now we have refrained from "imposing" any substantive visions of the good life with respect to family, marriage, and sexuality, for example. We've given people room to pursue both their sincerely held convictions and their passions for pleasure. We (allegedly) haven't "imposed" a normative vision of human social arrangements except the maxim "Be autonomous." The result? Erosion of family stability (especially for the poor) and widening inequality, exposing the

44. Ibid.

45. O'Donovan's observation is relevant here: "Much Christian enthusiasm for 'pluralism' has less to do with a relation to the state than with the church's yearning to sound in harmony with the commonplaces of the stock exchange, the law-courts, and the public schools. It is simply the modern Western version of 'Water-buffalo theology'" (*The Desire of the Nations: Rediscovering the Roots of Political Theology* [Cambridge: Cambridge University Press, 1996], 226). In chap. 4 I will address the challenge of pluralism directly. Here my interest is in the way Mouw and Griffioen's proposal exhibits a common Reformed tendency to be "directionally" agnostic at the macro level of society.

46. Mouw and Griffioen, *Pluralisms and Horizons*, 118. "Prima facie" appeals are always a bit of a weasely move, a way to say "obviously" when you don't have an argument.

47. Ironically, their proposal brings to mind an important critique of neutrality by a fellow Neocalvinist philosopher, Roy A. Clouser, in *The Myth of Religious Neutrality: An Essay on the Hidden Role of Religious Belief in Theories*, rev. ed. (Notre Dame, IN: University of Notre Dame Press, 2005).

most vulnerable to even more social threats, eviscerating the working class, and amplifying inequality—none of which looks very just, even if it is the result of observing a kind of procedural justice.[48] Once again, what Mouw and Griffioen underestimate is the *formative* aspect of our public policy and political configurations. They still tend to think of this "public" space as one occupied by "thinking things" who are looking for permission to hold certain *beliefs*. In other words, while they take themselves to be rejecting Rawls, they still end up sharing some fundamental assumptions with Rawls. Setting up society in this way doesn't just give permission to *think* what you want and *believe* what you will; it also becomes an incubator of virtues and vices. Every society *makes* a "people"; every *polis* breeds character. Laws function as "nudges" that are habit-forming.[49]

Mouw and Griffioen invoke eschatological waiting as the reason to become liberals in the meantime, as if this were counsel to adopt a merely *pen*ultimate stance with respect to justice. But in fact such a model of justice is ultimately loaded, and when it is inscribed in the warp and woof of a society, it becomes the ethos that shapes a people. A biblical passion for justice as shalom might be precisely what pushes us to refuse this merely procedural standard of justice. That is not license to confuse the state with kingdom come, but it is an impetus to bear witness to—and lobby for—substantive visions of the good *for the sake of* our neighbors. Our eschatological orientation should change our expectations, not our goals. We shouldn't shrink from hoping to bend our policy and public rituals in the direction of rightly ordered love, not so we can "win" or "be in control," but for the sake of our neighbors, for the flourishing of the poor and vulnerable, for the common good.

Democracy, Tradition, and Liturgy

I've tried to show that we should be skeptical of any neat-and-tidy distinction between the ultimate and the penultimate as a way to compartmentalize "religion" and "politics"—in part because the penultimate is not content to

48. See Charles Murray, *Coming Apart: The State of White America* (New York: Crown, 2012), and Robert Putnam, *Our Kids: The American Dream in Crisis* (New York: Simon & Schuster, 2015).

49. I have in mind here the important work of Cass Sunstein and Richard Thaler on "nudging." For a relevant and recent articulation, see Cass Sunstein, *The Ethics of Influence: Government in the Age of Behavioral Science* (Cambridge: Cambridge University Press, 2016). For a "hits-the-ground" discussion of similar themes, see David Halpern, *Inside the Nudge Unit: How Small Changes Can Make a Big Difference* (London: WH Allen, 2015). I hope to take up these themes in more detail elsewhere.

remain penultimate but also because our ultimate visions are not neutral with respect to penultimate decisions and policies that have to be made. This is another way of trying to suggest how the state and other public institutions have a kind of religious character while at the same time emphasizing that the gospel is not apolitical.

Eventually I will argue that this does not mean we have to choose between the church and the state. Although the state has its disordered liturgies, I will not thereby conclude that we can simply "check out" of the project of statecraft and public life. Indeed, eventually I will argue that it is precisely the cultural mandate coupled with the second Great Commandment—to love our neighbors as ourselves—that propels us to responsibility for the public life of the nations and communities in which we find ourselves as pilgrims and sojourners. Even when the city is Babylon, we are called to seek the welfare of the city (Jer. 29:7).

But before we get to that positive, constructive endeavor, I think it is equally important to cultivate a healthy suspicion of our Babylons. Too many Christian public theologies, rightly fending off an apolitical and anticultural pietism, end up with overly sanguine accounts of how and why Christians can embrace public and political engagement.[50] This stems, I think, from a failure to see our public institutions as *liturgical* bodies, a failure to see the *rites* that suffuse the state. When we fail to recognize the liturgical nature of our public institutions, we also fail to recognize their (de)formative power.[51] The state is not just a neutral, benign space I can stride into with my ideas and beliefs. The state isn't just the guardian of rights; it is also a nexus of rites that are bent on shaping what is most fundamental: my *loves*. The state doesn't just ask me to make a decision; it asks me to pledge allegiance. Governing isn't just something you do; it does something *to* you. And as I've tried to show above, the rites of the earthly city are not only managed by the state or government; the ethos of the *polis* is fostered in stadiums and arenas too. The "political" is wider than the government.[52]

50. I'm thinking primarily of arguments in my own Reformed tradition, which is why the subtitle of this book is *Reforming Public Theology*.

51. My neologism "(de)formative" is trying to honor the fact that the rites of the earthly city are not always and only deformative. Even earthly-city liturgies can run with the grain of the universe in such a way that they are conduits of what Abraham Kuyper liked to call a "common" grace. In this context, however, I will tend to highlight their underappreciated *de*formative capacities.

52. I take it this is why, especially in the United Kingdom, critics talk about "neoliberalism" as something that encompasses the configuration of both the state and the market, which have been, as it were, captured by the logic of capitalism. In her provocative book *Market Citizenship: Experiments in Democracy and Globalization* (London: Sage, 2007), Amanda Root tries to

Thus it is crucial to cultivate a healthy suspicion and discerning distance from the machinations of the state and the litanies of our public institutions (which, let me note up front, is different from a stance of disengagement and withdrawal). And I think it is just this sort of suspicion about the formative power of the *rites* of democracy that has been cultivated by a certain school of political theology that we could identify with Alasdair MacIntyre, Stanley Hauerwas, and John Milbank.[53] While my project lands in a different place, it nonetheless was forged in and by the proposals of MacIntyre, Hauerwas, and Milbank and retains some of their DNA.

In *Democracy and Tradition*, surely one of the most important works of political theology in the past generation, Jeffrey Stout criticizes this cohort of "new traditionalists" for encouraging faith communities to effectively withdraw from collaborating in our common life together. While eventually I will circle back to sympathy with some of Stout's critique, I first want to point out why Stout is wrong. As I hope to show, it hinges on the fact that he, too, misses the liturgical nature of the rites of democracy. In other words, Stout underappreciates the ways that liberalism wants to shape my *loves*.

In *Democracy and Tradition*, Stout articulates a trenchant critique of what he describes as the "new traditionalism" of MacIntyre, Hauerwas, and Milbank.[54] Characteristic of the new traditionalism is the sort of project that Milbank describes as "postmodern critical Augustinianism," which tends to look for *political* insights in Augustine's ecclesiology.[55] The picture of Augustine yielded by this project is one of a more "antithetical" Augus-

---

leverage this "market-ization" of society in order to improve democratic participation. Thus her project confirms the way in which "the political" as we experience it in late modernity involves much more than government or the state.

53. For a fuller account, see James K. A. Smith, *Introducing Radical Orthodoxy: Mapping a Post-Secular Theology* (Grand Rapids: Baker Academic, 2005), esp. chap. 7.

54. See Jeffrey Stout, *Democracy and Tradition* (Princeton: Princeton University Press, 2004), 2, for the first reference to "new traditionalism." I would prefer not to adopt Stout's term, since it is so clearly loaded. Nonetheless, I will adopt the phrase because it has worked its way into the literature. In what follows I will tend to focus on Stout's critique of Milbank, since Milbank is most explicit about situating his project in an Augustinian tradition.

55. See John Milbank, "'Postmodern Critical Augustinianism': A Short *Summa* in Forty-Two Responses to Unasked Questions," in *The Postmodern God: A Theological Reader*, ed. Graham Ward (Oxford: Blackwell, 1997), 265–78. This alternative "postmodern" Augustine is suggested in John Milbank, *Theology and Social Theory* (Oxford: Blackwell, 1990), chaps. 10–12; Graham Ward, *Cities of God* (London: Routledge, 2000); Michael Hanby, *Augustine and Modernity* (London: Routledge, 2003); and many of the studies collected in Doody, Hughes, and Paffenroth, *Augustine and Politics*, esp. contributions by David C. Schindler, Michael C. Hanby, and Eugene McCarraher. One could include here Stanley Hauerwas, *After Christendom: How the Church Is to Behave If Freedom, Justice, and a Christian Nation Are Bad Ideas* (Nashville: Abingdon, 1991), in which he engages Augustine at key points.

tine who exhibits a cultivated suspicion and antipathy toward the earthly city. This stance worries Stout because it seems to be providing theological warrant for Christians to withdraw from the practices and processes of democratic life.[56]

Stout's argument provides a helpful catalyst for articulating what I will describe as Augustine's political phenomenology. His account and response runs something like this:

1. Stout affirms the new traditionalists' critique of secular*ism*, which has attended modern liberal theories of justice purveyed by the likes of Rawls. With the new traditionalist, Stout rejects the notion that liberalism is a neutral, objective disclosure of "pure reason" or could otherwise remain untainted by religious, nonrational commitments.[57] So in this respect he is in common cause with MacIntyre and Milbank in rejecting the distinctly "liberal" version of the political that has "endorsed a theory of the modern nation-state as ideally neutral with respect to comprehensive conceptions of the good" and proposed that deliberative reason is "free" and "independent of reliance on tradition."[58]

2. However, Stout disagrees with MacIntyre and Milbank's prescription since the target of the new traditionalist critique is not just "liberalism" but modern democracy as such. "New traditionalism," according to Stout, entails a "total" critique of modern democracy because (a) the new traditionalists take claims to a-traditionality to be "definitive of modern democracy"[59] and (b) they also take such a-traditionality to

56. It is interesting to note, however, that in this project of looking to Augustine's *ecclesiology* as a resource for politics, the "new traditionalists" are very close to one of Stout's heroes in *Democracy and Tradition*, Sheldon Wolin. Wolin suggested that early Christianity's contribution to political thought was not in its direct attempts to address "the political" but rather in the "new and powerful ideal of community" it articulated in its vision of the *ekklēsia*. See Sheldon S. Wolin, *Politics and Vision: Continuity and Innovation in Western Political Thought* (Boston: Little, Brown, 1960), 97.

57. Stout, *Democracy and Tradition*, 294–96. Nevertheless, Stout affirms that there is a kind of therapeutic value to going through a "Rawlsian" exercise: "It is a very good thing for such people to spend a few weeks of their young adulthood imagining themselves behind 'the veil of ignorance' in 'the original position.' . . . But as Rawls gradually came to realize, the egalitarian arguments of *A Theory of Justice* were themselves expressions of a comprehensive view of life not widely shared by the general population" (294–95).

58. Ibid., 2. For a similar critique of the alleged neutrality of Rawlsian liberalism (at least as articulated in *A Theory of Justice*), see Nicholas Wolterstorff, "The Role of Religion in Decision and Discussion of Political Issues," in Robert Audi and Nicholas Wolterstorff, *Religion in the Public Square* (Lanham, MD: Rowman & Littlefield, 1997), 67–120. See also Wolterstorff, "Engagement with Rorty," *Journal of Religious Ethics* 31 (2003): 129–39.

59. Stout, *Democracy and Tradition*, 2.

be an impossible ideal. Therefore, the only way to be "political" is to be "traditioned" (though new traditionalism recognizes a plurality of traditions operative in a pluralistic political context). And since democracy and tradition are mutually exclusive, according to these new traditionalists, democracy is a fatally flawed political project.[60]

3. Stout contests this final claim, arguing (a) that democracy is *not* essentially "secularist"[61] and (b) that democracy is itself a *tradition* and therefore can nourish virtues and practices that contribute to political flourishing.[62] Stout thinks the American pragmatic tradition, hearkening back to Emerson and Thoreau, through James, is the best way to enact democracy *as* tradition.[63]

Thus Stout sees himself fighting on two fronts: "I have tried to define an acceptable path between the liberalism of Rawls and Rorty, on the one hand, and the traditionalism of MacIntyre and Hauerwas on the other."[64]

I want to briefly focus on what I perceive as Stout's underestimation of the new traditionalist critique of liberal democracy. As Stout puts it, the reason MacIntyre and Milbank criticize democracy is not that it fails to be a tradition and therefore fails to provide the resources necessary for the formation of political virtue. Stout takes the new traditionalist critique of liberal democracy to revolve around the claim that "we simply lack the virtues required to sustain an admirable way of life."[65] And so, if Stout can show that democracy *is* a tradition and that it *does* inculcate virtue, then democracy evades the new traditionalist critique.

But this misses a more substantive aspect of their critique. The problem isn't that liberal democracy is not a tradition; rather, the problem is something

---

60. One can see starker, more animated versions of such a thesis in more recent books. See Ryszard Legutko, *The Demon in Democracy: Totalitarian Temptations in Free Societies* (New York: Encounter Books, 2016), which has found enthusiastic reception in Rod Dreher, *The Benedict Option: A Strategy for Christians in a Post-Christian Nation* (New York: Sentinel, 2017). Cf. also Patrick J. Deneen, *Conserving America? Essays on Present Discontents* (South Bend, IN: St. Augustine's Press, 2016).

61. Stout, *Democracy and Tradition*, 11, 130.

62. Ibid., 3: "Democracy, I shall argue, *is* a tradition." He later continues: "Because traditionalists see democracy as an essentially negative, leveling force—as the opposite of a culture—they tend to underestimate the capacity of democratic practices to sustain themselves over time. . . . Democracy is a culture, a tradition, in its own right" (12, 13). In chap. 4 below we will note an irony in Stout's later book, *Blessed Are the Organized*—namely, that it is churches, in fact, that do the most work of forming citizens for liberal democracy.

63. Stout, *Democracy and Tradition*, 13: "To put the point aphoristically and paradoxically, *pragmatism is democratic traditionalism*."

64. Ibid., 296.

65. Ibid., 118.

more like the fact that it is (or has become)[66] an *insidious* tradition.[67] Or, to put it otherwise, the problem isn't that liberal democracy fails to inculcate virtues, but rather that it *does*, and (at least some of) these virtues are oriented to a *telos* that is, in some fundamental ways, antithetical to citizenship in the city of God (i.e., Christian discipleship).[68]

Stout seems to operate with a curious nonteleological or nonnormative notion of tradition and virtue—as if merely having a history and built-up set of "practices" were enough to qualify as a virtue-forming "tradition."[69] Or, to

66. On this point, Oliver O'Donovan regularly distinguishes between what he calls "early Christian" liberalism and "late" (contractarian) liberalism. See his discussion of George Grant's "modernity criticism" in *Desire of the Nations*, 271–84.

67. On this point, I think Milbank's critique is more nuanced than MacIntyre's.

68. Stout's confusion of Richard John Neuhaus and Milbank is illustrative here. Stout tends to simply identify the two as coming from the same camp. But he concedes that "Neuhaus is more favorably disposed toward modern democracy than Milbank is." What Neuhaus bemoans is "a religious evacuation of the public square" (*Democracy and Tradition*, 92). But this is precisely the crucial difference: Neuhaus does not really contest some of the core features of liberal, capitalist society; he just thinks those features require the nourishing resources of "religion" (cf. Elshtain as discussed by Stout [307]). In other words, Neuhaus doesn't see any *deep* antithesis (or at least not in the "temporal" sphere); instead, he is out to *source* democratic capitalism. Milbank, on the other hand, is more critical of liberal democracy precisely because he sees the fundamental antithesis of *teloi*. But that is also why Milbank is *not* out to revive Christendom. In other words, Stout seems to think that Milbank isn't a pluralist; but this is clearly mistaken. In fact, Milbank would accept what Stout describes as a situation of "secularization" (vs. secular*ism*): "What makes a form of discourse secularized . . . is not the tendency of the people participating in it to relinquish their religious beliefs or to refrain from employing them as reasons [that would be secular*ism*]. The mark of secularization, as I use the term, is rather the fact that participants in a given discursive practice are not in a position to take for granted that their interlocutors are making the same religious assumptions they are" (97). Stout's definition, we might note, is a tad stipulative and arbitrary; why not just call this a situation of *pluralism*? Cf. William Connolly's antisecularist account (that resonates in important ways with Stout) in *Why I Am Not a Secularist* (Minneapolis: University of Minnesota Press, 2000), and *Pluralism* (Durham, NC: Duke University Press, 2005).

In any case, a truly "nostalgic" stance (Stout, *Democracy and Tradition*, 115) would lament not just secularism but secularization as Stout has defined it. But *that* is true of Neuhaus, not Milbank. Milbank is protesting secularism as a ruse and wants to call it into question precisely in order to call into question the supposed "neutrality" and de facto status of the capitalist organization of late modern society. Stout seems to have missed the fact that Milbank is a socialist but not a *statist* socialist. To sum up, Milbank's "postmodern critical Augustinianism" does *not* "resent" secularization (as defined by Stout); to the contrary, it argues that such is *always* the situation of pluralist public discourse. Both theocracy *and* secularism resent secularization.

69. One finds a similar nonnormative, nonteleological notion of "practices" in Joseph Rouse, *How Scientific Practices Matter* (Chicago: University of Chicago Press, 2002). The common denominator to both Stout and Rouse is Robert Brandom's pragmatist account of practices; see *Making It Explicit: Reasoning, Representing, and Discursive Commitment* (Cambridge, MA: Harvard University Press, 1998) and *Articulating Reasons: An Introduction to Inferentialism* (Cambridge, MA: Harvard University Press, 2001). Thus it seems that it is the commitment to pragmatism that precludes a more robust teleology. But is a noncommunitarian account of

put it otherwise, Stout seems to focus on what's "behind" or "before" public discourse and democratic practice as sufficient to qualify as a "tradition" of virtue, but is blind to what that supposed tradition is oriented *toward*—that a tradition is virtue forming only insofar as it is oriented toward a *telos* that defines "excellence." Stout seems to imagine tradition and virtue without a *telos*—or at least his purview leads him to downplay the differences between the *telos* of democratic liberalism and that of Christian faith. Thus he argues that even a "secularized" democracy does not de facto exclude citizens from engaging in public discourse *as* religious persons, or even from invoking religious "reasons" (though, in a situation of "secularization" as defined by Stout, it would be "imprudent").[70] Democracy, Stout has argued, should not be confused with liberalism or secularism. And since democracy does not entail the exclusion of religious discourse, religious communities should not be critical of democracy.[71] So democracy is a "tradition," democracy instills "virtue,"[72] and democracy does not exclude "thick" religious commitments. What's not to love?[73]

Stout's evaluation of the compatibility between democracy and catholic Christianity (of the new traditionalists) is based on too limited a purview. As I have tried to indicate, Stout's pragmatic, nonteleological notion of tradition, practices, and virtue makes him blind to just what MacIntyre, Milbank, and Hauerwas are interested in: the competing and mutually exclusive *teloi* of

---

community viable (cf. Stout, *Democracy and Tradition*, 301)? Stout seems to think that it is sufficient for a group to have "shared activities" in order to qualify as a "community" (301). This is because he holds a minimalist definition of community as "a group that holds something in common" (300; cf. Augustine's definition of "a people"). But when he begins to explicate this a little more, he falls into teleological language: talking about his neighborhood, he concludes that "what we hold in common, what we have going for us as a community, are valued social practices and the *forms of excellence* they involve" (302, emphasis added). But talk of excellence requires the articulation of a *telos*.

70. Stout, *Democracy and Tradition*, 98.

71. There is another, loaded layer to this, which is Stout's general presupposition that democracy is the *only* way to think fruitfully and generously and justly about the common good. So whenever new traditionalists oppose some injustice, Stout claims that they are operating with "lingering democratic sentiments" (ibid., 119)—as if *only* democracy can oppose injustice.

72. "I am making for the conclusion that democratic culture is best understood as a set of social practices that inculcate characteristic habits, attitudes, and dispositions in their participants" (ibid., 203).

73. Thus Stout suggests that Milbank, who wants to claim "fidelity to Augustine's *City of God*," runs into trouble and "finds himself struggling against Augustine's evident ambivalence toward pagan 'virtue'" (ibid., 103). But Stout seems to take Augustine's "ambivalence" as if it were a ringing endorsement of pagan "virtue," and thus a precursor of what Stout wants from religious communities in their affirmation of democratic virtue. But as we'll note below, Augustine's "ambivalence" can be read along the lines of Milbank's suspicion rather than Stout's affirmation.

practices that give them their identity-forming capacities. Because Stout seems to imagine practices and virtues without *teloi*, he misses exactly the site of antithesis between liberal democracy and Christian discipleship.

Stout is arguing for a commensurability between democracy and Christianity based on what falls within his purview: both draw on tradition for formative practices that inculcate virtue, both inhabit a similar "space" and "time," and both share practical interests (e.g., in a neighborhood). But because of the limited purview of Stout's nonteleological account, he fails to recognize the ultimate incompatibility of the two.[74] This also means that, within a limited scope, what from a distance might appear to be intersecting or convergent lines are, when we track them out further, actually divergent.[75]

In a sense, then, I worry that Stout's account remains overly formalist and procedural: he is bent on demonstrating *that* democracy is a tradition and *that* it inculcates virtue, but he is largely inattentive to questions about *what kind* of tradition it is and *what sorts* of people it forms and creates. It is formally the case that democracy constitutes a tradition, a handing-on of practices, and that such practices are formative. But that is not sufficient to deflect the new traditionalist critique of liberal democracy, because the critique is not one of *a*-traditionality (that democracy lacks tradition) but rather one of *mis*-traditionality (that democracy is a "loaded" set of practices that form people for ends that are incommensurate with the vision of the good life articulated by the gospel).[76] Stout's formalist reply ends up with the vestiges of a kind of *secularism* because he fails to honor the identity-forming role of these ultimate *teloi*—which are ultimately "objects of love." Instead, he tries to persuade new traditionalist Christians to get over (ultimate) differences and get back into the game of a shared public discourse (as if they ever left it).

But the result is almost Rawlsian, because Stout seems to underestimate the degree to which our ultimate loves constitute our identities and shape *how* we participate in this public, shared space.[77] Thus he advocates with "great

74. Augustine describes the two cities as "different and mutually opposed" (*City of God* 14.4); these are not Gouldian "non-overlapping magisteria."

75. Or, alternatively, as MacIntyre points out in *After Virtue: A Study in Moral Theory* (Notre Dame, IN: University of Notre Dame Press, 1981), depending on the *telos* of the tradition, the same habit can be described as either a virtue or a vice; the identification of virtues is tradition dependent.

76. At least, this is the critique articulated by Milbank and Hauerwas; MacIntyre could be read as a different case.

77. At times Stout seems to suggest that the new traditionalist account simply precludes any interest in or concern with a shared, public space. This takes on a remarkable caricature when he suggests that "many of Hauerwas's readers probably liked being told that they should care more about being the church than about doing justice to the underclass. At some level they knew perfectly well how much it would cost them to do justice" (*Democracy and Tradition*, 158; cf.

urgency" a "general project of cultivating identifications that transcend ethnicity, race, and religion."[78] But what if *religious* identity is a properly *ultimate* identity? Would not "transcending" then amount to "trumping" such that, once again, despite all his critique of liberalism, Stout is requiring religious folk to minimize the particularity of their religious identity in order to serve democracy? And doesn't this picture still seem to carve out a kind of functional, pragmatic neutrality—as if one could leave one's religious identity at the door (the same requirement we ran into with the veil of ignorance)? What if it is precisely our religious identity—particularly as a *people*—that unveils deep (but not total)[79] incommensurability even at the level of the penultimate?[80]

Stout's misunderstanding of the new traditionalist critique of democracy stems from (1) his failure to adequately appreciate the substantive teleological nature of habits and practices, and hence (2) his failure to recognize the cases of fundamental incompatibility between the democratic "tradition" and the Christian tradition ("thickly" conceived).[81] We might encompass both elements by saying that Stout misses the nuance of the new traditionalist project

---

115). But this is just false, and irresponsible, since Hauerwas's point is clearly that the church will only "be" the church to the extent that it is hospitable to the underclass, by welcoming *all* into the body of Christ. See, for example, his contributions to Stanley Hauerwas and Romand Coles, *Christianity, Democracy, and the Radical Ordinary* (Eugene, OR: Cascade Books, 2008). This is, once again, an indication of Stout's assumption that *only* democracy can motivate interest in the common good. Aquinas, I think, would be surprised to hear that.

78. Stout, *Democracy and Tradition*, 302. In what follows it becomes clear that this means one's identity should be conditioned by a commitment to "the Constitution" (303). But what if, from a religious perspective, the Constitution is seen as unjust? Or could one worry that such constitutionalism could become its own kind of nationalism or tribalism?

79. That is, the new traditionalist project need not require a "total" critique of modernity or liberal democracy. It can offer an ad hoc evaluation of particular elements. Here I think the new traditionalist critique is well "disciplined," we might say, by the insights of Oliver O'Donovan, whose work is engaged in more detail in chaps. 2 and 3 below. My thanks to Hans Boersma for several conversations on this point.

80. Against Stout's rather rosy assumptions about the commensurability of democracy and Christian discipleship, I find William Connolly's agonism or deep pluralism to be more nuanced (and more Augustinian)—despite what I take to be Connolly's misreadings of Augustine in both *The Augustinian Imperative: A Reflection on the Politics of Morality*, new ed. (Lanham, MD: Rowman & Littlefield, 2002), and *Pluralism* (Durham, NC: Duke University Press, 2005). For a discussion along these lines, see Kristen Deede Johnson, *Theology, Political Theory, and Pluralism: Beyond Tolerance and Difference* (Cambridge: Cambridge University Press, 2006).

81. There is a third element that we cannot pursue here—namely, Stout's lack of attention to the "conditions" of the *agents* who inhabit a political community and what is required for them to be *able* to live justly. Here there will be a marked contrast between an Augustinian account of "virtuous" agency requiring *grace* as a necessary condition and Stout's continued confidence in the resources of immanence ("That stream is in us and of us" [Stout, *Democracy and Tradition*, 308]). For a relevant discussion, see James K. A. Smith, "Formation, Grace, and Pneumatology: Or, Where's the Spirit in Gregory's Augustine?," *Journal of Religious Ethics* 39 (2011): 556–69.

because he lacks an *intentional* account of political actors and communities, and more specifically misses the fundamental intentional mode of *love* as that which defines "citizens" and "peoples." In sum, in order to properly appreciate the new traditionalist critique of liberal democracy, we need to articulate a political phenomenology of love.

On (Mis)Understanding the "Earthly City"

Now, what does all this have to do with Augustine? I am suggesting that considering Augustine's account of the political as a proto-phenomenology will help illuminate the central dynamic of love in *City of God*, and also help to discern a fundamentally (though not absolutely) "antithetical" stance in Augustine's account of "the political" as it is embodied in the earthly city in general and the empire in particular. While Augustine's account of the relation between the city of God and the earthly city does not entail a withdrawal or isolation from the common tasks of political life, he nevertheless does offer a stinging critique of imperial "virtue" that calls into question the extent or posture of the Christian community's participation in common political tasks. Or more pertinently (vis-à-vis Stout), Augustine is concerned about the *formation* that takes place if the Christian community is too sanguine about its involvement in the political practices of the earthly city. In sum, I will argue that a phenomenological reading of *City of God* points to a more antithetical Augustine.

In this respect, I will push back on pictures of a more "accommodating" Augustine, one that reads Augustine *as if* the distinction between the heavenly and earthly cities were a distinction between the ultimate and the penultimate, a division of labor between the temporal and the eternal, the spiritual and the political. This misreading is the fruit of two failures of exegesis: (1) it downplays or misses altogether the core dynamics of *love* in Augustine's account of the political, and particularly the interplay of love, worship, and justice in his account of the "two cities"; and (2) because of this, it yields an Augustine who looks like a scholastic Thomist,[82] affirming the supposedly "natural" and "temporal" ends of the earthly city but pointing up its failure as a lack or inability to attend to supernatural, eternal ends.

82. I use the qualifier "scholastic" to indicate that this common picture (caricature?) of "Thomism" is not necessarily to be identified as the position of Aquinas. Rather, it is a picture that emerged from "manual" Thomism and continues to have influence today, particularly in the political revival of natural law ideologies in the United States. In contrast to this bifurcated Thomas, cf. Henri de Lubac.

One can find such a reading of Augustine in Todd Breyfogle's critique of Milbank's "postmodern critical Augustinianism."[83] Breyfogle, who wants to contest Milbank's more antithetical reading of Augustine, does so by reading Augustine's distinction between the two cities as if it were a distinction of "levels"—a neo-scholastic distinction between nature and grace, temporal and eternal, philosophy and theology. Breyfogle is critical of Milbank's rejection of "secular reason" precisely because Breyfogle thinks this forfeits the ability to have an "autonomous" account of the political—which, of course, is exactly what Milbank wishes to critique ("That's not a bug; it's a feature!"). But Breyfogle, who (like Wayne Hankey) can only imagine philosophy *as* autonomous and basically secular, suggests that "the political" can only be affirmed insofar as it is affirmed as the truth of a rational, "natural" sphere.[84] And he seeks to attribute this to Augustine by suggesting that Augustine distinguishes between that which can be "rationally discerned" about the political and that which can be "discerned by faith" regarding salvation.[85] This then translates into a picture of Augustine as affirming the earthly city as a proper custodian of "natural ends"[86] and attributing to Augustine a tidy carving up of the world into "spheres"—as if the distinction between the two cities were a relation of subsidiarity.[87]

83. Todd Breyfogle, "Is There Room for Political Philosophy in Postmodern Critical Augustinianism?," in *Deconstructing Radical Orthodoxy*, ed. Wayne J. Hankey and Douglas Hedley (Aldershot, UK: Ashgate, 2005), 31–47. I will not, in this context, attend to Breyfogle's numerous and sometimes stunning misreadings of Milbank.

84. When Breyfogle asks whether there is any room for "political philosophy" in Radical Orthodoxy, what he means is, Is there any room for a neutral, autonomous, and secular account of the "natural" realm of politics? This is because he continues to cling to a widely questioned picture of Thomism as affirming an autonomous realm of "natural, un-aided human reason"—which he then attributes to Augustine! At least Wayne Hankey, who also continues to cling to this vision of a universal, secular reason, has the good sense to recognize that this is exactly where Augustine and Aquinas differ. See Hankey, "Why Philosophy Abides for Aquinas," *Heythrop Journal* 42 (2001): 329–48. For a critique, see Smith, *Introducing Radical Orthodoxy*, 48–60. Because of this lack of nuance and imagination, Breyfogle and Hankey think that any critique of the *autonomy* or supposed secularity of philosophy constitutes a *rejection* of philosophy per se. Thus Hankey has described me as an "anti-philosophical theologian." For a brief reply, see James K. A. Smith, "Remythologizing Heidegger: A Response to Hankey," in *The Influence of Augustine on Heidegger: The Emergence of an Augustinian Phenomenology*, ed. Craig J. N. De Paulo (Lewiston, NY: Edwin Mellen, 2006).

85. Breyfogle, "Is There Room?," 35. Granted, one could perhaps find fodder for this reading in *De libero arbitrio*, but it does not seem to be a persuasive account of Augustine's more mature thought. My thanks to Steve Wykstra and Christina Van Dyke for discussions on this point.

86. Breyfogle, "Is There Room?," 44.

87. Ibid., 41. This picture seems to emerge from Breyfogle's curious distinction (again, attributed to Augustine) between "ontology" and "history," and more specifically between an "original creation" and a "historical creation"—as if the "original" creation were not historical (35–36).

Similarly, David VanDrunen reads Augustine's two cities as a "precursor" of later "two kingdoms" theory. VanDrunen rightly notes that Augustine distinguishes the city of God from what he variously describes as the "city of this world," the "earthly city," and the "city of man."[88] For Augustine, these two cities or societies[89] or "peoples" are marked by the standards by which they live: the earthly city lives by the standard of the flesh, whereas the city of God lives by the Spirit.[90] And while in the opening of *City of God* he distinguishes them by their animating virtues and vices (humility and charity vs. domination and pride),[91] he later emphasizes that what ultimately distinguishes the two cities are their *loves*:[92] "We see then that the two cities were created by two kinds of love: the earthly city was created by self-love reaching the point of contempt for God, the Heavenly City by the love of God carried as far as contempt of self."[93]

VanDrunen rightly notes that Augustine's analysis here is starkly *antithetical*, that there is no dual citizenship for Augustine.[94] "Each individual member is a member of one city, and one city only."[95] But then VanDrunen quickly begins to elide what Augustine distinguishes. In particular, the city of man increasingly becomes identified simply with "broader society" and (anachronistically) "the state," which are then identified with "the world" and "this life."[96] It is just such elisions that lead to strange translations when Augustine is invoked by two-kingdom theorists. Thus when VanDrunen expounds Luther's doctrine of two kingdoms, he claims that it "closely resembles key features of Augustine's two cities."[97] Indeed, he reads Luther as an extension of Augustine: "Luther's doctrine clearly must be distinguished from a straightforward Augustinian two cities doctrine, not so much in contradicting it as in *supplementing* it

88. David VanDrunen, *Natural Law and the Two Kingdoms: A Study in the Development of Reformed Social Thought* (Grand Rapids: Eerdmans, 2010).

89. By describing the city of God as a *city*, a *civitas*, Augustine has already made it political (note his reference to Phil. 3:20 in *City of God* 14.1). And though two-kingdom theorists often emphasize that the city of God is not identified with the church, in fact Augustine does suggest this in 16.2: "Christ and his Church, which is the City of God."

90. Augustine, *City of God* 14.1–4. It should be noted that in *City of God* 14.2–5 Augustine strenuously distinguishes "flesh" from the body and materiality per se.

91. Ibid., 1.1, 14.3.

92. Ibid., 19.24–26.

93. Ibid., 14.28.

94. It is perhaps important to clarify that Augustine means there is no dual citizenship between the earthly and heavenly city. This shouldn't be confused with him suggesting that citizens of the heavenly city (i.e., Christians) cannot be citizens of states and nations. My Canadian citizenship, on Augustine's reading, is something different from being a citizen of the earthly city.

95. VanDrunen, *Natural Law and the Two Kingdoms*, 22.

96. Ibid., 22, 27, 28.

97. Ibid., 59.

with certain significant ideas. To some degree, Luther's adding the nuance of two governments to the two kingdoms template accounts for this constructive development of Augustinian thought. For example, Luther's two governments framework gives the two kingdoms an institutional expression—in church and state—that lurks just below the surface in the *City of God*."[98] Describing this reading as a "supplemental paradigm," VanDrunen sees Luther as simply extending Augustine, going "beyond" him by complexifying the picture and thus giving Christians permission, even encouragement, to "embrace their roles in the civil realm" and see themselves "genuinely as citizens of an earthly domain." In short, they've been granted permission to hold "citizenship."[99]

But is this really just a "supplement" to Augustine? Is Luther just adding another layer of complexity to Augustine's account? If so, this is strange math, because the sum *undoes* key aspects of Augustine in the process. So what looks like a gradual, incremental translation is actually a transposition: notice that Augustine's earthly "city" (*civitas*) has now been spatialized into a "civil *realm*" and "earthly *domain*."[100] But whence comes this spatialization? And what gets lost in such a "translation"? By the end of this supplement, we're back to the notion of "dual citizenship" that Augustine clearly rejects—but now in the name of Augustine!

In a similar vein, in popular discourse it is increasingly common to hear calls for Christians to be invested in the "earthly city," or to hear that we are simultaneously citizens of both the heavenly city and the earthly city. These affirmations of the earthly city are rightly meant to displace our lingering otherworldliness, pushing us to see that God is not only interested in saving souls *from* the city but desires to see the flourishing *of* the city. The invocation and affirmation of the earthly city is meant to reflect Scripture's robust theology of creation and affirm our embodied, material, social, and cultural life. This is sound, biblical theology—and a much-needed corrective to our otherworldly ways. However, because the history of the term means something different, talking about the "earthly city" in this way can be confusing.

As we've noted, for Augustine the earthly city begins with the fall, not with creation. The earthly city is not coincident with creation; it originates with sin. This is why Augustine sets the city of God in opposition to the earthly city: they are defined and animated by fundamentally different loves. So the earthly city should not be confused with the merely "temporal" city or the material world. It is not identical to the territory of creation; rather, for Augustine the

---

98. Ibid., 60.
99. Ibid., 60–61.
100. Ibid., 61, emphasis added.

earthly city is a systemic—and disordered—configuration of creaturely life. However, this does *not* mean that Augustine cedes material, cultural, creaturely life entirely to the evil one. The city of God is not just otherworldly; it is that "society" of people—that *civitas*—who are called to embody a foretaste of the social and cultural life that God desires for *this* world.

Augustine doesn't invoke the earthly city in order to motivate Christians to care about this-worldly cultural life. His theology of creation already does that. The analysis of the earthly city is instead cautionary, pressing Christians to recognize that cultural systems are often fundamentally *dis*ordered, in need of both resistance and reordering by Christian labor in all streams of culture. And as we can see from his letters, Augustine involved himself in such work. There you'll find the bishop invested in the concrete realities of politics and civic life.[101]

Augustine doesn't use the term "earthly city" to carve up reality into a "heavenly" second story and an "earthly" first floor. No, both the earthly city and the city of God are rival visions of heaven *and* earth. So the "earthly city" is more like Babylon than the Garden. But even this fundamental antithesis doesn't give us permission to retreat into holy huddles or simply castigate the earthly city. Citizens of the city of God who find ourselves exiled in the earthly city (in Augustine's technical sense) are called, as Jeremiah counsels, to seek the welfare of the city precisely because we are called to cultivate creation. We will seek the welfare of the earthly city by seeking to annex it to the city of God, thereby reordering creaturely life to shalom.

Misreadings like Breyfogle's and VanDrunen's try to account for Augustine's tempered affirmation of the earthly city through the register of a kind of reified "Thomistic" distinction between nature and grace.[102] On this reading, the earthly city is affirmed as that which properly administers "temporal" goods oriented toward "natural" ends, whereas the city of God is concerned with eternal goods and supernatural ends. But this fails to do justice to the radicality of Augustine's critique of the earthly city, and Rome in particular.[103] We can see this in two ways:

101. For a representative sampling of Augustine's letters and sermons that intersect with political life, see Augustine, *Political Writings*, ed. E. M. Atkins and R. J. Dodaro (Cambridge: Cambridge University Press, 2001).

102. For a helpful discussion that distinguishes Aquinas and Augustine on this point, see Jesse Covington, "The Grammar of Virtue: Augustine and the Natural Law," in *Natural Law and Evangelical Political Thought*, ed. Jesse Covington, Bryan McGraw, and Micah Watson (Lanham, MD: Lexington Books, 2013), 167–93. My thanks to Micah Watson for reminding me of this helpful essay.

103. Breyfogle contends that Milbank "undervalues Augustine's assessment of the earthly peace" ("Is There Room?," 39). I would suggest Breyfogle—like other advocates of the "accommodationist" or "liberal" Augustine—*over*estimates Augustine's assessment.

1. The earthly city, for Augustine, is not merely "temporal"; it is a decidedly postlapsarian phenomenon (see *City of God* 11.33–34, 14.4). The
   "temporal/natural" reading of Augustine makes the earthly city coincident with "the political"; or to put it otherwise, it makes the earthly
   city coincident with *creation*. But Augustine traces the genealogy of
   the earthly city to the fall, which permits him a nuance that makes it
   possible to affirm the political as inherent to creation (and so rightly
   embodied in the city of God) but also to criticize the misdirection of
   the political in the fallen earthly city.
2. Augustine's critique of the earthly city is not merely that its love is
   insufficient, falls short, and thus doesn't reach "far" enough; rather,
   the love that animates the earthly city is *dis*ordered and *mis*directed
   (by loving creatures *as if* they were the Creator).[104] It is precisely the
   "intentional" account of love in phenomenology that will highlight
   this aspect of Augustine's critique.

So the "accommodating" Augustine, we could argue, is the fruit of a reading
that misses the central dynamics of love; that is, it misses what I will describe
in the next section as the "phenomenological" framework of Augustine's
notion of love. There we will note that his picture of the individual subject
(which I've explored in more detail in *Desiring the Kingdom*) mirrors his
account of a "people."

Augustine's Political Phenomenology

Augustine suggests a social, communal, political correlate to the erotic phenomenology of the person I've sketched in *Desiring the Kingdom*. In the same
way that the individual "soul" intends[105] the world "in love" and thus is identified by the object of that love, so too we find that Augustine, not surprisingly,
says that a "people" or "commonwealth" is defined in the same way: by the
objects of their love. As already noted, Augustine defines a people as "the
association of a multitude of rational beings united by a common agreement
on the objects of their love," so that in order to "observe the character of a
particular people" we must examine "the objects of its love" (*City of God*
19.24). Now, it is important that Augustine takes up this "intentional" defi-

104. This is why the "essence" of the earthly city is intimately linked to idolatry.
105. As outlined in *Desiring the Kingdom*, 48–49, we are using "intends" in the phenomenological sense of Husserl and Heidegger. To intend (from *intentio*) is to aim, to "mean"
the world in a certain way. When I see the object on the desk before me *as* a coffee mug, the
phenomenologist would say I "intend" it as a coffee mug.

> ### To Think About: A Stance for the Journey
>
> Anyone who has ridden a subway standing up will appreciate how important one's *stance* can be. Whether it's the Tube in London, the Metro in Paris, or the subway in Toronto, the standing rider faces a universal challenge: to remain upright despite the jolts and shocks of the typical train ride. And we can all recall scenes from film or television of the benighted bumpkin from the provinces who steps on the subway for the first time: harried and hurried, crushed then ignored, losing the race to secure a seat and hence left standing in the middle of the car as it lurches forward, our protagonist finds herself on the floor, flustered and embarrassed. (If it's a rom-com, at this point Hugh Grant reaches down to help her up and, well, you know how the story goes.)
>
> Contrast this with the seasoned veteran who glides through the crowd, assumes the position, and nonchalantly braces himself for the journey without missing a beat on his smartphone. The difference is his *stance*, one he now assumes without thinking about it. Feet shoulder-width apart, slightly staggered, our urbanite is ready for whatever the jarring track might throw at him. This posture grants a kind of 360-degree strategy of resistance: it is one that is ready for the lurches of starting and stopping as well as the side-to-side sway of twists and turns.
>
> In a way, we might say that the wisdom of Augustine's *City of God* is like a stance lesson for the church as it journeys through the *saeculum* toward its destination, kingdom come. Augustine doesn't advise us to stay at home; he counsels us to buy a ticket for the journey. To be a subject of Christ the King is to be *on the way*. Neither does Augustine advise that we look for "safe" ways there, only traveling with "our own" in holy huddled packs of pilgrims who walk on some hidden "spiritual" path above the fray. His admonition is to learn *how* to share the terrain with others as we're on the way. Indeed, for Augustine, the *saeculum*—the age between the fall and kingdom come—is one that is essentially *permixtum*, an age where church and world are thrown together, intermingled and mixed up in overlapping territory (*City of God* 19.26). What Augustine offers, then, is not a secret map or some Harry-Potter-like floo-powder network that excuses us from mingling with Muggles. Instead, he offers wisdom about how to cultivate a good stance and posture for the challenges of the journey. This is how to stand if you're a pilgrim.

nition of a people as an alternative to Scipio's definition of a people as "a multitude 'united in association by a common sense of right and a community of interest'" (19.21). On Scipio's definition, Augustine contends, there never was a Roman commonwealth because there was no "true justice," since true justice requires true *worship*, and that is impossible for any configuration of the earthly city. "Justice is found where God, the one supreme God, rules an obedient City according to his grace, forbidding sacrifice to any being save himself alone" (19.23).

However, Augustine revises his definition of a people from Scipio's more static conception to a more dynamic, intentional one that makes *love* central to that which constitutes a people *as* a people. His next question is whether, under this new definition, Rome will qualify as a people or commonwealth. Here the result is quite different: on this new definition, "the Roman people is a people and its state is indubitably a commonwealth" (19.24). Some tend to hastily conclude from this that Augustine offers a basic affirmation of Rome.[106] But this is certainly not the case, precisely because Augustine's proto-phenomenology is interested in the intentional *objects* of this animating love. And here the conclusion is similar but more nuanced. If we follow the static categories of Scipio, we'll conclude that Rome was not a people because it was not just. If, instead, we take up this more intentional and "erotic" definition of a people, we will have to conclude that, indeed, Rome is a people. However, Augustine still concludes that, while Rome (and other empires of the earthly city) can be formally described as "peoples," they are nevertheless *unjust*. As Augustine puts it,

> By this definition of ours, the Roman people is a people and its estate is indubitably a commonwealth. But as for the objects of that people's love . . . for all this we have the witness of history. . . . And yet I shall not make that a reason for asserting that a people is not really a people or that a state is not a commonwealth, so long as there remains an association of some kind or other between a multitude of rational beings united by a common agreement on the objects of its love. *However*, what I have said about the Roman people and the Roman commonwealth I must be understood to have said and felt about those of the Athenians and of any other Greeks, or of that former Babylon of the Assyrians, when they exercised imperial rule, whether on a small or large scale, in their commonwealths—and indeed about any nation whatsoever. For God is not the ruler of the city of the impious, because it disobeys his commandment that sacrifice should be offered to himself alone. . . . And because God does not rule there the *general characteristic* of that city is that it is devoid of true justice. (19.24, emphases added)

To these imperial configurations of the earthly city Augustine grants the formal status of "peoples," but substantively he judges them to be "generally" or basically unjust precisely because they are not (and cannot be) animated by a rightly ordered love aimed at worship of the Triune God. Augustine recognizes the perduring structural aspect of a people animated by love and even suggests

---

106. For a critique of such tendencies, see Timothy P. Jackson, "*Prima Caritas, Inde Jus*: Why Augustinians Shouldn't Baptize John Rawls," *Journal of Peace and Justice Studies* 8, no. 2 (1997): 49.

that such an erotic orientation of a community is ineradicable. But what's at issue is not *whether* a people loves but *what* that people loves. Augustine is interested in the *objects* of love as that which indicates the "character" of a people (19.24). It is the *telos* of a people's love that defines a people, and thus Augustine's political phenomenology, while recognizing a common, formal, intentional structure of a people, zooms in on what *distinguishes* them— namely, the intentional objects of these communities. It is what-is-aimed-at, the *teloi* of the communities, that distinguishes them. It is in their different intentional objects that Augustine locates the *antithesis*.

The only proper object of love for a rightly ordered political community is the Triune God (just as the only "thing" that is to be enjoyed is the Triune God).[107] This is just to say that the rightly ordered *political* community must be oriented by right *worship*; and insofar as the earthly city is essentially idolatrous (recall that it is not just the "temporal" city), it cannot be so ordered. The earthly city's different political configurations qualify as "commonwealths" but fail to be just because they are aimed at the wrong objects of love (that is, they wrongly *constitute* objects of love). Augustine's phenomenology of love enables him to be attentive to this difference precisely because it yields a sufficiently complex account of subjects and communities that allows him to distill and focus on the intentional objects as constituted by different communities.

It is this kind of Augustinian sensibility that is at work in Hauerwas and Milbank, who are suspicious of liberalism (and democracy) not because it doesn't form virtue but precisely because it does. More specifically, the concern is that liberal democracy is a repertoire of rites that quite successfully form a people to *love* certain ends and goods. It is a theological evaluation of those specific goods—the *telos* of the rites of democracy—that engenders their critique and hesitation. In this respect, it is Augustine's political phenomenology that enables him to be attentive to an antithesis that Stout's limited purview does not recognize: that at stake in participation in the political configurations of the earthly city are matters of *worship*. The public practices of the empire are not "merely political" or "merely temporal"; they are "loaded," formative practices aimed at a *telos* that is often antithetical to the goods of the city of

107. See Augustine, *Teaching Christianity* [*De doctrina christiana*], trans. Edmund Hill (New York: New City Press, 1994), bk. 1. This is why I think Wolin rightly suggests that the church is not apolitical but alternatively political (*Politics and Vision*, 99–100). For those who would quickly contend that this confuses the church with the city of God, see Augustine's identification of the two in *City of God* 16.2. We also need to recall that the "earthly city" is not simply to be equated with "the political."

God.[108] The public practices of the earthly city (including its modern outposts that find expression in liberal democracy) are *idolatrous* practices because embedded in them is a *telos* that is other than the Triune God. However, as we will see below, this is not a recipe for dismissal or retreat.

This now propels the next two chapters. First, if it is the substance of the *telos* that distinguishes the heavenly and earthly cities, then we need to attend to the substance of the *ekklēsia*'s *telos*. In other words, it is not merely the "formal" reality of having rituals, liturgies, and tradition that distinguishes the church; what distinguishes the church is the *substance* of the *telos* that is carried in those rituals and liturgies. So in chapter 2 we will revisit the church as a *polis* and unpack the substance of that *telos* and tease out why the eschatological orientation inherent in Christian worship is essential to the "politics" of the church.

Second, we need to consider whether this antithesis between the earthly and heavenly cities is total or absolute. As I hope to show in chapter 3, a fundamentally antithetical critique of the earthly city (including liberal democracy) need not—and should not—entail a wholesale rejection, dismissal, or withdrawal. Once we appreciate what Augustine calls the *permixtum* of the church and our political heritage—that all of our attempts to tidily distinguish church and world are fraught—and couple this with a historical appreciation of the gospel's impact on even the rites of democracy, we'll then consider how we *can* collaborate in the public sphere for the common good, which will be the focus of chapters 4–6 and the conclusion.

---

108. "Often" is a key qualification. We will expand on this point in chap. 3 below.

2

Revisiting the Church as *Polis*

Cultivating an Ecclesial Center of Gravity

Chapter 1 reframed the political as a way of life, not merely a space or sphere or square. The political is not reducible to parties or procedures, as if political life were merely a procedural channel for what we believe. The political is not merely an outlet for my beliefs or a forum for expressing my commitments. The public space of the *polis* is a shared, formative space of action. I participate as an agent, and yet my participation also shapes how I exercise my agency and to what ends my action is directed. Politics isn't just my vote; it's the allegiances I learn by rote.

If we have so far tried to see a football game or a pilgrimage to the National Mall as an exercise that is *liturgical* in nature, it is equally important that we see Christian worship as *political* in nature—not in the sense of its being "partisan" or tied to "earthly city" special interest groups, but precisely insofar as it is the enactment of a public ritual centered on—yea, led by—an ascended King. As I've already shown in chapter 5 of *Desiring the Kingdom*, the rites of worship—confession, offering, baptism, communion—carry a social imaginary that is an inescapably "political" vision of a people called as a *royal* priesthood and sent as ambassadors of the King above all kings.[1]

---

1. See James K. A. Smith, *Desiring the Kingdom: Worship, Worldview, and Cultural Formation*, Cultural Liturgies 1 (Grand Rapids: Baker Academic, 2009), 155–214. This exegesis of the social imaginary of Christian worship is crucial to—and assumed by—the argument of the current chapter and won't be repeated here.

The repertoire of historic Christian worship carries in it a "social imaginary" that constitutes the biblical vision of flourishing for creation and culture. Implicit in the practices of Christian worship is an economics, a sociology, a politics. The goal of this chapter, then, is to delineate how Christian worship carries the scriptural vision of the church as *polis* in order to then discern what that means for Christian political engagement in the *saeculum*, in this "era" between the fall and parousia in which we find ourselves in the territory of a contested creation.

In doing so, we will also revisit just what it means to see the church as *polis*—particularly since this formulation, championed by Hauerwas's reading of MacIntyre, has been so often misunderstood (even by its advocates) to be a recipe for disengagement from the common life that constitutes the "public" of our cities, states, and nations.[2] To see the church as an "alternative" *polis* does not entail the superlative claim that Christian citizens in the *saeculum* ensconce themselves in *only* the church. Resident aliens are *resident* where they are alien. It is not a question of *whether* we engage in common life but *how*. To appreciate the church as *polis* is to see the body of Christ as a political body that centers our political identity and shapes our habits of solidarity. As Hauerwas emphasizes, this is to see the church as "a body constituted by the disciplines that create the capacity to resist the disciplines of the body associated with the modern nation-state and, in particular, the economic habits that support that state. For the church to *be* a social ethic, rather than to *have* a social ethic, means the church must be (is) a body politic. The crucial question is how the church can be such without resorting to mirroring the nation-state and/or being tempted to use the nation-state for the disciplining it so desires and needs."[3]

---

2. This is certainly the worry articulated by Jeffrey Stout, despite Hauerwas's explicit protests to the contrary; see Stout, *Democracy and Tradition* (Princeton: Princeton University Press, 2004), 147–48. Stout sees the effects of Hauerwas's argument outstripping his own intentions, a kind of chemistry experiment run amok when one combines Yoder and MacIntyre: "One cannot stand in a church conceived in Yoder's terms, while describing the world surrounding it in the way MacIntyre describes liberal society, without implicitly adopting a stance that is rigidly dualistic in the same respects that rightly worried Hauerwas in 1974" (149). I'm not convinced that the "resident aliens" trope of Willimon and Hauerwas (*Resident Aliens: Life in the Christian* Colony [Nashville: Abingdon, 1989]) at all entails the proverbial "sectarian withdrawal" their critics have contended. Indeed, as we'll see below, the "resident aliens" trope is important for Augustine as well. Nonetheless, the way Willimon's and Hauerwas's work has been appropriated, coupled with a certain quasi-monastic accent and a millennial despair about politics as such, has generated more simplistic demonization of "the state" per se and withdrawals from the common life of nation-state politics. We can see this being replayed by the so-called Benedict Option.

3. Stanley Hauerwas, *In Good Company: The Church as* Polis (Notre Dame, IN: University of Notre Dame Press, 1995), 26. In a footnote to this point Hauerwas cites Wendell

So Hauerwas's concern is not to prevent heavenly citizens from acting amidst and alongside citizens of the earthly city but rather to correct a "spiritual" understanding of the church as *a*political. The point of seeing the church as *polis* is not to posit it as an otherworldly island in the midst of the nation-state but rather to resist the temptation to see only the earthly city as political, ceding "politics"—and hence our political formation—to the habits and disciplines of the state. But this in no way precludes getting our hands dirty in "the world."[4] To the contrary, being centered in the formative disciplines of the heavenly *polis*, we are then *sent* to labor in the contested terrain of creation in the *saeculum*. This isn't about permission; it is about preparation. It's not about sequestering the church from the messiness of "engagement"; it's about intentionality with respect to the church's formation *for* engagement.[5] As Richard Bauckham concludes his remarkable study of the book of Revelation:

> Revelation does not respond to the dominant ideology by promoting Christian withdrawal into a sectarian enclave that leaves the world to its judgment while consoling itself with millennial dreams. . . . It is in the public, political world that Christians are to witness for the sake of God's kingdom. Worship, which is so prominent in the theocentric vision of Revelation, has nothing to do with pietistic retreat from the public world. It is the source of resistance to the

---

Berry, *Sex, Economy, Freedom, and Community* (New York: Pantheon, 1993), 114: "Modern Christianity has become willy-nilly the religion of the state and the economic status quo. Because it has been so exclusively dedicated to incanting anemic souls into Heaven, it has been made the tool of much earthly villainy. It has, for the most part, stood silently by while a predatory economy has ravaged the world, destroyed its natural beauty and health, divided and plundered its human communities and households. It has flown the flag and chanted the slogans of empire."

4. See my discussion of the multiple scriptural connotations of "world" in *Desiring the Kingdom*, 187–90.

5. This is how I understand James Davison Hunter's model of "faithful presence." "As to our spheres of influence," Hunter summarizes, "a theology of faithful presence obligates us to do what we are able, under the sovereignty of God, to shape the patterns of life and work and relationship—that is, the institutions of which our lives are constituted—toward a shalom that seeks the welfare not only of those of the household of God but of all" (*To Change the World: The Irony, Tragedy, and Possibility of Christianity in the Late Modern World* [New York: Oxford University Press, 2010], 254). Thus he envisions the church forming people who are sent into the contested terrain of the earthly city: "The vocation of the church is to bear witness to and to be the embodiment of the coming Kingdom of God." This outpost of the "new creation" comprises "a different people and an alternative culture that is, nevertheless, integrated within the present culture" (95–96). This is why "beyond the worship of God and the proclamation of his word, the central ministry of the church is one of formation; of making disciples," and that means equipping the people of God so they can "learn to live with and reflect in life the dialectical tension of affirmation and antithesis" (236–37).

idolatries of the public world. It points representatively to the acknowledgment of the true God by all the nations, in the universal worship for which the whole creation is destined.[6]

In this sense, because worship is so central to the drama of the book of Revelation, what Bauckham says about the book of Revelation is equally true of worship:

> One of the functions of Revelation [or of worship] was to purge and to re-furbish the Christian imagination. It tackles people's imaginative response to the world, which is at least as deep and influential as their intellectual convictions. It recognizes the way a dominant culture, with its images and ideals, constructs the world for us, so that we perceive and respond to the world in its terms. Moreover, it unmasks this dominant construction of the world as an ideology of the powerful which serves to maintain their power. In its place, Revelation offers a different way of perceiving the world which leads people to resist and to challenge the effects of the dominant ideology. Moreover, since this different way of perceiving the world is fundamentally to open it to transcendence it resists any absolutizing power or structures or ideals within this world. This is the most fundamental way in which the church is called always to be counter-cultural.[7]

Building on my exegesis of the "social imaginary" carried in Christian worship in *Desiring the Kingdom*, this chapter will articulate the dynamics of the church/world, the kingdom/nation dynamics that are rehearsed in worship—which is itself a rehearsal of the biblical narrative. I will do so by offering a summary commentary on Oliver O'Donovan's seminal work, particularly *The Desire of the Nations*, in dialogue with Bernd Wannenwetsch's *Political Worship*. The animating conviction here is that worship is its own well for public theology. We don't need to come up with a theological "justification" for connecting worship and public life, because worship narrates an understanding of public life *internal* to its practice. Our task is simply to make explicit what is already implicit in the liturgy.

6. Richard Bauckham, *The Theology of the Book of Revelation* (Cambridge: Cambridge University Press, 1993), 161. It is therefore interesting to also see Hunter highlight the importance of imagination in this context (*To Change the World*, 42).

7. Bauckham, *Revelation*, 159–60. Bauckham goes on to note that "Revelation's prophetic critique is of the churches as much as of the world. It recognizes that there is a false religion not only in the blatant idolatries of power and prosperity, but also in the constant danger that true religion falsify itself in compromise with such idolatries and betrayal of the truth of God. Again, this is the relevance of Revelation's theocentric emphasis on worship and truth. The truth of God is known in genuine worship of God" (162).

To Think About: The Unveiling of a King

Because the political language of kingship, citizenship, and "reign" is so woven into the Scriptures and the language of Christian worship, it is easy for its political import to slide past our attention. This requires a renewed liturgical catechesis that wakes us up to the political claims embedded in our worship. Think of such an exercise as being like the "decoder" games that children used to find in cereal boxes: the pictures on the back of the box carried "hidden messages" that couldn't be seen with the naked eye, but the treasure inside was a decoder device that, when used to magnify the images on the cereal box, unveiled the hidden messages and scenes.

We do well to run a kind of "political decoder" over the familiar language and practices of Christian worship. The goal of the exercise is to "reveal" what's been right in front of us all along: a gospel that revolves around a Lamb on a *throne* who has made a *people* "from every tribe and language and people and nation" to be "a *kingdom* and priests to serve our God, and they will *reign* on the earth" (Rev. 5:9–10). This is not the language of a merely "spiritual" message that promises escape from the vicissitudes of political life; it is the good news of another politics. We are not liberated *from* politics; we are liberated by a King who makes us citizens of a *polis* whose lamp is the Lamb (Rev. 21:23).

This sensibility is woven into our worship, even our daily worship. For example, during Epiphany—a season of unveiling, recalling the three kings who paid homage to Herod's infant rival—I was struck by the opening passages in the Book of Common Prayer's morning prayer rite:

> Nations shall come to your light, and kings to the brightness of your rising. *Isaiah 60:3*

> I will give you as a light to the nations, that my salvation may reach to the end of the earth. *Isaiah 49:6b*

> From the rising of the sun to its setting my Name shall be great among the nations, and in every place incense shall be offered to my Name, and a pure offering: for my Name shall be great among the nations, says the Lord of hosts. *Malachi 1:11*[a]

As we awake, this rite awakens us to the cosmic politics of Jesus's reign. Our morning prayers are also political rites, by which we participate in what the King is doing, praying "thy kingdom come," looking forward to the time when the nations will walk by the light of the Lamb and the nations of the earth will be welcomed into the heavenly *polis* (Rev. 21:24–26).

a. "Daily Morning Prayer: Rite One," *Book of Common Prayer . . . according to the Use of the Episcopal Church* (New York: Oxford University Press, 1990).

Worship as an Irruption *in* and *for* the World

We don't have to undertake any intellectual acrobatics to link the church and politics; we don't need to extrapolate "applications" to connect worship with citizenship. Political practice and intervention are "internal to the practice" of Christian worship (as Pierre Bourdieu would say).[8] Christian worship is already, inherently a *political* act. The proclamation of the Word is the rehearsal of a liberation narrative for a royal priesthood, the announcement of a *euangelion* that rivals Caesar's. The Table is a revolutionary meal in which even the "are nots" (1 Cor. 1:28) are invited to sit at the King's table. The weekly gathering of the saints is a rite that rehearses their heavenly citizenship.

And the church's worship is not just an "alternative" *polis* of a secluded enclave; it is always already a political *intervention* in "the world." The doxological claim "Jesus is Lord!" (*Iesus kyrios!*) is also a political act in its refusal to say "Caesar is Lord!"[9] In the mundane reality of Christians gathering to worship, Bernd Wannenwetsch observes,

> men and women repeatedly disengage from the comings and goings of the world, with its inextricably tangled web of the moral and the immoral, so as to enter into God's rest; and this witnesses to the fact that the world may revolve on its axis, but its life does not depend on its own frenetic activity. The future of the world cannot be secured by morality, nor can immorality destroy it. The external testimony of worship is intrinsic to its very existence as an interruption of the course of the world, and this testimony subjects all total claims to an ultimate criticism.[10]

We undergo the transformative "spiritual work" of *leitourgia* (Rom. 12:1) in order to be transformed, rather than being conformed to the world; and yet even this is *for the sake of the world*.[11] Formed for the hard work of discernment and judgment, we are to see through what the world calls "good" in order to discern what is truly good, true, and beautiful. Thus "devoted service on behalf of the world includes the criticism that tests the world."[12]

Indeed, the church's worship has political spillover effects for those who might never darken the door of the sanctuary. Not only does worship shape heavenly citizens who are sent to love their neighbors; there is also an important sense in which Christ's redemptive work in the body of Christ renews

8. See James K. A. Smith, *Imagining the Kingdom: How Worship Works*, Cultural Liturgies 2 (Grand Rapids: Baker Academic, 2013), 153–54.

9. See my discussion of N. T. Wright in James K. A. Smith, "Christian Worship as Public Disturbance," in *The Devil Reads Derrida: And Other Essays on the University, the Church, Politics, and the Arts* (Grand Rapids: Eerdmans, 2009), 71–77.

10. Bernd Wannenwetsch, *Political Worship: Ethics for Christian Citizens*, trans. Margaret Kohl (Oxford: Oxford University Press, 2004), 5.

11. Wannenwetsch rightly notes that the "mind" (*nous*) that is transformed here is "the organ of perception in the widest sense—practical judgment" (ibid., 37).

12. Ibid., 38.

society in more systemic ways. The Spirit-ed, sanctified, sacramental renewal of practical judgment includes, as Joan Lockwood O'Donovan describes it, "the renewal of moral agency" that has a spillover effect: "The renewal of moral agency and action in sinful human society springs from the practice of evangelical proclamation centered in common worship, and not from the practice of political judgment."[13] The church's *political* work is exercised in "proclaiming rather than judging."[14] Thus the proclamation of the Word constitutes a "public legal pedagogy": "The architects of English church establishment . . . made a distinctive contribution to the safeguarding of evangelical freedom in their discernment of the paradigmatic role of public worship in the renewal of human moral community. Archbishop Cranmer and his reforming circle, who designed a vernacular liturgical order for the reformed church in England, understand that human goods are decisively appropriated where the community hears and receives God's revealed judgments in their manifoldness, encompassing all the intentions, decisions, and actions by which he determines his human and non-human creatures."[15] The renewal of moral agency is not moral training for a rapture launch; it is the formation of a people who, in the *saeculum*, share terrain—and political responsibility—with their neighbors:

> The English liturgies take seriously the petition of our Savior's prayer: "Thy kingdom come. Thy will be done on earth, *as it is* in heaven." For they set forth as a present hope a communion of persons whose equality resides in their liberty and their liberty in their single obedience to God's will. In all their acts of obedient proclamation, the faithful stand along side one another as equal beneficiaries of God's merciful and saving judgments; they do not stand above their fellows, exercising judgment on them. They also stand along side those who have not yet heard or received God's saving judgment in Christ, to whom they are commissioned, as servants of the Spirit's work, to speak God's word of grace. With these neighbors they share equally in the universal vocation of all humanity to recover its full being, dignity and glory through communion with God in Christ, the everlasting *imago dei*.[16]

The church's worship does not "become" political when it is translated into policy or hooked to partisan agendas. The politics of worship is tied to the renewal of moral agency of the people of God, who are formed to be

13. Joan Lockwood O'Donovan, "The Liberal Legacy of English Church Establishment: A Theological Contribution to the Legal Accommodation of Religious Plurality in Europe," *Journal of Law, Philosophy and Culture* 4, no. 1 (2011): 31.

14. Ibid., 32.

15. Ibid., 33.

16. Ibid., 38.

sent. In this sense, the very fact of Christian worship is a twofold political act involving the formation of political agents and the proclamation *to* legislators and lawmakers that the created order of culture is subject to a higher law.[17]

> In displaying the eschatological determination of human moral agency and action by God's word of judgment given in Jesus Christ, the church's public worship also defines and empowers the secular determination of moral community by the practice of political judgment. The church's central liturgical act of such defining and empowering is the ordered reading of the Scriptures,[18] which provide the ultimate measure, not only of true proclamation, but of just political judgment in ecclesiastical and secular polity. For the mainstream English Reformers, the authority, purposes and limitations of political judgment, as well as the principles of communal right, justice and obligation have been definitively revealed to God's chosen people: to the "Old Israel" by God's appointed giver and interpreters of His law, and to the "New Israel" by the example, commands and judgments of Christ and his apostles.[19]

Worship is not a rehearsal of a "natural law" that can be known by reason or conscience; it is the restor(y)ing of a renewed humanity who are liturgically schooled. The index and criterion for justice and the right ordering of society is not some generic, universal, or "natural" canon but rather the revealed, biblical story unfolded in God's covenant relationship with Israel and the church. It is to the lineaments of this story that we now turn.

The Desire of the Nations

What is rehearsed in worship is, primarily, the ongoing story of God's covenant with his people.[20] This is why Christian worship is a re-narration of

17. "When the work of coercive jurisdiction, whether at the national or international level, does not acknowledge its determination by the eschatological renewal of human freedom through the church's proclamation, it inevitably becomes . . . an instrument of humanity's enslavement to the law of sin and condemnation rather than an instrument of God's preserving judgment" (ibid., 31).

18. O'Donovan emphasizes the way in which Cranmer's lectionary was a work of renewed moral agency and public legal pedagogy: "Cranmer planned his lectionary to cover the bulk of the *Old Testament* in the course of one year, the *New Testament* (excepting the *Book of the Apocalypse*) every four months, and the *Psalter* every month" (ibid., 36n55).

19. Ibid., 38. O'Donovan notes that while "late scholastic and renaissance theories of natural law (right, justice) . . . gave epistemological priority to unassisted reason over Biblical revelation," such strategies "were not much in evidence among Cranmer's clerical reforming colleagues" (38).

20. See Michael Horton's account of worship as a "covenant renewal" ceremony in *A Better Way: Rediscovering the Drama of God-Centered Worship* (Grand Rapids: Baker Books, 2003), 19–25. Given my focus on O'Donovan in what follows, I should note that Jonathan Chaplin

To Think About: The Lectionary as Political Drama

At the heart of the imagination-forming practices of Christian worship is the Story of God in Christ reconciling the world to himself (2 Cor. 5:19). Thus the narrative spine of Christian worship is Scripture itself. But this isn't just the *preached* Word—a sermon-centric claim that prioritizes the didactic. Rather, in historic Christian worship, Scripture is woven through the entirety of the liturgy: from the call to worship, through confession; in the promise of the gospel in the assurance of pardon; in psalms sung; in readings from the Old Testament, New Testament, and Gospels; in the rehearsal of the passion in the Eucharist; even in the benediction. Unlike sermon-centric congregations that profess "high views of Scripture" but leave the reading of the Bible to the preacher's whim and circumscribe it within "sermon time," in catholic Christian worship the Bible isn't just the focus of preaching; it is the lexicon of the entire service of worship.

"How, then, does the Church submit itself to the authority of Scripture?" Oliver O'Donovan asks. "In the first place—and forgive me if this sounds too simple, but it is of cardinal importance—the Church *reads* Holy Scripture. Faith expressed in *reading* is the discipline by which the Holy Spirit binds our lives and their practical questions into the central drama of history."[a]

This is why, O'Donovan continues, "liturgical practice can be no better than the lectionary that supports it." Thus one of the key historic disciplines of the catholic liturgical heritage is some form of a lectionary (*kalendar*) whereby worshiping congregations would be taken through the whole of Scripture, hearing the whole counsel of God, including those parts that challenge our own preferences and haunt our learned political leanings. Any congregation whose worship is governed by the lectionary will be confronted by widows, orphans, and strangers all year long. Thomas Cranmer, for example, in his work creating the Book of Common Prayer, was most interested in liturgical reform precisely as a means of renewing the reading of Scripture. "Indeed," comments Alan Jacobs, "one could argue that Cranmer's chief reason for implementing standard liturgies was to provide a venue in which the Bible could be more widely and more thoroughly known."[b] Insofar as hearing the whole counsel of God is a political discipline, the lectionary is a rite of the kingdom of God.

a. Oliver O'Donovan, "What Kind of Community Is the Church?," *Ecclesiology* 3 (2007): 190–91.
b. Alan Jacobs, *The "Book of Common Prayer": A Biography* (Princeton: Princeton University Press, 2013), 26–27.

who we are and whose we are. Liturgy is the enactment of the Story in a way that sinks into our imagination.[21] It is the *specifics* of that story—and that

has rightly asked why the theological notion of covenant plays so little role in O'Donovan's theological genealogy of Western liberalism. See Jonathan Chaplin, "Political Eschatology and Responsible Government: Oliver O'Donovan's 'Christian Liberalism,'" in *A Royal Priesthood? The Use of the Bible Ethically and Politically: A Dialogue with Oliver O'Donovan*, ed. Craig Bartholomew, Jonathan Chaplin, Robert Song, and Al Wolters, Scripture and Hermeneutics 3 (Grand Rapids: Zondervan, 2002), 265–308, esp. 272–73.

21. This is the focus of my argument in *Imagining the Kingdom*, chaps. 3–4.

history—that distinguish the unique "political" imaginary of the people of God. The *substance* of the story is what delineates the ethos of this Christ-following, Spirit-empowered *polis*.

Oliver O'Donovan's groundbreaking work *The Desire of the Nations* is an extended exegesis of that story and history, teasing out the political imagination that is carried in the Scriptures and, in turn, forms the spine of the church's liturgical practice. So my primary goal in this chapter is to unpack the political imaginary of Christian worship by means of a summary exposition of O'Donovan's own exegesis. As we do so, our task is to make explicit the political theology that is implicit in Christian worship.

But to do that we have to overcome two common temptations. First, we have to avoid the temptation to look at worship—and the Scriptures that enliven worship—as fuel that simply underwrites "politics as we know it." Worship doesn't somehow *become* political when we think we hear some "application" to a pressing matter of current policy concern. Worship isn't political only to the extent that it can be marshaled and invoked in contemporary partisan debates; it is always already political insofar as liturgy is the rite of citizens of the heavenly city. Second, we have to avoid the temptation of limiting our definition of the "political" to what we have experienced in the nations, states, and municipalities of this earthly sojourn. What counts as politics is older than both our democracies and tyrannical dictatorships. There are more kingdoms in heaven and earth than are dreamt of in our political philosophies. "The Kingdom of God," O'Donovan points out, "is not a mere kingdom, but it is a real kingdom." So we need to be careful "not to reduce the semantic range of speech about God's acts to the limits of our commonplace political discussion . . . but to push back the horizon of commonplace politics and open it up to the activity of God."[22] This is at the very heart of O'Donovan's project: discerning the activity of God in our "commonplace politics." With this opening move, O'Donovan is pushing back on our tendency to merely "naturalize" politics.[23]

---

22. Oliver O'Donovan, *The Desire of the Nations: Rediscovering the Roots of Political Theology* (Cambridge: Cambridge University Press, 1996), 2 (hereafter cited in text as *DN*).

23. This is a dynamic, historical equivalent of emphasizing, per Abraham Kuyper, that there is not a single square inch of creation over which Christ does not say "Mine!" Indeed, one could suggest that Kuyper's methodology in his Stone Lecture on politics was somewhat akin to O'Donovan's methodology here: discerning and narrating the activity of God in the unfolding of political realities of the West (though Kuyper's story, for understandable reasons, was narrowly focused on Calvinism as the engine of God's renewing activity). See Abraham Kuyper, "Calvinism and Politics," in *Lectures on Calvinism* (Grand Rapids: Eerdmans, 1943), 78–108. My sense, however, is that later Neocalvinism would be less comfortable with such an unapologetically providentialist account of political development. In

Thus a crucial methodological conviction undergirds O'Donovan's exercise in political theology: that there is a fundamental *analogy* between the political vocabulary of salvation—terms like "kingdom," "nation," "liberation," and "people"—and the secular use of the same political terms. They don't mean exactly the same thing, but there is a resonance and overlap—"an analogy grounded in reality—between the acts of God and human acts, both of them taking place within the one public history which is the theatre of God's saving purposes and mankind's social undertakings" (*DN*, 2). This is a reminder of something at the heart of the gospel that is rehearsed in every gathering for Christian worship: we celebrate and remember the acts of a living Lord who breaks into history, who called to himself covenant partners in the "public history" of humankind, from Adam to Abraham to Jesus and even the gentiles. A political theology is not just the application of ideals; it is learning how to inhabit this history of divine action that—in scandalous particularity—is tethered to particular times and places ("in the time of Herod king of Judea," in the days that "Caesar Augustus issued a decree," "under Pontius Pilate"). So the acts of God in history, rehearsed and celebrated in worship, are themselves *political* acts, providing analogical signals and clues as to what God's rule looks like, and what it might mean to hope and pray "thy kingdom come." If in the meantime of our "secular" waiting we hope to see earthly politics bent, if ever so slightly, toward the kingdom of God, our imaginations will need to be bathed in this history of God's acts in order to discern what is kingdom-like in the continued providence by which God *still* acts in history.[24] God's saving actions in history are the canon and criterion by which we make political judgments today.[25] So we read and absorb biblical history in order to be able to discern what God is doing.

At the same time, we read this "public history" of human sociopolitical life ("mankind's social undertakings") as an arena in which God also acts. So while the canonical Scriptures are the canon and criterion of our political imagination, we also "read" political history more broadly in order to discern how God's in-breaking into history has impacted and continues to impact our bottom-up political experiments. The strategy here is *analogical* because it postulates an overlap (not an identification) between God's saving acts and

---

this respect, an encounter with O'Donovan might be a catalyst to remember themes we've forgotten.

24. This is why providence is so central to both O'Donovan's project and its progenitor, Augustine's *City of God*. Cf. Stephen H. Webb, *American Providence: A Nation with a Mission* (New York: Continuum, 2004).

25. Cf. William Abraham, *Canon and Criterion in Christian Theology: From the Fathers to Feminism* (New York: Oxford University Press, 1998).

human political endeavors. As O'Donovan summarizes, "Earthly events of liberation, rule and community-foundation provide us with partial indications of what God is doing in human history; while, correspondingly, we must look to the horizon of God's redemptive purposes if we are to grasp the full meaning of political events that pass before our eyes. Theology needs more than scattered political images; it needs a full political conceptuality. And politics, for its part, needs a theological conceptuality. The two are concerned with the one history that finds its goal in Christ, 'the desire of the nations'" (*DN*, 2).

Christian political theology is scriptural not only because it is interested in a "canonized" political entity like Israel but also because it is a biblical imagination that enables us to discerningly "read the signs of the times" in our own political contexts. Historic Christian worship rehearses the canon of Scripture *and* the drama of God's saving action in its own dramatic performance, providing a way for this scriptural narrative to sink into our bones and become the social imaginary by which we "read" the political.[26] This is not a matter of using "hard-edged political concepts to illuminate [so-called] spiritual realities," as if we merely move "from 'core' political concepts to the Kingdom of God as from the known to the unknown" (*DN*, 119). That would be to take earthly politics as the standard. "Precisely the opposite movement is called for," O'Donovan counsels. "Can we not be introduced to a kind of rule that is unlike, as well as like, the kind of rule with which we are familiar? And can we not be taught to conceive of living within law in a manner unlike, as well as like, the litigious culture we associate with lawcourts? The first assumption of political theology must be that these analogies are valid, and that through them the Gospel of the Kingdom offers liberation to an imprisoned political culture. Political aspirations find their true satisfaction in these unlikely likenesses" (*DN*, 119).

Political theology—and, one hopes, faithful political action—must be "prophetic," he concludes, but not merely in the sense of being critical, denouncing false prophets. The judgment of "true prophets . . . consists precisely in what they have to say of God's purposes of renewal, his mercy towards even such weak and frangible societies as Israel and Judah" (*DN*, 11). Thus "Christian theology must assume the prophet's task, and, accepting history as the matrix in which politics and ethics take form, affirm that it is the history of God's action, not sheer contingency but purpose." Any truly prophetic critique and identification of purpose, then, needs what we've called a canon and criterion:

26. Indeed, I would argue that O'Donovan's singular, seminal work in *Desire of the Nations*—with its astounding blend of biblical exposition, theological discernment, political acuity, and historical insight—was made possible, in no small part, by O'Donovan's own liturgical formation.

some outline of the substance of how things *ought* to be, some delineation of what "kingdom come" looks like. "The prophet needs a point of view from which it is possible to criticise without criticism becoming a mere form, empty of substance. The prophet is not allowed the luxury of perpetual subversion. After Ahab, Elijah must anoint some Hazael, some Jehu" (*DN*, 12).[27]

This is also why political theology must be *Christian* and not merely theistic or governed by the lower bar of "natural law."[28] The political is not a merely temporal, earthly reality that can be understood as a feature of "nature" apart from the reign of the risen Christ. The political falls within the scope of "all things" that Christ creates, redeems, and rules (Col. 1). Again, this cuts both ways. "Theology must be political if it is to be evangelical," O'Donovan asserts. "Rule out the political questions and you cut short the proclamation of God's saving power; you leave people enslaved where they ought to be set free from sin—their own sin and others'" (*DN*, 3). Conversely, the political must be read in light of God's acts, not least the cross, resurrection, and ascension of Jesus Christ. "Israel's history must be read as a *history of redemption*, which is to say, as the story of how certain principles of social and political life were vindicated by the action of God in the judgment and restoration of the people" (*DN*, 29). So political theology can't merely traffic in the naturalized conceptions of the political that have been rendered believable in the immanent frame of modernity. Political theology must be underwritten by the specificity of the scriptural narrative of God's saving work in Israel and Jesus, "attesting the claim that Yhwh reigns." It is precisely because Christian political theology is historical that it is both specifically christological and specifically missional, rooted in what we know of the history of redemption revealed in the Scriptures. "Its subject is God's rule demonstrated and vindicated, the salvation that he has wrought in Israel and the nations. Unless it speaks in that way it can only advance a theological type of political theory, not an evangelical political theology, a 'Law,' in the theological sense, rather than a 'Gospel'" (*DN*, 81).

A gospel-ed political imagination draws on the wells of God's covenantal history with Israel, Jesus, and his body, the church. The only proper frame for a political theology is the "canonical history" of Israel, a history that culminates in the life of Christ, who recapitulates the calling of Israel (*DN*,

---

27. See Roger Stronstad, *The Prophethood of All Believers: A Study in Luke's Charismatic Theology* (Sheffield: Sheffield Academic Press, 1999), and Amos Yong's commentary in *In the Days of Caesar: Pentecostalism and Political Theology* (Grand Rapids: Eerdmans, 2010), 239–44.

28. This will be discussed in much more detail in chap. 5 below.

21).[29] And it is this canonical history that we absorb in Christian worship. To exegete the narrative arc of Christian worship is to sketch the outline of the *substance* of this (hi)story of redemption that is political.

O'Donovan unpacks this in terms of "political concepts": political concepts shape our descriptions of political realities, which, in turn, prime and direct our political action and policy making. So it is crucial that we discover "true political concepts" that will govern all of this. If we believe that Christ has been revealed as King of kings (Rev. 17:14), that before him every knee shall bow (Phil. 2:10), then the revelation of the Son is the disclosure of true kingship that is also revealed insight into the nature and calling of the political. Thus a self-described Christian political theology, O'Donovan emphasizes, must find true political concepts in the revelatory history of the canonical Scriptures (*DN*, 15). And such concepts are first tacitly absorbed on the register of the imagination.[30] The sources for such an imaginary are found in the Scriptures, of course, but they are absorbed through the performed enactment of that redemptive history in the liturgies of Christian worship. So we need to be immersed in such formative worship in order to curate a Christian political imagination that primes us to *see* the world through a kingdom lens. On the other hand, the task of a political *theology* is to make explicit the political vision that is implicit in the scriptural narrative of worship. O'Donovan's *Desire of the Nations* amounts to a reading of this covenantal history of God and his people, culminating in Christ, as a reservoir for political concepts. It is to this reading that we turn as a way to hear the same (political) story in Christian worship.

The Reign of God

At the heart of this covenantal history is "the reign of God." In worship, when we rehearse the drama of Scripture, we are learning to place "political

29. On this point, O'Donovan's reading resonates with N. T. Wright's reading of the Israel-Jesus-church relationship in *The New Testament and the People of God* (Minneapolis: Fortress, 1992). J. Kameron Carter rightly points out what happens when this covenant history is forgotten and "Christianity" is abstracted into an ahistorical "belief system." It is precisely when that happens that we also see the emergence of "whiteness" as the new default paradigm. "Its accomplishment," Carter remarks, "was one in which Eastern, mainly Gentile, Christians no longer had to interpret their existence inside another story—Israel's. Rather, its accomplishment was to make Israel's story a moment within understanding the story of Western civilization as the story of white accomplishment. In this sense, Israel's story was made white: was made a moment within the mythical-poetic imagination of the West" (*Race: A Theological Account* [New York: Oxford University Press, 2008], 261). We will return to these themes in chap. 6 below.

30. See *Imagining the Kingdom*, chap. 4.

history within the history of God's reign" (*DN*, 19). This central and political reality is as old as creation. Indeed, "the history of divine rule safeguards and redeems the goods of creation. . . . When we speak of divine rule, we speak of the fulfilment promised to all things worldly and human. To judge politics in the light of the divine rule is to be assured of its world-affirming and humane character" (*DN*, 19). God's rule is not an antinatural tyranny but more like the authority of the gardener who husbands creation to its fullness.[31] Indeed, all the subsequent history of God's relationship with his people is continuous with this original covenant with creation such that now the only appropriate lenses to truly see creation are Israel and Jesus. The reign of Christ is the restoration, realization, and intensification of this "creational" rule: "The moment of resurrection does not appear like an isolated meteor from the sky but as the climax of a history of the divine rule" (*DN*, 20).

But this means that, even though divine rule originates with creation and applies to human history in its entirety, insight into creation—including politics—is now dependent on God's special revelation and his scandalously particular covenant with Israel that culminates in Jesus. True political concepts are not generic or generally available via "nature" or "reason" or common grace. As O'Donovan puts it, "The hermeneutic principle that governs a Christian appeal to political categories within the Hebrew Scriptures is, simply, Israel itself. Through this unique political entity God made known his purposes in the world." So the "governing principle" of a Christian political theology is "the kingly rule of God, expressed in Israel's corporate existence and brought to final effect in the life, death and resurrection of Jesus" (*DN*, 27). This canonical, covenantal history is the well from which normative political insights must be drawn in order to then "read" the contingent political histories within which we find ourselves.[32] But our first task is to understand the *whole* of this canonical history. "We may not appeal to the Exodus for the deliverance of the poor," as liberation theologians do, "and then avoid mention of the conquest of Canaan" (*DN*, 27). Rather, "Israel's history must be read as a *history of redemption*, which is to say, as the story of how certain principles of social and political life were vindicated by the action of God in the judgment and restoration of the people" (*DN*, 29).[33] We need to discerningly read the *whole*

31. This is why the only appropriate lens for reading human political history is the lens of special revelation; any "natural" concepts will be proven inadequate, even untrue. To naturalize the political is to obfuscate it.

32. "Failure to attend to Israel is what left Christian political thought oscillating between idealist and realist poles" (*DN*, 27). Cf. Carter's persistent cautions about the dangers of forgetting the Jewishness of Jesus in *Race*, e.g., 167–87.

33. O'Donovan recognizes that this is an act of *theological* interpretation of Scripture, a confessional project: "To turn to Israel is already a step of faith on the theologian's part"

of this history to identify the political imaginary that is authorized by it—not merely looking for biblical license for our contemporary political sensibilities, but also being open to our political predilections being challenged by what God has done with and through Israel, realized in Jesus. "This means that any question about social forms and structures must be referred to a normative critical standard: do they fulfil that will of God for human society to which Israel's forms authoritatively point us?" (*DN*, 25). The criteria here are revelational, canonical, and scriptural and are rehearsed in the repertoire of historic Christian worship.

Picturing Political History Otherwise: *Hidden Figures*

If CNN were reporting from Jerusalem in the first century, it's not at all likely that yet another criminal, crucified on the outskirts of town, would have even registered on its radar of newsworthy events. The drama of Jesus before Pilate—the riveting, world-changing story that is the culminating passion narrative of the four Gospels—would, at the time, have been a skirmish of a religious minority and of little concern to the machinations of the empire. Indeed, the drama of the passion only makes sense if we realize it is the defining episode in the ongoing drama of Israel's covenantal relationship with God. And these first-century events only register on the historical radar now because the one who would have appeared to be a disdained criminal or disruptive zealot to our mythical ancient CNN cameras would go on to become a risen, ascended King. Retrospect, and the retrospective frame of faith in revelation, transform what we recognize as world changing.

Cinema of late has reflected this. While there is a long-standing tradition that focuses on winners, heroes, and fortune's favorites, reinforcing our official grand narratives and textbook histories, over the past generation we have become attuned to those overlooked by "history"—or by, at least, our *telling* of history. While our textbook histories have focused on men, it has often been novels and film that have told the heretofore ignored stories of women; while our standard accounts have focused on white, European actors, cinema and literature have ventured to remind us of the persons of color they either ground underfoot *or*, in fact, depended upon; while we have constructed histories so that the usual suspects occupy center stage and a host of characters are relegated to the margins, revisionist cinema has not only shone a light on the margins, but it has challenged the very typesetting of our collective stories and put the marginalized in the center of the page where they belong.

(*DN*, 28). This is also why the reading of Israel's history is always an exercise in christological theological interpretation. For relevant discussion of such a hermeneutic, see Richard B. Hays, *Reading Backwards: Figural Christology and the Fourfold Gospel Witness* (Waco: Baylor University Press, 2016).

An early example of this ploy is Tom Stoppard's 1990 play-become-film *Rosencrantz and Guildenstern Are Dead*. In this retelling of *Hamlet* from the margins, Rosencrantz and Guildenstern, two minor characters in Shakespeare's tragedy, become the stars of Stoppard's comedy. While the movie intersects with Shakespeare's drama "on stage," so to speak, it mostly zooms in on the otherwise hidden lives and desires of Rosencrantz and Guildenstern as the main action. And when these "minor" characters make a fateful decision onboard a ship bound for England, they end up making an impact on the world-historical stage.

But perhaps better examples are more recent, precisely because they are dramatic retellings of actual historic events rather than the restaging of something that was already staged. Consider, for example, *The Imitation Game*—a very different kind of World War II movie, one that doesn't focus on Winston Churchill or D-Day commanders or daring Air Force dog fighters but instead on an awkward Cambridge mathematician named Alan Turing. Turing is the sort of character who is not only ignored; he is shunned, disdained, and suppressed because of his sexual orientation in a world that would have still felt "Victorian." But for months the Allied Forces have suffered heavy casualties and repeated military failures simply because the Germans have developed a way to encrypt their communications that is "unbreakable." The Enigma machine translates all Nazi communiques into a secret code that no one from the vast arsenal of intellectual firepower in England, France, Russia, or the United States has been able to break. As a result of this intelligence failure, countless lives are being lost. And so British mathematician Turing asks for a shot. A problem solver who is only energized when he's told something is impossible, Turing works with a team to create an anti-Enigma machine, The Bombe, that is finally capable of cracking the code. As a result, a mathematician achieves a military victory that rivals any of the masterful logistics of generals or the death-defying courage of soldiers. But it is not the sort of story that has traditionally been celebrated in our cinematic histories of war. And yet *The Imitation Game* brings a different lens, a different kind of focal attention, to the same history and shows us something we wouldn't have known otherwise, even awakening us to our debts to a lonely, persecuted mathematician.

Interestingly, mathematicians are the stars of another historical reframing movie: the Academy Award–nominated *Hidden Figures* (based on a *New York Times* bestseller of the same name). The story takes us back to the 1960s space race. Endeavoring to send its first man into orbit, NASA has trouble calculating launch and re-entry trajectories. The brains and talent they need—the "human computers" who solve the problem—are found in "figures" who have been hidden and doubly marginalized by American society: black women. Enduring heartbreaking discrimination from the white men who dominate the halls of NASA, these talented mathematicians—particularly the prodigy Katherine Johnson—are the lifeline for John Glenn as he blasts from the launch pad. While the Mercury space program has been heralded for years, these key players in the world-changing story were ignored, relegated to the silent sidelines of history just as these women were relegated to the segregated West Area Computers section of Langley. Margot Lee Shetterly's book, and the ensuing movie, reframed history to show us the influence of figures previously hidden.

We might think of O'Donovan's exercise in *Desire of the Nations* as a similar reframing of history. In writing a theologically inflected political history, O'Donovan is inviting us to see the hidden figures in the story of Western liberal democracy. While we might expect a political history to focus on kings and emperors, revolutionaries and governors, O'Donovan argues that, in fact, it is the sources of special revelation and the history of God's relationship to his people that are the keys to unlocking the nature of the political. Hence, his focus on Israel and Jesus as the lenses for disclosing the nature of political authority: despite our habit of secularizing and naturalizing the political, in fact it is what we know on the basis of revelation and God's relationship with humanity that is fundamental to understanding the political vocation of humanity.

The same year that *Hidden Figures* was nominated for an Academy Award, actress Viola Davis won the Oscar for Best Supporting Actress for her role in *Fences*. In her acceptance speech, Davis appealed to film's unique ability to shine a light on the underside of history. "You know, there is one place that all the people with the greatest potential are gathered and that's the graveyard," she began. "People ask me all the time—what kind of stories do you want to tell, Viola?," she recalled. "And I say exhume those bodies. Exhume those stories." Recent film has done that: it has dug up stories of the forgotten, exhuming the influence of those we forgot or ignored or actively repressed. Oliver O'Donovan is doing something similar: he is digging up a political story we've buried. But in Israel's story, one of the bodies is gone. The King has risen from the dead. This changes everything. That's why O'Donovan has to tell the story.

-ℓℓ℘-

So what are the features and marks of Yahweh's kingly rule? What "true political concepts" are embedded in this history? What can we learn about politics from Yahweh the King's covenantal relationship with Israel? And what does this tell us about the political per se?[34]

34. As we'll see in the next chapter, this is not just the whimsical attempt of a Christian theologian to find political concepts in Israel's history or some kind of biblicist endeavor to uncover biblical justification for Christians to engage in politics. To the contrary, O'Donovan reads Israel's canonical and political history both for normative insights into the nature of the political and because Israel's history turns out to be *our* history. The political institutions and assumptions of Western constitutional liberalism are a legacy of this history. Cf. Eric Nelson, *The Hebrew Republic: Jewish Sources and the Transformation of European Political Thought* (Cambridge, MA: Harvard University Press, 2010). It's worth noting that Jürgen Habermas, in no way a Christian philosopher, makes the same point. In "A Conversation about God and the World," in *Time of Transitions* (London: Polity, 2006), he comments: "Egalitarian

Contrary to what we might expect, this is *not* a legitimation narrative in the spirit of "the divine right of kings." To the contrary, O'Donovan agrees with Martin Buber: one can "interpret Yhwh's kingship as an anti-monarchical idea" (*DN*, 35).[35] It is not a straightforward deduction from the reign of God to an inherently "conservative" politics that secures the rights and powers of the ruling class.[36] But neither does it license an inherently revolutionary model that demonizes such rule with equal simplicity. Instead, we need to look at the features and terms associated with Yahweh's rule in order to discern just what God's will is for flourishing human society. Thus O'Donovan highlights the "leading political terms that are habitually grouped" with God's kingship. He sees three:

1. *Salvation.* Yahweh is a liberator, a defender, a victor, a protector. Yahweh is the God and father who delivers his people, a history rehearsed over and over again in the Psalms, the hymnbook of the people of God ("The king rejoices in your strength, Lord [Yahweh]. How great is his joy in the victories you give!" [Ps. 21:1]). A political society is one that enjoys security and protection.

2. *Judgment.* As king, God exercises juridical authority as a righteous judge. "When 'judgment' is present, it is not a state of affairs that obtains but an activity that is duly carried out." So "when Amos calls for *mishpat* to 'roll on like a river,' he means precisely that the stream of juridical activity should not be allowed to dry up" (*DN*, 39). Yahweh will carry out righteous judgment on behalf of the fatherless, the widow, the alien and stranger. We can hear in this an echo of "fairness" given the stability of God's faithfulness and "divine decisiveness" (*DN*, 40). A society in which judgment is carried out justly, on behalf of the vulnerable, is a society that reflects the political norms of Yahweh.

---

universalism, from which sprang the ideas of freedom and social solidarity, of an autonomous conduct of life and emancipation, of the individual morality of conscience, human rights and democracy, is the direct heir of the Judaic ethic of justice and the Christian ethic of love. This legacy, substantially unchanged, has been the object of continual critical appropriation and reinterpretation. To this day, there is no alternative to it. And in light of the current challenges of a postnational constellation, we continue to draw on the substance of this heritage. Everything else is just idle postmodern talk" (150–51).

35. Cf. Peter Leithart's discussion of "monster ingratitude" in *Gratitude: An Intellectual History* (Waco: Baylor University Press, 2014), 99–120. It was, in a sense, the revelation of the Kingship of God that undermined the claims of earthly kings.

36. For a related discussion, see J. Richard Middleton, "Is Creation Theology Inherently Conservative? A Dialogue with Walter Brueggemann," *Harvard Theological Review* 87 (1994): 257–77.

3. *Possession.* While Yahweh gives Israel a possession and an inheritance ("the land"), this is "an assertion that Israel itself is Yhwh's possession. Possessing the gift, she is possessed by the giver" (*DN*, 41). What O'Donovan sees in this are the parameters that make it possible for a people to have an identity, an ethos, to be "a people." A people's inheritance is its tradition, the Story that governs its self-understanding and provides a fund for its moral imagination.

Now, why does this matter for us? Is this just an antiquarian endeavor? Given the methodology outlined above, this now becomes a lens for reading politics as such: "The unique covenant of Yhwh and Israel can be seen as a point of disclosure from which the nature of *all* political authority comes into view. Out of the self-possession of this people in their relation to God springs the possibility of other peoples' possessing themselves in God. In this hermeneutic assumption lay the actual continuity between Israel's experience and the Western tradition" (*DN*, 45, emphasis added).[37] In this respect, O'Donovan highlights two "theorems" about political authority as such.

The first is a descriptive or phenomenological observation about how political authority works: "Political authority arises where power, the execution of right and the perpetuation of tradition are assured together in one coordinated agency" (*DN*, 46). This is like a three-legged stool, and a political regime cannot stand without all three. Thus authority—and hence politics as such—is threatened by shifting social conditions that would jeopardize any one of these three conditions. Later O'Donovan says this is why individuals can be engines of social and political renewal: "To generalise . . . we may say that *the conscience of the individual members of a community is a repository of the moral understanding which shaped it, and may serve to perpetuate it in a crisis of collapsing morale or institution.* It is not as bearer of his own primitive pre-social or pre-political rights that the individual demands the respect of the community, but as the bearer of a social understanding which recalls the formative self-understanding of the community itself. The conscientious individual speaks with society's own forgotten voice" (*DN*, 80).[38]

The second is a normative claim (taking Israel's history as revealed salvation history): "That any regime should actually come to hold authority, and should continue to hold it, is a work of divine providence in history, not a

---

37. I will consider this history of Western democracy's debts to Israel in more detail in chap. 3 below.

38. Granted, this is also why the generational loss of such formative communities is a wider social threat; see the scenario of collective amnesia that opens MacIntyre, *After Virtue: A Study in Moral Theory* (Notre Dame, IN: University of Notre Dame Press, 1981), 1–2.

mere accomplishment of the human task of political service" (*DN*, 46). This is not synonymous with a divine *endorsement* of any and all enduring political regimes, but more an account of the conditions for a regime's perdurance. "Behind every historically successful regime, there is the divine regime of history. The continuity achieved by the one presupposes the operation of the other, because it does not lie within the power of political orders to secure the social conditions for their own indefinite prolongation" (*DN*, 46).

O'Donovan then adds a third pivotal theorem: "In acknowledging political authority, society proves its political identity." In other words, "Acknowledgement is the fundamental relation that obtains between a society and its own political authority" (*DN*, 47).

Picturing Resistance in Cormac McCarthy's *The Road*

As we noted, O'Donovan points to a *social* role for the individual. So a critique of in-dividual*ism* is not undertaken in the name of effacing the individual. At the heart of the gospel is a personal relation between God and individual that is sacred, and the individual formed by the Spirit can sometimes be a carrier of prophetic memory. As O'Donovan puts it, the individual can be "the bearer of a social understanding which recalls the formative self-understanding of the community itself. The conscientious individual speaks with society's own forgotten voice" (*DN*, 80).

We see this dynamic of social memory "carried" by an individual illustrated in the ruthless, postapocalyptic world of Cormac McCarthy's *The Road*, an exploration of human relationships after the destruction of the world. In *The Road* we see a reduction to what Giorgio Agamben calls "bare life." And what's left? Liturgy. Humanity reduced to "bare life," to *zōē*, remains a liturgical animal. If one begins to read the novel with these eyes—through this lens—even the barren landscape of this "bare life" has a litur-gical echo about it.[39]

> It's snowing, the boy said. He looked at the sky. A single gray flake sifting down. He caught it in his hand and watched it expire there like the last host of christendom.

> The boy sat tottering. The man watched him that he not topple into the flames. He kicked holes in the sand for the boy's hips and shoulders where he would sleep and he sat holding him while he tousled his hair before the fire to dry it. All of this like some ancient anointing. So be it. Evoke the forms. Where you've nothing else construct ceremonies out of the air and breathe upon them.

39. I'm not making any claims about authorial intent here. At the least, these aspects might be chalked up to the "afterimage" of McCarthy's Catholic upbringing.

The boy didn't stir. He sat beside him and stroked his pale and tangled hair. Golden chalice, good to house a god. Please dont tell me how the story ends.

Then they set out upon the road again, slumped and cowled and shivering in their rags like mendicant friars sent forth to find their keep.[40]

What's at stake in *The Road* is not just sacramentality but the matter of formation, and more specifically *moral* formation. Where did these characters come from who shine like lights in this brutal darkness? What were the father and son before this holocaust such that they are now these kinds of people, "carrying the fire," as the narrator puts it? What practices formed and shaped them? What rituals birthed in them certain moral boundaries, even shades of hope? What has the father passed on to the son? And how? Whence come their reservoirs of resistance?

I don't think McCarthy is suggesting that they have a kind of "natural" goodness about them. The humans who have become monsters all around them prove otherwise. Whether it is the father and son, or the family who finally welcome the boy into their care,[41] these characters are human animals who have been *formed* differently. This is not a return to a "state of nature" but a winnowing that shows up the effectiveness or ineffectiveness of practices and rituals that induce character formation. These characters are bearers of a prior formation, carrying the fire of a vision and a civilization that has been obliterated, and so their "individual" resistance is the legacy of what now looks like a foreign people. Perhaps this is what it means to be a people of a heavenly *polis* amidst the ruins of late modernity, "children of God without blemish in the midst of a crooked and twisted generation, among whom you shine as lights in the world" (Phil. 2:15 ESV).

Here is where O'Donovan identifies the intersection of politics and worship: just as Israel is Yahweh's "people" precisely because they acknowledge him in praise, so any political community will be constituted by a kind of acknowledgment that is worshipful, ascribing worth to some authority. "The community is a political community by virtue of being a worshiping community" (*DN*, 47). There is no politics without praise (*DN*, 48). This insight is both revelatory and cautionary. As O'Donovan asks,

Shall we conclude, then, that within every political society there occurs, implicitly, an act of worship of divine rule? I think we may even venture as far as that. . . . And it allows us to understand why it is precisely at this point that political

40. Cormac McCarthy, *The Road* (New York: Vintage, 2006), 16, 74, 75, and 126, respectively.
41. Ibid., 282.

loyalties can go so badly wrong; for a worship of divine-rule which has failed to recollect or understand the divine purpose can only be an idolatrous worship which sanctions an idolatrous politics. It sheds light, too, on the nature of the impasse into which a politics constructed on an avowedly anti-sacred bias has now come. For without the act of worship political authority is unbelievable, so that binding political loyalties and obligations seem to be deprived of any point. (*DN*, 49)[42]

Embedded in Israel's narrative is a transcending of tribalism—the conviction that because Yahweh is "a great king over all the earth" (Ps. 47:2 ESV), his "law can be extended in principle to other nations than Israel" (*DN*, 65). "The political structures of other nations had the same vocation to exercise just judgment as Israel's did" (*DN*, 68). Israel was called to model this, to show them how, not through colonial rule, but through witness.[43] Whether or not Israel succeeded in this (spoiler alert: Israel failed), this entails a *responsibility* of the nations. The nations are expected to obey God's rule, which is precisely why the prophets call the nations to account. It's also why, as we'll see, nations are still called to obey God's rule and, after the resurrection of Jesus, some will answer that call, albeit fallibly and imperfectly.

Jesus Is King

In the fullness of time, Jesus, born of a woman, arrives as the Son of David who will fulfill Israel's vocation. But the advent of the King also changes everything. We can see the clues of this in Jesus's own response to the regnant political authorities. O'Donovan's close reading of the synoptic episode regarding the census tax (Mark 12:13–17)—"Render unto Caesar what is Caesar's"—is illuminating. O'Donovan is critical of *spatialized* readings that imagine Jesus

42. He goes on to note the danger of political regimes not owning up to the necessity of worship: "The doctrine that *we* set up political authority, as a device to secure our own essentially private, local and unpolitical purposes, has left the Western democracies in a state of pervasive moral debilitation, which, from time to time, inevitably throws up idolatrous and authoritarian reactions" (*DN*, 49).

43. Here, O'Donovan notes, "we find a developing critique of empire" (*DN*, 70). Surveying the postexilic vision, we see that "the order of the future, when Israel shall have returned to her home, will be an internationally plural order, free from the unifying constraints of empire. The events of Israel's overthrow by the empire and her subsequent restoration will serve as a lesson and a model by which Yhwh will instruct the nations of the world. A family of humble nations will creep out from under the wreckage of the empires" (*DN*, 71). For more on international pluralism, see *DN*, 72.

is carving up distinct jurisdictions of authority.[44] "The census-tax story . . . allows us to rule out the view that Jesus assigned Roman government a certain uncontested sphere of secular right" (*DN*, 92). Instead, Jesus's announcement of his kingdom is one that is caught up in the dynamism of *time*. We must hear his announcement diachronically, not synchronically. In this sense, to give Caesar what is his is a bit like granting someone the right to occupy a building that has been condemned to demolition, or giving someone currency that is going to be decommissioned in the near future. O'Donovan articulates this by means of a modern parable:

> Imagine an official of the Russian Government in October 1991, confronted with some demand from the foundering Soviet authorities. "This is ridiculous!", he thinks to himself. "We will be running that ourselves by next week!" Yet to display open contempt would give the impression that the new authorities did not believe in constitutional government at all. So confident is he of the shape of the coming [post-Soviet] order, that he has no need of an insolent gesture to assert it against the order that is vanishing. Jesus, similarly, believed that a shift in the locus of power was taking place, which made the social institutions that had prevailed to that point anachronistic. His attitude to them was neither secularist nor zealot: since he did not concede that they had any future, he gave them neither dutiful obedience within their supposed sphere of competence nor the inverted respect of angry defiance. He did not recognize a permanently twofold locus of authority. He recognized only a transitory duality which belonged to the climax of Israel's history, a duality between the coming and the passing order. (*DN*, 92–93)

Note again the displacement of a *spatialized* politics to a politics of *time*. The question at issue in this episode is not jurisdictional (who rules what?) but temporal (who rules *now?*). The "Two Cities" are, in fact, "Two *Eras*" (*DN*, 93, emphasis added). The advent of the kingdom in Jesus is the dawn of a new age.

Jesus was not a zealot, because his focus wasn't the displacement of Rome but the renewal of Israel. "Jesus' concern," as O'Donovan puts it, "was with the reauthorising of Israel rather than with the deauthorising of Rome. The Temple, not the praetorium, was the seat of Yhwh's authority among his people. The appearance of true authority in Israel meant the unity of political and religious spheres under the rule of God. Obedience and worship were to be one and the same. . . . The Two Kingdoms period, in which Temple without power and praetorium without worship coexisted in some kind of parallel,

---

44. As O'Donovan puts it, the criterion for a proper reading of this episode is "to decide what the trap was that his answer avoided so successfully," since his audience was "astonished" (*DN*, 91).

> ### To Think About: The *Saeculum* as Pregnant Widow
>
> In Martin Amis's 2010 novel *The Pregnant Widow*, an aging hedonist reconsiders an Italian bohemian romp in the summer of 1970, zooming out to assess the so-called sexual revolution on a larger scale. Constructed around the story of Narcissus as told in Ted Hughes's rendering of *Tales of Ovid*, the conceit is the perfect platform for Amis's cutting humor and curmudgeonly criticism. The image of the "pregnant widow" is itself suggestive of a strange transition: impregnated by a man no longer alive, the widow will birth her child into a world fundamentally different from the one in which he was conceived. The image is taken from the Russian writer Alexander Herzen, in a passage Amis includes as an epigraph to the novel: "The death of the contemporary forms of social order ought to gladden rather than trouble the soul. Yet what is frightening is that the departing world leaves behind it not an heir, but a pregnant widow. Between the death of the one and the birth of the other, much water will flow by, a long night of chaos and desolation will pass."
>
> While Herzen and Amis invoke this image for quite different applications, it might also be suggestive as a way to understand the unique time of the *saeculum*, this long transition in which the whole world lies under the sway of the evil one (1 John 5:19) *and* Christ has overcome the world (John 16:33). In a way, the church is the new *polis* waiting to be born, the kingdom gestating amidst its rivals until the parousia when the present age will pass away and the advent of the King will be realized.

was declared closed" (*DN*, 117). The Christ-event that rent the temple curtain in two also obliterated the line demarcating these prior jurisdictions. Caesar's authority is "secular" not because he's in charge of the earth and Jesus reigns in heaven, but rather because, in light of the comprehensive reign of the ascended King, Caesar's authority in the *saeculum* is passing away. He's yesterday's ruler.

If the kingdom is embodied *in* the Son, then in Jesus we see a renewal of those features of political authority that Yahweh instituted in his covenant with Israel. But this requires that we resist what O'Donovan calls the lure of "Jesuology," the tendency to read Jesus as a political actor without situating him in the providential, redemptive *history* of which he is the culmination, or to separate the message of Jesus from the acts of God in his life, passion, cross, resurrection, and ascension. "Every political Jesuology offers a helpful illusion: let us model ourselves on Jesus, ignoring Caiaphas and Pilate; then we will at least achieve something" (*DN*, 121). But a "secure" political theology, O'Donovan counsels, "must base itself on 'the hidden counsel of God' which worked also through Caiaphas and Pilate" (*DN*, 122)—that is, through the providential institutions and actors that are also subject to the reign of God. Thus political theology has two modes. "Political theology in its liberal mode" is prophetic and critical: "Ideas of what government is must be corrected in the light of that imperious government which the Spirit wields through the conscience of each worshiper . . . attacking and overcoming the pretentiousness of the autonomous political order" (*DN*, 123). But there is also political theology in a constructive, ecclesiological mode that shows "how the extension of the Gospel of the Kingdom into the Paschal Gospel elevates, rather than destroys, our experience of community." Political theology in this ecclesiological mode "takes the church seriously as a society and shows how the rule of God is realized there. The independence, then, of the individual believer"—which political theology in its liberal mode may assert—"is not antisocial. It arises from the authority of another community, centred in the authority of the risen Christ" (*DN*, 123). This means that not only the life and teaching of Jesus have political relevance; also relevant is a full-orbed *Christology*, a robustly theological understanding of the Christ-event that comprises the life, death, resurrection, and ascension of the Son of God who is the Prince of Peace. "The Christological tradition belongs to the proclamation of the Kingdom of God" (*DN*, 123).[45] (And insofar as this event makes a dent on history, Christ's rule and authority also become "templates" of a sort for subsequent political history that we'll explore in chapter 3.)

So Christ's death, resurrection, and ascension signal something about the political features of the kingdom of God: *mediation* and *representation*. Christ is the King and Priest who mediates the relation of Israel—and now humanity—to God precisely by representing them before God. There are, in turn, four "moments" of Christ's representative act: advent, passion, restoration, and exaltation (*DN*, 133).[46] His exaltation in the ascension is a

45. Anticipating the sort of argument that N. T. Wright makes in *How God Became King: The Forgotten Story of the Gospels* (New York: HarperOne, 2012), O'Donovan remarks: "If Christian theology as a whole has sometimes allowed the careless or skeptical to conclude that the church changed its proclamation from Kingdom to Christ somewhere around AD 50, it is the special task of political theology to efface that impression" (*DN*, 123).

46. Advent is the act of divine authorization of Jesus as Son of God; the kingdom arrives in Jesus. The passion is the moment of judgment—of the world, of Israel—but as such it cannot really be distinguished from the resurrection, which is the moment of restoration: "Fulfilling the promises that Abraham believed in, Christ represents Israel equally in both moments of the Paschal crisis, and becomes a new focus of identity for those who inherit Abraham's faith. But the form which this rejection and affirmation take is the conquest of death; and this makes Israel's restoration representative of the wider human hope, a restoration to be claimed by the human race as a whole" (*DN*, 141). However, O'Donovan makes an important qualification: "What is achieved is more than a simple restoration of Adam's life. There is a difference between what was first given, described as 'soul' and 'dust,' and what will be given, which is 'spiritual' and 'from heaven'" (*DN*, 142). For a helpful discussion of why redemption is always "something more" than mere restoration, see Jon Stanley,

royal coronation, the vindication of Jesus's reign. Indeed, "the Ascension is the *foundation* which determines all future time" (*DN*, 145).[47] O'Donovan makes an important point about the political significance of the ascension as a *historical* reality:

> The political expectations of Jesus, denied validation within the immediate course of Israel's history, have to be laid aside as altogether ill-founded unless some validation for them is to be found within the history of Jesus himself. But if the story of this validation is said to be not a history of event but a myth of interpretation, then those political expectations were, after all, insubstantial. There has been no political achievement; the hope of it has merely become the conceptual material out of which is spun a religious validation for a life of frustrated efforts and fruitless self-sacrifice. . . . But without the Exaltation such vindication can only be a personal affair, not in the realm of public achievement. This demythologizing of the Gospel is, inevitably, a depoliticizing of it. (*DN*, 144–45)

Because (and only if) the Christ-event is taken to be true and historical, political ramifications for the earthly city cascade from this. The historical reality of the ascended King casts an eschatological light of hope over the present age (or, if you are Babylon, the long shadow of an assured demise [Rev. 18:21–24]). In short, the political is now inherently eschatological. Christ has disarmed the powers, made a public show of them, and delegitimized their claims to be mediators of ultimacy. "That must be the primary eschatological assertion about the authorities, political and demonic, which govern the world: they have been made subject to God's sovereignty in the Exaltation of Christ. The second, qualifying assertion is that this awaits a final universal presence of Christ to become fully apparent." These two assertions—already and not yet—are the parameters for a complete reconfiguration of the place and status of political authority. "Within the framework of these two assertions there opens up an account of secular authority which presumes neither that the Christ-event never occurred nor that the sovereignty of Christ is now transparent and uncontested" (*DN*, 146). The result is what O'Donovan de-

---

"Restoration and Renewal: The Nature of Grace in the Theology of Herman Bavinck," *The Kuyper Center Review*, vol. 2, *Revelation and Common Grace*, ed. John Bowlin (Grand Rapids: Eerdmans, 2011), 81–104.

47. This is why the absence of the ascension from Scot McKnight's *Kingdom Conspiracy: Returning to the Radical Mission of the Local Church* (Grand Rapids: Brazos, 2014) is so puzzling. Cf. Douglas Farrow's comment: "I do not see how any theologian can neglect political theology altogether. In my own case, work on the ascension made it unavoidable, for that doctrine is incomprehensible without its political dimension" (*Desiring a Better Country: Forays in Political Theology* [Montreal: McGill-Queen's University Press, 2015], x).

To Think About: The Christian Year as the Life of the King

In his wonderful primer to the Christian liturgical calendar, *Ancient-Future Time*, Robert Webber shows that the source and focus of "Christian-year spirituality" is Christ himself. To inhabit time according to the liturgical calendar is not just to keep time with the church; it is to retrace the life of Jesus Christ—his incarnation, life, passion, resurrection, and ascension. The practice of Christian timekeeping counters the egoistic tick-tock of the consumerist calendar by constantly inviting us to rehearse the life, death, and resurrection of Jesus, the exemplar we are called to imitate. And when we remember that he is the ascended King and recall O'Donovan's account of the political implications of Jesus's reign, then the spirituality of the Christian year becomes a political rite of the city of God. Just as the Lamb is the lamp of the new Jerusalem (Rev. 21:22–23), so the Son shines as the sun of the city of God, the one around whom our calendar revolves. In rehearsing the life of this King, we are reminded of the peculiar reign of the heaven-sent Prince of Peace, whose advent takes place in a feed trough in a forgotten barn; who apprentices with a carpenter and is shaped by a woman whose "Let it be" changed history; whose birth attracted kings from the Orient but threatened the rule of the governor at home; whose triumphal entry was a contested, makeshift procession with cloaks thrown down before the donkey foal he rode upon; whose "coronation" took place with a crown of thorns and mockery; whose ascension was witnessed by fishermen and scorned women; and who, in what must sometimes seem like a kind of divine madness, has named the likes of us to be vice-regents and co-heirs of this kingdom. The Christian year is a political rite that invites us to reinhabit the life of our King and learn what it might look like to imitate the strange politics of his kingdom here in the meantime.

Christian-Year Spirituality at a Glance

Season	Emphasis	Spiritual Challenge
Advent (coming)	Readiness for the coming of Christ at the end of history and at Bethlehem (the four Sundays before Christmas day).	Repent and be ready for the second coming of Christ. Allow an eager longing for the coming of the Messiah to be birthed in your heart.

scribes as the "'desacralisation' of politics by the Gospel": "Secular authorities are no longer in the fullest sense mediators of the rule of God. They mediate his judgments only. The power that they exercise in defeating their enemies, the national possessions they safeguard, these are now rendered irrelevant by Christ's triumph" (*DN*, 151). Hence the "cry from heaven which John heard at the seventh trumpet, 'Sovereignty over the world has passed to our Lord and his Christ'" (*DN*, 156). It is this eschatological in-breaking—the same eschatology that informs Augustine's *City of God*—that radically reconfigures the Christian's political posture.

Season	Emphasis	Spiritual Challenge
Christmas	The fulfillment of Israel's longing. The Messiah has come. The prophecies have been fulfilled. The Savior of the world has arrived (from December 25 through January 5).	Embrace an incarnational spirituality. Let Christ be born within in a new way.
Epiphany (manifestation)	The manifestation of Jesus to all as Savior not only for the Jews but for the whole world (January 6).	Make a new commitment to allow Jesus to be manifest in and through your life.
After Epiphany	A journey with Christ in his ministry as he manifests himself as the Son of God through signs and wonders (the period after January 6 to the beginning of Lent).	Learn to manifest the life of Christ through the witness of life and deeds.
Lent (spring)	A time to travel with Jesus toward his death. Although Jesus is under constant attack, he ministers effectively to the crowds. Lent follows the gathering storm (begins Ash Wednesday, six-and-a-half weeks before Easter; includes Palm Sunday and ends at sunset on Thursday of Holy Week).	Lent is a time for repentance through self-examination and renewal through identification with the journey of Jesus. A time for prayer, fasting, and almsgiving.
The Great Triduum (the three great days)	The most crucial time in the history of salvation. The church recalls in its worship the events of Maundy Thursday and Good Friday. The Great Paschal Vigil of Saturday night concludes with the resurrection Eucharist (the Thursday, Friday, and Saturday of Holy Week).	The three great days are a time for fasting and prayer. We commit to live in the pattern of Jesus' death and resurrection, the pattern of life into which we have been baptized.
Easter (the Christian Passover—known as the paschal mystery in the early church)	A celebration of the great saving event of the death and resurrection of Jesus for the salvation of the world. The most crucial event of the Christian year and the source of all Christian-year spirituality (extends for fifty days after Easter, includes Ascension Day, and ends on Pentecost).	Here is the source of the spiritual life. We are called to die to sin in the death of Jesus and to rise to the life of the Spirit in resurrection spirituality.
After Pentecost	The church is born on Pentecost Sunday with the coming of the Holy Spirit. After Pentecost the gospel spreads and the early church experiences growth and trials (from Pentecost Sunday to the beginning of Advent—about a six-month period).	A time to embrace the teaching of the church and to go deeper into the truths of God's saving events in history.

From Robert Webber, *Ancient-Future Time* (Grand Rapids: Baker Books, 2004), 16–17. Used with permission.

Naturalizing Shalom: The Temptations of a Kuyperian Secularism

As O'Donovan reminds us, Christian eschatology is an essential aspect of a Christian political theology.[48] We rehearse this week after week in the very observance of the Lord's Supper, being reminded that "as often as you eat this bread and drink this cup you proclaim the Lord's death *until he comes*

48. See also Graham Ward's discussion of "the eschatological remainder" in *Political Discipleship: Becoming Postmaterial Citizens* (Grand Rapids: Baker Academic, 2009), 167–80.

again." The Eucharist is, in a sense, a *secular* meal insofar as its celebration is a reminder that we live in the meantime of our waiting (the *saeculum*). This eschatological reminder does not engender an apolitical quietism but rather functions as both a discipline on our political pretensions and a reminder that the political is haunted by the "to come" of expectation. To lose this eschatological reminder is to abandon the call of a distinctly Christian "politics."

But the forces of eschatological forgetting are legion, and their effects on Christian political witness are myriad, spawning both theocratic, "Eusebian" agendas and Pelagian endeavors to instantiate justice without waiting. Resisting such eschatological forgetting is a primary pastoral task for shaping citizens of the city of God to be faithfully present amidst the earthly city in the *saeculum*. Since I've gone through my own phases of eschatological forgetting, allow me a testimony in this respect.

About a dozen years ago I was on the campus of the University of San Francisco as a participant in "Western Conversations in Jesuit Higher Education," an annual gathering of Jesuit universities west of the Mississippi devoted to exploring the issues of mission and identity. Though an evangelical Protestant, I was teaching at Loyola Marymount University in Los Angeles at the time and had been recruited to be part of the team taking up issues of liberal arts education in the Catholic tradition.

It turned out to be an opportune moment for us to be at the University of San Francisco since they were rolling out a new mission statement that same week. So here we were, professors from Jesuit universities, discussing the mission of Jesuit Catholic higher education, hosted by a Jesuit university rolling out a new articulation of its own mission. It was a case study unfolding right under our noses. However, it didn't take long for some of us to notice: the mission statement seemed to have a curious blind spot. Although long on talk of justice, diversity, and service, nowhere in the document did the word *God* appear. *Jesus* never makes an appearance in the mission of this Jesuit university. (This is the sort of thing that led my friend, a devout Roman Catholic, to quip: "I like teaching at a Jesuit university. But I would *love* to teach at a *Catholic* university!")

For the longest time, I thought of this as "their" problem—just one more indicator of the secularization of Catholic higher education in North America. But since then I've come to realize that this is *our* problem. In strange, often unintended ways, the pursuit of "justice," shalom, and a "holistic" gospel can have its own secularizing effect. What begins as a gospel-motivated concern for justice can turn into a naturalized fixation on justice in which God never appears. And when that happens, "justice" becomes something else altogether—an idol, a way to effectively naturalize the gospel, flattening it to a social amelioration project in which the particularity of Jesus as the revelation of God becomes strangely absent. Given the newfound appreciation for justice and shalom among evangelicals, we do well to see such trajectories as a cautionary tale, like a visitation from the ghost of Christmas future showing us where we could end up.

If this feels like I'm pointing my finger at others, there are three more pointed back at me. In fact, consider this a letter to my younger self. As a former fundamentalist, I was taught the biblical vision of a holistic gospel by heirs of Abraham Kuyper.[49] But I've come to realize that if we don't attend to the *whole* Kuyper, so to speak—if we pick and choose just parts of the Kuyperian project—we can end up with an odd sort of monstrosity: what we might call, paradoxically, a "Kuyperian secularism" that naturalizes shalom, precisely because it naturalizes the political and sequesters it from the specifics of Jesus's reign.

Before I recount my own foray into Kuyperian secularism, let me provide some context. Behind this story is a much bigger backstory told by Charles Taylor in his mammoth tome, *A Secular Age*.[50] You might think of this as a tale about the Frankensteinish effects of the Protestant Reformation. As Taylor so winsomely puts it, one of the world-changing consequences of the Reformation was "the sanctification of ordinary life." This was a refusal of the two-tiered Christianity in the late medieval ages that extolled priests and monks and treated butchers and bakers and candlestick makers as if they were merely second-class citizens in the kingdom of God. *Nein!*, shouted the Reformers in reply. If all of life is lived *coram Deo*, before the face of God, then all vocations are holy. Everything can and should be done to the glory of God (1 Cor. 10:31) and as an expression of gratitude to God (Col. 3:17). In sum: there will not be a single square inch in all of creation over which Christ does not say, "Mine!"[51]

This also transforms how we think about salvation, redemption, and restoration. On this picture, God is not interested just in "soul rescue," saving souls *from* and *out of* the world. He is redeeming *this* world. Jesus announces a kingdom that is characterized by justice: for the poor, for the oppressed, for

---

49. As an example, consider Chuck Colson's *How Now Shall We Live?* as a kind of "gateway drug." For the backstory on this, see my interview with Richard Mouw in *Comment*: "Learning from Kuyper, Following Jesus: A Conversation with Richard Mouw," September 13, 2013, https://www.cardus.ca/comment/article/4044/learning-from-kuyper-following-jesus-a-conversation-with-richard-mouw/.

50. See my summary and discussion in *How (Not) to Be Secular: Reading Charles Taylor* (Grand Rapids: Eerdmans, 2014), 35–40.

51. This is Abraham Kuyper's famous phrase. For a helpful introduction, see Richard Mouw, *Abraham Kuyper: A Short and Personal Introduction* (Grand Rapids: Eerdmans, 2011), 86–90.

the vulnerable, for all. The scope of God's salvation includes the material. Christ doesn't just redeem souls; he puts the world to rights. This is why Jesus heals bodies and feeds the crowds. And insofar as justice—shalom, flourishing—is God's concern, it should also be ours. Christians should be "this-worldly" in the best sense of the term: participating in God's renewal and redemption of *this* world, and hence passionately devoted to the cause of justice and propelled into the messiness of politics.

However, Taylor points out an unintended, Frankensteinish turn that was the result: by unleashing a new interest and investment in "this-worldly" justice, the Reformation also unleashed the possibility that we might forget heaven. By rejecting the dualism of two-tiered Christianity, the Reformation opened the door to a naturalism that cared *only* about "this world." Taylor describes this in terms of an "eclipse"—an eclipse of a "further purpose" or a good that transcends mere human flourishing. As he puts it elsewhere, "For Christians, God wills human flourishing, but 'thy will be done' doesn't reduce to 'let human beings flourish.'"[52] In premodern Christianity, both agents and social institutions lived with a sense of a *telos* that was eternal—a final judgment, the beatific vision, and so on. And on Taylor's accounting, this "higher good" was in some tension with mundane concerns about flourishing that entailed a sense of obligation "beyond" human flourishing. In other words, this life is *not* "all there is"—and recognizing that means one lives this life differently. It will engender certain ascetic constraints, for example: we can't just eat, drink, and be merry because, while tomorrow we may die, that's not the end. After that comes the judgment.

But Taylor sees an important shift in this respect, made possible by the Reformation but really taking hold in the work of Adam Smith and John Locke among others. Whereas historically the doctrine of providence ensured a benign *ultimate* plan for the cosmos, with Locke and Smith we see a new emphasis: providence is primarily about ordering the world for mutual benefit, particularly *economic* benefit. Humans are seen as fundamentally engaged in an "exchange of services," so the entire cosmos is seen anthropocentrically as the arena for this economy. What happens in the "new Providence," then, is a "shrinking" of God's purposes, an "economizing" of God's own interests. So even our theism becomes humanized, immanentized, and the *telos* of God's providential concern is circumscribed within immanence. And this becomes true even of "orthodox" folk: "Even people who held to orthodox beliefs were influenced by this humanizing trend; frequently the transcendent

---

52. Charles Taylor, "A Catholic Modernity?," in *Believing Scholars: Ten Catholic Intellectuals*, ed. James L. Heft, SM (New York: Fordham University Press, 2005), 17.

dimension of their faith became less central."[53] Because eternity is eclipsed, the this-worldly is amplified and threatens to swallow all.

What Taylor is talking about amounts to ancient history for us. But I have to confess that it cuts pretty close to the bone for me. It's a history that I feel like I've relived in my own lifetime, and it's a story I see repeating itself among a younger generation.

My own rendition of this story is a "Kuyperian" variation. I was converted and nurtured in a largely dualistic stream of North American evangelicalism, complete with a robust dispensational view of the end times and a very narrow understanding of redemption. It was very much a rapture-ready, heaven-centric piety that had little, if anything, to say about how or why a Christian might care about urban planning or chemical engineering or securing clean water sources in developing nations. Why worry about justice or flourishing in a world that is going to burn up?

So when I heard the Kuyperian gospel, so to speak, I was both blown away and a little angry. I was introduced to a richer understanding of the biblical narrative that included not only sin and soul-rescue but also creation, culture-making, and a holistic sense of redemption that included concerns for justice. I realized that God is not only interested in immaterial souls; he is redeeming all things and renewing creation. Christ's work also accomplishes the redemption of *this* world. The good news is not the announcement about an escape pod for our souls; it is the in-breaking of shalom.

You might say I finally received an understanding of Christianity that gave me "this world" back. Again, in Kuyperian terms, here was an account of the biblical story that not only emphasized the church as *institute* (the body of Christ gathered around Word and sacrament) but also emphasized the church as *organism* (Christians engaged in cultural creation, caretaking, and justice). Because I felt like this more robust, comprehensive understanding of the gospel had been kept a secret, I harbored a kind of bitterness and resentment toward my fundamentalist formation. Having been given back the world, I was almost angry that my teachers had only and constantly emphasized heaven.

As a result, my Kuyperian conversion to "this-worldly" justice and culture-making began to slide into its own kind of immanence. In other words, as Taylor notes in the shifts of modernity, even believers, in the name of affirming "this world," can unwittingly end up capitulating to a social imaginary that really values *only* this world. We become encased and enclosed in our own affirmations of the "goodness of creation," which, instead of being the

53. Charles Taylor, *A Secular Age* (Cambridge, MA: Harvard University Press, 2007), 222.

theater of God's glory, ends up being the echo chamber of our own interests. In sum, I became the strangest sort of monster: a Kuyperian secularist. My Reformed affirmation of creation slid toward a functional naturalism. My devotion to shalom became indistinguishable from the political platforms of the "progressive" party. And my valorization of the church as organism turned into a denigration of the church as institute.

Of course, this isn't really "Kuyperian." It's more like a slice of Kuyper, a side of Father Abraham. It was a very selective appropriation, as if concern for shalom could be separated from the resurrection of Jesus that subjects the principalities and powers; as if culture-making could be unhooked from sanctification and liturgical formation; as if the biblical vision of justice could be detached from justification by faith. As Rich Mouw has shown in his marvelous little book *Abraham Kuyper: A Short and Personal Introduction*, all of these hang together in Kuyper. We are the ones who detach and distort them into a functional "secularism."

Kuyper has been inherited in different ways in North America, yielding different Kuyperianisms. While Henry Zwaanstra suggests that "ecclesiology was the core of [Kuyper's] theology,"[54] one quickly notes that it is the church as *organism* that is the "heart" of his doctrine. This emphasis, coupled with some other emphases in Kuyper, led to a strain of Kuyperianism that actually had little place for the church as *institute* in its understanding of Christian engagement with culture. Indeed, there have even been strains of Kuyperianism that have been quite *anti*-ecclesial.

But Kuyper himself clearly saw a crucial role for the church as institute and devoted a great deal of his time, energy, and gifts to its welfare and reform.[55] The fact that he did this signals that there might be a different way to inherit Kuyper on this score. This idea invites us to reread Kuyper with new eyes, and I'd like to briefly offer such a rereading here. Let's take, as an example, his classic statement of sphere sovereignty and the institute/organism distinction in *Common Grace*.[56] In order to get to the heart of the matter, permit me a brief detour into his argument. We should first appreciate that he's doing battle on two fronts. On the one hand, he is opposing the model of a "national church" (which was then still a sort of live option in the Netherlands); on the other hand, he is battling "sectarianism," which is the ecclesiological

---

54. Henry Zwaanstra, "Abraham Kuyper's Conception of the Church," *Calvin Theological Journal* 9 (1974): 150.

55. Abraham Kuyper, *Our Worship*, ed. Harry Boonstra (Grand Rapids: Eerdmans, 2009).

56. Abraham Kuyper, "Church and Culture," in *Common Grace*, quoted in *Abraham Kuyper: A Centennial Reader*, ed. J. Bratt (Grand Rapids: Eerdmans, 1998), 187–201 (hereafter cited in text as CG).

outworking of the pietism he has already criticized. Let's pick this up in his critique of the national church.

Note, first, where Kuyper says that he *agrees* with the national church "party": "We and they agree that Christ's church and its means of grace cover a broader field than that of special grace alone" (*CG*, 189). In other words, they both agree that the church, as the body of Christ, is called to have an impact beyond merely "spiritual" matters. The body of Christ is to be the agent by which the "significance" of Christ for "nature" is made manifest. "We both acknowledge that the church does two things: (1) it works *directly* for the well-being of the elect, lures them to conversion, comforts, edifies, unites, and sanctifies them; but (2) it works *indirectly* for the well-being of the whole of civil society, constraining it to civic virtue" (*CG*, 189–90). So the church is called to have a "leavening" effect on society, impacting all the spheres of human cultural production.

With that agreement in mind, we can appreciate the difference; they differ "in how to reach that good goal." Kuyper's disagreement with the "national church" model, in other words, is about strategy. The national church party thinks that the way to have this impact is to "include civil society in the church." Kuyper, in contrast, emphasizes that the church *as institute* should be a "city on a hill amid civil society" (*CG*, 190) *from which* the church as organism infiltrates and leavens civil society. As he'll later put it, "This institute does not cover everything that is Christian. Though the lamp of the Christian religion only burns within that institute's walls, its light shines out through its windows to areas far beyond, illumining all the sectors and associations that appear across the wide range of human life and activity." Thus, he suggests that we picture these as concentric circles, with the church as institute—administering the sacraments, exercising discipline, forming disciples—nourishing a vibrant core of believers who, as an organism, infiltrate and leaven civil society (*CG*, 194–95).[57]

With this model in mind, we can see Kuyper's critique of both the national church and sectarianism. Because the national church model "recognizes only one circle," so to speak (*CG*, 194)—because it can only imagine the church as institute and thus absorbs civil society into the institute—it thereby dilutes the vibrant core that is needed to be leavening. In other words, by baptizing everyone, the national church admits into the church a host of nonconfessors and unbelievers, and by failing to exercise church discipline, it loses any

57. Kuyper, in a mode of Protestant flourish, actually claims that the church as organism *precedes* the church as institute—and could even "manifest itself" where the church as institute has ceased to function (*CG*, 195).

purifying or sanctifying animus with which to impact society. By effectively taking "the world" (i.e., civil society; *CG*, 194) into the church, the church just becomes worldly (*CG*, 196). It lacks any Christ-disciplined center from which to be a means of making Christ "significant" for the rest of society.[58]

However, if the national church goes wrong by losing its center, *sectarianism* goes wrong by retreating into and fortifying itself within a pure "center" and thereby neglecting responsibility for "nature." "Sects," for Kuyper, are those configurations (or rather, *disfigurations*) of Christianity that effectively put themselves "outside the context of *human life*." A sect is "a tiny holy circle that has remained on earth by mistake and really has nothing to do with the life that is lived down here" (*CG*, 191). Sectarians are also critics of the national church, but they criticize both the *strategy* and the *goal*; on their account, the gospel is not concerned with the institutions and practices of civil society. Politics, economics, the arts, and education are "worldly" matters not of their concern. In short, sectarianism rejects what God affirms as good—namely, creation in all its facets; thus, it also rejects any notion of common grace.[59] Or, to use Kuyper's earlier language, sectarians reject "nature."

What does this distinction between the church as institute and organism have to do with our concern—the relationship between worship and politics, the eschaton and the *saeculum*? What's at stake is not only how we make the distinction between the two but also how we understand the *relation* between the two. So while Kuyper certainly emphasizes that "the institute does not cover everything that is Christian" (*CG*, 194), he goes on to note, recalling the concentric-circle metaphor, that "aside from this first circle of the institute *and in necessary connection with it*, we thus recognize another circle whose circumference is determined by the length of the ray that shines out from the church institute over the life of people and nation" (*CG*, 195, emphasis added). It seems to me that it is precisely Kuyper's claim that there is a *necessary connection* between institute and organism that has been lost in certain strains of Kuyperianism. And why does Kuyper propose a necessary connection between the two? He does so precisely because it is the wor-

58. Kuyper also generates a theological account for a principled pluralism in this context: "What we want is a strong confessional church but *not* a confessional civil society *nor* a confessional state." Thus, he advocates a certain kind of "secularization of state and society"—one that makes space for confessional pluralism in the state and civil society—as "one of the most basic ideas of Calvinism" (*CG*, 197). (This should be distinguished from an aggressive secular*ism* that would seek to "nullify the church's influence on civil society" [*CG*, 196].) We will return to these themes in chap. 4 below.

59. Kuyper's argument is a tad circular here. He chastises the sectarians for refusing to recognize common grace and therefore refusing to affirm the goodness of civil society (*CG*, 192). We also need to (later) distinguish pietistic sectarianism from antithetical critique.

ship of the church as institute that *forms* those who will be the rays of light in civil society. It is in the formative worship of the church—rehearsing the biblical drama whose *telos* is the eschaton—that we learn both the norms for flourishing *and* how to wait.

But even those who know nothing of Abraham Kuyper would do well to consider *how* we pursue justice. When we "naturalize" shalom, it is no longer shalom. For the new Jerusalem is not a product of our bottom-up efforts, as if it were constructed by us. The new Jerusalem descends from heaven (Rev. 21:2, 10). And the light of the holy city is not a "natural" accomplishment but is the light radiating from the glory of the risen, conquering Lamb (Rev. 21:22–25). The holistic affirmation of the goodness of creation and the importance of "this-worldly" justice is not a *substitute* for heaven, as if the holistic gospel were a sanctified way to learn to be a naturalist. To the contrary, it is the very transcendence of God—in the ascension of the Son who now reigns from heaven, and in the futurity of the coming kingdom for which we pray—that disciplines and disrupts and haunts our tendency to settle for "this world." It is the call of the Son from heaven, and the vision of the new Jerusalem descending from heaven, that pushes back on our illusions that *we* could figure this all out, that *we* could bring this about. Shalom is not biblical language for progressivist social amelioration. Shalom is a Christ-haunted call to long for kingdom come.[60]

Christian worship is a unique gift in this respect, a strange sort of reminder since it reminds us of not just a past but a future. Thus Bernd Wannenwetsch says the discipline of Christian worship gifts us with a unique sort of *inertia* that is a political virtue: "Worship again and again interrupts the course of the world. Through worship the Christian community testifies that the world is not on its own. And this also means that it is not kept alive by politics, as the business of politics, which knows no Sabbath, would have us believe. This is why the celebration of worship is not directed simply against this or that totalitarian regime; it is directed against the totalization of political existence in general."[61] In this sense, "Lift up your hearts!" is a political admonition we hear week after week.

---

60. For a helpful caution in this respect, see Bethany Hanke Hoang and Kristen Deede Johnson, *The Justice Calling: Where Passion Meets Perseverance* (Grand Rapids: Brazos, 2016).
61. Wannenwetsch, *Political Worship*, 126–27.

3

The Craters of the Gospel

Liberalism's Borrowed Capital

Unacknowledged Legislation

"Poets are the unacknowledged legislators of the world." So concluded Percy Bysshe Shelley in his famed essay "A Defence of Poetry." This Romantic vision of the poet as maker par excellence, as one who calls worlds into being and thus remakes the world as he finds it, is no doubt a tad hyperbolic—a strident defense of the poet against the long line of Platonic philosopher-kings who would prefer to see the poets exiled outside the walls of the *polis*. The poets, Shelley says, "apprehend the true and the beautiful . . . the good which exists in relation." The poets are like prophets with insights into the eternal and divine; they are intrepid explorers of a transcendent order who journey to what the world might be and come back to us with reports and blueprints.

> Poets, or those who imagine and express this indestructible order, are not only the authors of language and of music, of the dance, and architecture, and statuary, and painting: they are the institutors of laws, and the founders of civil society, and the inventors of the arts of life, and the teachers, who draw into a certain propinquity with the beautiful and the true that partial apprehension of the agencies of the invisible world which is called religion. Hence all original religions are allegorical, or susceptible of allegory, and, like Janus, have a double face of false and true. Poets, according to the circumstances of the age and nation in which they appeared, were called, in the earlier epochs of the world, legislators, or prophets: a poet essentially comprises and unites

both these characters. For he not only beholds intensely the present as it is, and discovers those laws according to which present things ought to be ordered, but he beholds the future in the present, and his thoughts are the germs of the flower and the fruit of latest time.[1]

So for Shelley the best defense of the poets is a recognition of society's debts to them: they are the "unacknowledged legislators" of the society we all take for granted. They are the "founders of civil society" whose courageous creativity and innovative insight have sketched the lineaments of law and the parameters of the earthly city we inhabit. The poets gave us the eschatological glimpses that helped us imagine how the world could be otherwise, launching revolutions and spawning reforms. We could only imagine challenging the divine right of kings because the poets helped us imagine a world in which we were not subjects but citizens.

But our liberal democracies owe debts not only to poets but also to theologians, another set of "unacknowledged legislators" whose insights have spawned revolutions and reforms. Or we might say that the church has been an unacknowledged legislator of the late modern *polis*, a body politic whose insights (revelation) and practices (liturgy) have spawned visions, theories, and rites that have spilled over into the rhythms of nations and the litanies of self-understanding we call "constitutions." So the state we encounter (and challenge) is, in some ways, a child of the *ekklēsia*.

Two key implications follow from this—one that has repercussions for our pluralistic, contested, democratic civil polities, and one that impinges on the church's understanding of its relationship to the state and the regimes of liberal democracy.

The Church's Public Political Pedagogy

First, part of the *public* task of a Christian political theology is a theologically inflected history of liberal democracy that unveils this unacknowledged legislation. "Notwithstanding the discontinuity of the West with its past in Christendom," Oliver O'Donovan points out, "there is a legacy still apparent in the institutions of Europe and America. Even if Christendom is not our tradition, we cannot forget that it was our great-grandfathers'. It lies in a fruitful constellation of social and political ideas which came together

---

1. Percy Bysshe Shelley, "A Defence of Poetry," in *English Essays, from Sir Philip Sidney to Macaulay*, ed. Charles W. Eliot, Harvard Classics 27 (New York: P. F. Collier & Son, 1909–14), 4, http://www.bartleby.com/27/23.html. I confess I wouldn't likely have known of Shelley's phrase were it not for Christopher Hitchens's caustic collection, *Unacknowledged Legislators: Writers in the Public Sphere* (London: Verso, 2000).

in a decisively influential way in the sixteenth and seventeenth centuries."[2] While there are obnoxious renditions of this history that would make liberal democracy the possession of Protestantism, and equally distorted histories that ignore this Christian inheritance in favor of a sui generis emergence of liberal democracy from Enlightenment rationalism, O'Donovan points to an uncontestable history that has emerged: "What has become clear . . . from half a century of research in political history, is that the roots of this new organisation of political priorities run deep into the centuries that preceded it, not only through the late scholastics who are recognisably forebears of the Reformation, but through the earlier scholastics back into the Carolingian and patristic eras; and not only through theologians and their disputations but through the various concrete forms of life in the Christian community: corporations, monastic communities, canon law, penance and so on" (DN, 226).[3]

Even granting the far-reaching effects of the Enlightenment, the French Revolution, and secularization, the history and legacy of these distinctly Christian and theological sources for the political regimes of the West cannot be effaced by wishing it so.[4] What comprises "late modern" liberalism, as O'Donovan calls it, is further removed from these sources, of course. "The 'democracy,' based on the twin institutions of ballot-box and stock-market, in which the late modern West takes such pride as to inflict misery and political disruption on the largest scale in order to export it, and even to threaten nuclear annihilation to avenge it, is not a simple prolongation of the principles enunciated in that crucial early-modern period" (DN, 226). The branches of political liberalism are a long ways from their Christian and theological roots. "Still," O'Donovan remarks, "behind the billboards set up by this brash ideology, certain habits and practices instilled by the formative traditions of the modern era can be discerned, at least in the traditional heartlands, and can provide, unacknowledged, much of the moral collateral that supports the giddy speculations of their offspring" (DN, 226–27). Thus political theology

2. Oliver O'Donovan, *The Desire of the Nations: Rediscovering the Roots of Political Theology* (Cambridge: Cambridge University Press, 1996), 226 (hereafter cited in text as *DN*).

3. For an anthology of primary sources that rehearses this history, see Oliver O'Donovan and Joan Lockwood O'Donovan, eds., *From Irenaeus to Grotius: A Sourcebook in Christian Political Thought* (Grand Rapids: Eerdmans, 1999).

4. Charles Taylor also documents how the "modern moral order" emerged from a certain formalization of the Christian tradition; see *A Secular Age* (Cambridge, MA: Harvard University Press, 2007), 234–59. The "new humanism," as he puts it, "has taken over universalism from its Christian roots" because it "supposes that we are motivated to act for the good of our fellow human beings" (246). But this supposition is rooted, in fact, in "Christian agape" as that "which can take us beyond the bounds of any already existing solidarity" (246).

has a public role to play simply by re-narrating to late modern liberal societies their religious and theological inheritance.

Political theology in this mode also has an important secondary function today: "It has an *apologetic* force when addressed to a world where the intelligibility of political institutions and traditions is seriously threatened. Christian theology sheds light on institutions and traditions, to address a crisis that is more pressing on unbelievers than on believers; and so it also offers reasons to believe."[5] In this sense political theology is *public* theology, and it serves the public by offering a *genealogy* of the public's own institutions (in the modern West). "Western civilization finds itself the heir of political institutions and traditions which it values without any clear idea why, or to what extent, it values them" (*WJ*, xiii). Here a distinctly Christian genealogy is a public offering: "Recovery of theological description enables us to understand not only what the goods of our institutions and traditions are, but why and how those goods are limited and corruptible, and to what corresponding errors they have made us liable" (*WJ*, xiv–xv). So this isn't a usurper's errand; it is, rather, part of the teaching ministry of the church: "Christian theology in these circumstances resumes its ancient role of educating a people in the practical reasonableness required for their political tasks" (*WJ*, xv).[6] (As we will see in the next section, this pedagogical role can also be a mode of prophetic critique that aims to protect individuals from an absolutization of politics.)

If I have argued that we need to see the liberal democratic state as a liturgical reality, a kind of rival *ekklēsia*, that is *not* to therefore conclude we should

---

5. Oliver O'Donovan, *The Ways of Judgment* (Grand Rapids: Eerdmans, 2005), xii (hereafter cited in text as *WJ*).

6. Joan Lockwood O'Donovan describes this as part of the church's "public legal pedagogy" in "The Liberal Legacy of English Church Establishment: A Theological Contribution to the Legal Accommodation of Religious Plurality in Europe," *Journal of Law, Philosophy and Culture* 6 (2011): 17–45, quotation on 19. As she points out, the proclamation and practices of the church have a public role that includes reminding society—particularly legislators, judges, and police—that their judgment is not ultimate. Hence, the church's public proclamation pushes back on a "legal perfectionism" that often entails a secularized statism (41–42). By reminding late modern liberalism of its sources, such a public legal pedagogy disciplines such perfectionism by transcendence. "When public law no longer attests the order of jurisdiction to proclamation, or in other words, when public law dissociates itself from God's law in its Trinitarian fullness, then, inevitably, it loses sight of its derivative, dependent and subordinate status in relation to the divinely ordained goods and rights of human moral community. It loses sight of the spiritually peripheral character of its work of protecting human freedom in its manifold social realizations, and assumes a false spiritual and social centrality, fostering a legalistic and juridical moral and social ethos that curtails and stifles practical judgement" (44). In short, the church's public legal pedagogy, far from being some covert theonomy, is rather an antidote to statist absolutism.

withdraw or retreat. In the spirit of Augustinian nuance and complexity, we need to undertake ad hoc analysis and critique, open to recognizing those aspects of our public life that can be affirmed, even celebrated, while rightly resisting those that are deformative and unjust. This requires a more nuanced historical account of how we got here, so to speak—an appreciation of the specific, contingent history of liberalism. In particular, following the work of Charles Taylor and Oliver O'Donovan, this chapter will point out the Christian legacy and imprint on Western liberalism, complicating any simple demonization or distance. In this sense, Taylor and O'Donovan echo Augustine's own close (yea, providential) reading of history in *City of God*.[7]

Sending: Discernment for Engagement

While on the one hand such a history is offered as something of a public service to secularized liberal democracies (even when it is a challenge), this history is equally crucial for the church's self-understanding of its "political" mission in modernity. Hence a second implication follows from this theologically inflected history of liberalism: Christian political theology will have to articulate a nuanced, even messy understanding—and *appreciation*—of aspects of liberal democracy that are, in crucial ways, the fruit of the gospel's impact on the West and now the world. In other words, there can be no simplistic antithesis between the church as *polis* and the liberal democratic *polis* in which so many of us find ourselves "mixed up."[8] Instead, what is necessary, as O'Donovan already suggested, is a Christian imagination capable of careful *discernment*: "By way of [a] closer view of the weaving of modernity, we

7. Augustine offers his "providential" history of Rome in books 4 and 5 of *City of God* (trans. Henry Bettenson [London: Penguin, 1984]). The account is at once a stinging critique of Rome's pagan idolatry and an account of "for what ends, the true God, in whose power are all kingdoms, deigned to assist the growth of the Roman Empire" (4.2) and "why God was willing that the Roman Empire should extend so widely and last so long" (5.preface).

8. If *Desiring the Kingdom* tended to paint what feels like an almost entirely antithetical stance vis-à-vis liberal democracy (and capitalism), I would note two qualifiers. First, the emphasis in that first volume was largely corrective and contextual, and hence tended to emphasize the need to recover a sense of antithesis, particularly in light of projects whose emphasis on "common grace" ended up simply baptizing the status quo. That particular, strategic emphasis, however, was never the whole story; see James K. A. Smith, *Desiring the Kingdom: Worship, Worldview, and Cultural Formation*, Cultural Liturgies 1 (Grand Rapids: Baker Academic, 2009), 17n2, for an early qualification. See also James K. A. Smith, "Worldview, Sphere Sovereignty, and *Desiring the Kingdom*: A Guide for (Perplexed) Reformed Folk," *Pro Rege* 39 (2011): 15–24. Second, I would also grant that my own thinking has shifted on precisely this point, largely because of sustained engagements with Augustine's *City of God* and the corpus of Oliver O'Donovan. So my argument here represents a more mature take on these matters that should supersede the more limited sketch in *Desiring the Kingdom*.

are free to discern both the triumph of Christ in liberal institutions and the coming of the Antichrist" (*DN*, 228).[9]

To frame this liturgically, we should note that because worship ends with sending,[10] Christian worship is less the rites of an enclave and more like the training ground for a *sent* people whose *missio* will take them into the contested space of markets and elections, corporations and council halls. The enacted narrative of Christian worship, as a rehearsal of both our creation and our recreation, culminates in the "Go!" of both Genesis 1 and Matthew 28. Thus the church is less a contrast society we retreat into than a re-centering community of practice that we are sent *from*. As an imagination station whereby our social imaginary is shaped by the gospel, the church isn't an end in itself, an alternative place, but rather a pedagogical community of the Spirit where we are equipped for *discernment*. But our discernment is not primarily protective, pitching us back on our heels on the watch for threats and dangers that push us into smaller and smaller corners of "safety" and "purity." To the contrary, the formation of our social imaginary in Christian worship equips us for an active discernment, the engaged wisdom and prudence that enables us to see openings for participation, collaboration, and critique within the wider contested spaces of the *saeculum*.

Integral to the biblical story—and the sacramental imagination fueled by the incarnation—is a unique attentiveness to, and embeddedness in, history and the vicissitudes of time ("when the fullness of the time came," "suffered under Pontius Pilate"). The Christian imagination, then, is not an idealism, a set of abstract principles thirty thousand feet above the zigzag of history with all its twists and turns.[11] To the contrary, the rehearsal of the drama of redemption in worship situates us in salvation history precisely so that we can be a people equipped for discernment that is temporal, historical, contextual, and revisable.[12]

---

9. While I disagree with some of the specifics, I think Nicholas Wolterstorff's work on justice fits in this same sort of project: a theologically inflected genealogy of liberal democratic concerns with justice, rights, and legal protections for the vulnerable. See Wolterstorff, *Justice: Rights and Wrongs* (Princeton: Princeton University Press, 2008) and *Justice in Love* (Grand Rapids: Eerdmans, 2011).

10. James K. A. Smith, *Imagining the Kingdom: How Worship Works*, Cultural Liturgies 2 (Grand Rapids: Baker Academic, 2013), 151–57.

11. As I will suggest below in "Excursus: Common Grace versus Providence," I think such idealism—a fixation on principles and ideas and theories that float above, and independently of, history—infects a range of other proposals in political theology including some versions of Kuyperianism, Hauerwas's unique form of "Catholic Anabaptism," and some natural law projects (including the specific version that calls itself "two kingdoms" theology).

12. Indeed, even my own project in this book is contextualized by the parameters of Western liberal democracy. While I hope there are insights here that are helpful to the church wherever it finds itself, I don't pretend to be able to encompass the range of histories beyond the influence of "the West." This is not because they are unimportant; to the contrary, the bulk of the church finds itself there! I am simply limiting myself to a cultural analysis where I have some relevant

In short, Christian political analysis and cultural exegesis needs to be informed by an adequate theology of providence.[13] So there are layers of discernment at work here. First, we discern the lineaments of the political vision carried in the gospel itself; that was the task of chapter 2. Second, we need to discern the unique history of those institutions and practices we call "liberal democracy," which is the water so many of us swim in if we live in North America, Europe, and other regions whose history is bound up with migrations (and conquests) from these places. This is the primary task of the current chapter and is meant to undercut any hasty conclusion that a liturgical politics is necessarily or entirely antithetical with respect to liberal democracy.[14] Finally, when we have been equipped with this theologically inflected genealogy of liberal democracy and shaped by the gospel through immersion in the biblical story in worship, there is the ongoing work of temporal discernment that Christian citizens need to carry out as ones who are *sent* into "the world." This is the chapter that the church writes in action, so to speak—in the ad hoc, contextualized work of discerning what faithful political presence looks like in *this* time, in *our* place, given *these* current challenges and *these* policy proposals and *this* political environment in parliament, and so on. Hence "the work of political theology," O'Donovan comments, "is to shed light from the Christian faith upon the intricate challenge of thinking about living in late-modern Western society" (*WJ*, x). The value of such an enterprise, he emphasizes, is that "it has, in the first place, pastoral importance: to give guidance to those who, believing the Christian faith or capable of suspending their disbelief, have to exercise political responsibilities." This is not just the domain of politicians and civil servants, however:

> The responsibilities are those which we all face, regardless of our views on political institutions and the propriety of taking a leading role in them. . . .

---

expertise, and don't presume to speak at all authoritatively into contexts beyond that. That said, in a world in which capitalism, liberalism, and expressive individualism are increasing globalized, even these contextual insights might have more global import than we'd expect—which is precisely why we can still profitably read Augustine's *City of God* even though his political environment was radically different from ours. (Or as O'Donovan notes: "Lactantius' *Institutes*, composed for a martyr-church at the height of Diocletian's persecution, was easily repackaged in a second edition, with a dedicatory preface to . . . Constantine!" [*DN*, 217]).

13. In an excursus below I will explain why I believe this requires a renewed theology of providence rather than the ahistorical abstractions of "common grace" so often invoked in the Reformed, Kuyperian tradition.

14. While my emphasis in chap. 2 was on the ways Jeffrey Stout has underestimated what is at stake in the liturgies of liberal democracy, in this chapter I am pushing back on the conclusions that Hauerwas and MacIntyre tend to draw from this by pointing out the legacy of Christian thought *in* liberalism; hence, I am undercutting a dismissive withdrawal from or antipathy toward the liberal state as such.

Hermit and politician both have to make up their minds as to whether they can acknowledge the institutions that claim to serve them (democratic elections, civil courts, or whatever), and whether they can or cannot defend some policy enacted in the name of the community of which they are part (decriminalizing cannabis, or going to war). We all have many occasions to decide whether to approve or disapprove. Insignificant as they may seem, such decisions are not inconsequential for our moral and spiritual integrity. (*WJ*, xi)

"Offering guidance from within the discourse of the church" is a succinct summary of our project here. So let us first turn to a discerning history of liberal democracy, drawing again on the work of O'Donovan.

The Ecclesial Roots of Democratic Liberalism

"Like the surface of a planet pocked with craters by the bombardment it receives from space, the governments of the passing age show the impact of Christ's dawning glory" (*DN*, 212). O'Donovan's cosmological image suggests a picture for our project: Where are the craters of the gospel's impact on Western liberal democracies? Even if we have articulated a trenchant critique of the rites of liberalism and the ethos of consumer capitalism, can we nonetheless also see legacies of the gospel that endure within this realm?[15] As we survey the landscape of late modern liberalism, can we discern overgrown craters of the gospel's impact, where gardens are growing, nourishing us in ways we might not realize? Are there features of our political institutions whose DNA shows they are heirs of the church? To discern such is not just an apologetic endeavor, a "defense" against an encroaching secularism that posits its own false antithesis between Christianity and liberal democracy; it also has an important pastoral function, particularly when a generation of influential Christian theologians and ethicists have demonized liberal democracy as simply reducible to "the world."

Picturing Political Genealogy: *Finding Your Roots*

In his PBS television series *Finding Your Roots*, Harvard literary historian Henry Louis Gates Jr. taps into our inbuilt longing to know where we came from. It seems as if we

---

15. O'Donovan's comment here is germane: "The triumph of Christ among the nations Hauerwas is not prepared to see" (*DN*, 216). For an exemplary contextual reading of "America" in this way—discerning both its providential role and its predilection for idolatry—see Peter Leithart, *Between Babel and Beast: America and Empires in Biblical Perspective* (Eugene, OR: Cascade Books, 2012).

are wired with genealogical curiosity. Gaps in our immediate family history unsettle us like a missing puzzle piece. People make pilgrimages to the places of their ancestors to understand their own story. Adoptees set out on quests to find their biological parents to quell a host of rumbling doubts and hungers, to explain the uncanny things they experience about themselves. These journeys are sometimes joyous, sometimes heart-breaking, with bright revelations and dark disclosures. But to face our genealogies is, in some sense, to come face-to-face with ourselves.

In *Finding Your Roots*, Gates and his team marshal all the tools they can to delve back into personal histories. Utilizing both the cutting-edge science of genomics and DNA research alongside the painstaking archival sleuthing of genealogical research, they traverse generations to introduce people to their own ancestors. Granted, the program also taps into our celebrity-worship culture and thus tends to focus on actors, musicians, and politicians; but these personal histories of famous people are merely illustrative of the patchwork of race, ethnicity, and immigration that makes up the stories of countless Americans.

Sometimes the genealogies are a peculiar mirror, like when Senator John McCain discovered that his ancestor, William Alexander McCain, was also a prisoner of war after deserting the Confederate Army in 1864. McCain's discomfort is visible when he, a decorated soldier, learns his ancestor committed the unpardonable military sin. But also visible is the flash of recognition when he learns about his ancestor's experience as a prisoner of war. When Gates digs into the story of sculptor Maya Lin, we learn why her young mother fled revolutionary China in 1949: because her own mother (Lin's grandmother) had committed suicide in front of her daughter, leaving her alone in the world. The actress and comedian Maya Rudolph learns that some of her enslaved ancestors had their freedom written into a will by one of their former owners—except that this was never honored by the surviving family. But then the remarkable disclosure: Rudolph's ancestor, a black man in a slave state, sued his white owners for freedom *and won*! Musical artist Sean Combs finds a surprising bright spot in his family's history: the remarkable fact that one of his ancestors was a free man in 1850s Maryland. Indeed, we learn that there were seventy-five thousand free people of color in the state at that time. But the perceived "threat" of so many free and freed African Americans engendered a backlash in draconian laws and oppressive policing. Then Combs learns of a story that is now only all too familiar to him: his third-great-grandfather was apprehended and thrown in jail for being a "runaway"—even though he was a free man. You can almost watch the shadow of angry recognition fall across Combs's face as he hears this story.

We are historical creatures, shaped by our legacies, heirs of the cultural snowballs that constitute our family histories. We come from somewhere, engendered by a con-stellation of someones who "made" us in all kinds of ways. Genealogy is always a voy-age of self-discovery.

Part of the work of public theology, Oliver O'Donovan suggests, is to offer a theologically inflected genealogy of our political institutions and rites in Western liberal
democracies. In this mode, the public theologian is an institutional genealogist,
uncovering the perhaps hidden (perhaps embarrassing?) history of secular society.
When and where the Christian theological impetus for political realities is shrouded in
ancient history, or actively forgotten for revisionist reasons, the public theologian can
be prophetic simply by being an organ of collective memory. The public theologian
unveils the family history of liberal democracy with all of its religious grandmothers
and Christian uncles. Perhaps this helps explain us to ourselves. Perhaps it even invites
us to imagine ourselves otherwise.

From Christ Our Representative to Capitol Hill

O'Donovan begins his excavation by suggesting that the very notion of "the
state" in modernity is a legacy of Christendom, a remnant of the displacement
of political authority by the first advent of the King. The announcement of
the kingdom of God and the resurrection of the King of the Jews are signs
that earthly kingdoms are passing away. The emperor is not God. Caesar is
not Lord. The empire is not the kingdom. Thus "the political doctrine that
emerged from Christendom is characterized by a notion that government is
responsible. Rulers, overcome by Christ's victory, exist provisionally and on
sufferance for specific purposes" (*DN*, 231). The governing authorities possess
a power that is only temporal, accountable to an order and law and King who
is eternal. In short, the "state" emerges when and because government comes
to see its authority as "secular," confined to the *saeculum*, circumscribed by
the eternal and ultimately passing away. The notion that government and those
who govern are accountable to something other, something higher, Someone
Other, is an irruption in Western political history whose effects continue to
reverberate at the heart of democracy in which rulers are held accountable.

"The state exists in order to give judgment," O'Donovan argues, "but
under the authority of Christ's rule it gives judgment *under law*, never as
its own law" (*DN*, 233). The revelation of God in Christ has a relativizing
effect on the powers that be: "The legislative activity of princes, then, was
not a beginning in itself; it was an answer to the prior lawmaking of God
in Christ, under which it must be judged. Christendom in effect refused the
classical commonplace that the ruler was a 'living law,' his personal authority indistinguishable from the authority of the law he gave" (*DN*, 234). So
whenever we hold government accountable—in elections, by impeachment

proceedings, in protests, or at town hall meetings—we are moving within a repertoire of political action that bears the legacy of the revelation of Christ the King, political gifts we should affirm and for which we should be thankful.

This tempering of temporal authority translates into an understanding of government as *representative*. This is why "constitutional reflection became one of the hallmarks of the Christian political tradition, following a course quite different from the classical reflection about what kind of government was best—democratic, oligarchic or monarchic. For Christian culture the question, rather, was how a government of any of these kinds can claim to be *the* government of a given people. In other words, how can a government be representative?" (*DN*, 234–35).[16] If Christendom was tempted, for a time, to imagine a "world empire" as the required "secular" expression of Christ's reign (see Dante's *De monarchia* for the nadir of this tradition), a fundamental biblical caution kept haunting this: "The presence of the Apocalypse within the canon did not allow Christians to forget that Antichrist, too, was perfectly expressed in world-rule" (*DN*, 236). Rather than look for the expression of Christ's universal reign in a world ruler in the *saeculum*, the political thought of Christendom located this universality in *law*: "The last and greatest of the legal accomplishments of Christendom was the conception that there exists, not merely as an ideal but in fact, an *international law*, dependent on no regime and no statute, but on the Natural Law implanted in human minds by God, and given effect by international custom and convention" (*DN*, 236). So rather than the entire "secular" world coming under the rule of a Christian emperor, all rulers—Christian or not—were to be held accountable to a law that was higher than them, not dependent on their fiats, and to which they were accountable.[17] And so from the matrix of Christendom "we witness the birth of constitutional law": "Law not only proceeds from the ruler; it precedes him. His own legitimation must be a matter of appeal to law" (*DN*, 236).[18]

16. As we saw in chap. 2, this dynamic of representation goes back to Christology itself, and even to Israel.

17. O'Donovan reminds us that "radical Calvinist theories of the late sixteenth century" formalized this to the extent that they "identified a particular office, supposedly implicit in any constitutional order, which bore the responsibility for restraining or removing the supreme magistrate" (*DN*, 238)—like Gandalf arriving to remind Denethor that he is merely the *steward* of Gondor. Later liberalism, which opted for immanentist contractarianism rather than accountability to divine law, fell prey to a "nationalist positivism" that is susceptible to the erosion of the state by individualism, anarchism, and absolutism of various stripes. But in a sense this isn't new, O'Donovan remarks: "On all sides pundits proclaim that the nation-state is in trouble. The truth is, it has been in trouble ever since Christ rose from the dead. The challenge issued to given, a priori political identities has been a persistent *Leitmotiv* of Christian thought" (*DN*, 241).

18. My colleague Micah Watson reminds me that one could have gained a similar insight from Sophocles's *Antigone* and that, in general, O'Donovan tends to ignore some of the Greek

This, despite all our frustrations in the West, is precisely the political ethos that distinguishes liberal democracy. To inhabit states where authorities are governed by law is, to some degree, to live in a political environment that has been dented by the gospel. And to the extent that liberal democracies *forget* this, specters of injustice reemerge.[19] "A failure to see that *society* requires the state's deference underlies a great deal of 'liberal tyranny' in the late-modern age" (*DN*, 241–42), which is precisely why a political theology that offers such a genealogy undertakes a *public* service.[20]

"In tracing the characteristic features of liberal society," O'Donovan says, "we need to show how it has been affected by the narrative structure of the church, which is itself a recapitulation of the Christ-event" (*DN*, 250). His genealogy thus highlights four aspects of liberal society that parallel the four moments of Christ's representation (discussed in the section "Jesus Is King" in chap. 2 above).

First, liberal society is, of course, characterized by *liberty*. But we need to appreciate that this discovery of freedom—contrary to secularist narratives— was first a gift of the church's witness. "For the voice of a prophetic church in its midst, which speaks with divine authority, loosens the hold of existing authorities and evokes the prospect of liberty" (*DN*, 252). It is the gospel that unleashes freedom, the Spirit of the Lord that secures liberty. "God has done something which makes it impossible for us any more to treat the authority of human society as final and opaque. He has sent the anointed one to rule; and wherever he has appeared—to John the Baptist by the Jordan, to the sick

---

antecedents to republican politics. My hunch is O'Donovan would concede the point and aver that *Desire of the Nations* is focused on a different genealogy for very specific reasons. Given limitations of space, I'll leave it to the two of them to hash this out elsewhere.

19. This is why O'Donovan is so critical of the United States Constitution, which he sees as "the symbolic end of Christendom," bearing "the marks of the Age of Revolution, reflecting a conception of society constituted from below" (*DN*, 244). He particularly highlights the implications of the First Amendment: "By denying any church established status in principle, the framers of the First Amendment gave away more than they knew. They effectively declared that political authorities were incapable of evangelical obedience. And with this the damage was done. It did not need the anti-religious line of interpretation pursued by twentieth-century courts to make this formula, from a theological point of view, quite strictly heretical. The creed asserts: *cuius regni non erit finis*; and the apostle, that 'at the name of Jesus every knee shall bow' (Phil. 2:10). The First Amendment presumes to add: 'except . . .' Excluding government from evangelical obedience has had repercussions for the way society itself is conceived" (*DN*, 246). The First Amendment effectively sequesters one of the "principalities and powers" from submission to the reign of Christ. The notion of governments, rulers, and states being called to *evangelical* obedience—submission to Christ's rule, announced as gospel—is also denied by natural law and "two kingdoms" political theologies.

20. I discuss this theme in more detail in "Revolutio*nism* and Our Secular Age," *Comment* 34, no. 3 (Fall 2016): 43–48.

in Capernaum, to the crowds in Jerusalem as he entered on an ass—he has loosed the claims of the existing authority, humbling them under the control of his own law of love" (DN, 253), even if there are countless ways this remains unrealized in the *saeculum*. In this sense, "evangelical liberty has proved to be the foundation of a more generalised freedom" (DN, 255). Thus, despite all the ways that freedom has morphed into autonomy in late modernity, we shouldn't demonize freedom or liberty as such.[21]

Second, precisely because the body of Christ was called to be a suffering church, it engendered a unique call to sympathy. In liberal society this found expression in terms of *mercy in judgment*. A society that recognizes its own judgment is under the judgment of God, aware of the grace received from the King who bore our judgment on the cross, is going to be aware of the evangelical demand to remember forgiveness received before administering punishment. Now, as O'Donovan recognizes, "It might have seemed that the only conclusion to be drawn from the proclamation of the cross must be that all human judgement is suspended"—judge not, lest you be judged (DN, 256). "But that would be to proclaim the cross without the resurrection," he points out, and would miss the fact that the resurrection signals a judgment that has led to reconciliation.

Furthermore, the redemption effected by this judgment is a restoration of creation, and hence a restoration of the capacity to judge well, even in the meantime of the *saeculum*. Judgment is reoriented in light of the cross, renewed by the resurrection, but also tempered by the eschaton: we judge even as we await an ultimate judgment. "Out of this sprang a highly dialectical set of ideas about human judgment," O'Donovan concludes, "in which the judicial paradigm for secular government, so far from being displaced by the judgment of the cross, was strengthened. The intelligibility of the secular authorities in the resurrection age depended on their being seen to carry forward what God had set himself to do. The secular function in society was to witness to divine judgment by, as it were, holding the stage for it; the church, on the other hand, must witness to divine judgment by no judgment, avoiding litigation and swallowing conflict in forgiveness" (DN, 259). Together these make up "society" and the possibility of a *Christian* society. The "secular," passing-away political authorities tasked with governing the contested territory of creation and the earthly city do so with an awareness of the penultimacy of their judgment, and thus reform their practices. "Christian liberalism taught judges to look over their shoulders when they pronounced on fellow-sinners'

---

21. One could worry that in our current moment, in which we witness an expanding libertarianism, the temptation is almost the opposite: to fetishize and idolize liberty *as* autonomy.

crimes. It taught them they were subject to the higher judgment of God, who would judge mercifully those that judged mercifully" (*DN*, 278).[22]

But in the same contested space, awaiting the realization of kingdom come, the church is that *polis* which judges not but rather extends the earth-shattering good news of forgiveness, mercy, and reconciliation. Bishops challenged emperors to forgo executions and wars of revenge, show leniency, grant clemency. And over time the penitential practices of the church reshaped judgment and punishment, giving us the departments of "corrections" that uphold modern liberal understandings of punishment and incarceration and hold out hope for conversions, reform, and sanctification.[23] "The church asserted its own evangelical justice in society's midst, and society, to a degree, had to defer to it" (*DN*, 260). Justice was "tempered" in the "penumbra of forgiveness" (*DN*, 262).

Third, the church's reluctance to judge was not born of timidity or tentativeness; rather, it was the reflection of a newfound, postresurrection "confidence in the security of the humane order"; God's mercy evinced in the cross and resurrection "issued in vindication of created being" (*DN*, 262). In other words, the "creational" theology that underwrites a Christian political imagination is not a merely nostalgic return to "creation order" or an ahistorical appeal to "natural law." To the contrary, it is first and foremost a living into a *resurrection of* the created order; it is a *christological* affirmation of creatureliness.[24] So the affirmation of *natural right* that emerges in modernity is not a rationalist, "natural" phenomenon but instead reflects a christological renewal of the face of the earth and the plane of the human. O'Donovan highlights three features of a doctrine of natural right:

1. an affirmation of *natural equality* "by which each human being may encounter any other as a partner in humanity, neither slave nor lord";
2. structures of *affinity* "by which homely communities are built," a solidarity that makes it possible to imagine common life and the very notion of a *common* good; and
3. a sense of *reciprocity*—whether "between homes or homelands"—which grants an integrity to each individual, community, and entity but also imagines a mode of interaction and "communication" that invests the exchanges of society with new hope and expectation (*DN*, 262).

22. In contrast, in late modernity "ex-Christian liberalism inherited all the hesitancy; but no longer grounded in religious humility, it became moral insecurity" (*DN*, 278).

23. Which isn't to say that these systems themselves are not in dire need of reform.

24. This account of the relationship between creation and redemption, nature and grace, is articulated more fully by O'Donovan in *Resurrection and Moral Order: An Outline for Evangelical Ethics*, 2nd ed. (Grand Rapids: Eerdmans, 1994), 54–55.

If these came to be realized in modernity under the rubric of "rights,"[25] and managed to secure protections and provisions for a wider and wider constellation of "all," this is because of *metaphysical* incursions into the Western political imaginary that began with the gospel. Even if this has morphed into identity politics and a certain fixation on championing the latest "right," O'Donovan sees in this an echo of a distinctly Christian legacy: "It seems to be a true Christian instinct to defend small and imperilled cultural and linguistic communities liable to be overwhelmed by the homogenising pressures of Western technological culture" (*DN*, 267).

A fourth feature of the liberal order with a distinctly Christian legacy is the *openness to speech* we associate with "freedom of speech." The fearless speech (*parrhēsia*) the church proclaims to the world, speaking the gospel to emperors and truth to power, unleashed habits of mutual address, prophetic challenge, and public confidence that began to seep into the expectations of citizens as well as those noncitizens—the underclasses, the plebs, the disenfranchised—who had found citizenship in the city of God. When coupled with the prior features, it is no accident that this openness to speech would amplify the voice of the people and underwrite the conditions of the democracy we see as integral to "the modern world."

This genealogical account of key features of modernity, unveiling its heritage in distinctly Christian revelation, convictions, and practices, undermines any theological account that would simply demonize the liberal order, just as it would equally challenge any lazy or enthusiastic blank-check baptism of our modern liberal societies. Such genealogical work is a model, on a historical scale, of the sort of *discernment* we have said is essential to Christian participation in the political. Such genealogies should cultivate a baseline stance of critical charity and discerning openness, looking for those practices, institutions, policies, and habits in late modern liberal societies that—even if they themselves do not recognize their "evangelical" family tree—carry within them convictions and inclinations that resonate with the gospel.

O'Donovan continues this important work in his follow-up book *The Ways of Judgment*, which once again sketches the church's nuanced relationship to "liberalism." In this book we see an example of a genealogy that both affirms the Christian heritage of liberal ideals and clearly articulates a theological critique of contemporary, "late modern" liberal expressions of those ideals. On the one hand, as he traced it in *Desire of the Nations*, many of the features we affirm in political liberalism are actually some of the "craters" of the gospel's

25. O'Donovan will distinguish the early modern doctrine of "natural right" from the late modern expression of autonomy and "inherent" rights (*DN*, 276).

To Think About: Mercy in Judgment

One could feel the reverberations of Christian mercy in judgment in the wake of World War II as France confronted the question of what to do with collaborators in the "intellectual culture" industry—writers, editors, journalists, and artists who had collaborated with the German occupiers. Many called for ruthless measures, even death, and saw anything less as continued complicity in the injustice of the Nazis. Among the most vociferous demanders of "justice" was the writer Albert Camus. Though he would eventually become uncomfortable with the death penalty as a judgment, he nonetheless argued for stringent punishment for such intellectual collaborators.

Camus saw any sign of weakness on this front as a compromise of justice itself. Mercy was only weakness, even a form of injustice. Thus he was drawn into a very public debate with fellow French writer François Mauriac (both Camus and Mauriac would later be awarded the Nobel Prize for Literature). Mauriac, a Catholic who had also been an active member of the Resistance, nonetheless argued for mercy and charity in how justice was carried out. Mocking him as "Saint Francis of the Assize Courts," Camus heard any invocation of charity or mercy as a cover for injustice and a de facto affirmation of the collaborators. "Until our last moment," Camus protested, "we will refuse a godly charity that cheats men of their justice."[a] Purification, Camus had concluded, demanded a stringent justice in the here and now. Olivier Todd, Camus's biographer, seems sympathetic to Camus's case. "Camus chose human justice," Todd comments, "whereas Mauriac thought of divine justice and therefore indulgence."

It is interesting to note, however, that Camus would later come to see things differently, that a justice that included charity, pardon, and mercy was the better way. In a talk at the Dominican monastery of Latour-Maubourg in 1948, Camus returned to the episode with a new frame. He began with a confession, a "declaration" as he called it: "I shall never start from the supposition that Christian truth is illusory, but merely from the fact that I could not accept it." As an example of how the truth of Christianity would press, even haunt, him, he returned to the episode with Mauriac: "I have not ceased meditating on what he said. At the end of this reflection . . . I have come to admit to myself, and now to admit publicly here, that for the fundamentals and on the precise point of our controversy François Mauriac got the better of me."[b]

a. This episode is recounted in Olivier Todd's masterful biography, *Albert Camus: A Life*, trans. Benjamin Ivry (New York: Knopf, 1997), 198–202.
b. This talk is included in Albert Camus, *Resistance, Rebellion, and Death*, trans. Justin O'Brien (New York: Vintage, 1960), 69–70.

impact that dot the political landscape of the West. Even our off-the-rails individualism in the West bears the marks of the gospel in important ways. Thus O'Donovan (rightfully) emphasizes that the individual needs to have some "transcendence" with respect to society: "There must come a moment at which the individual stands apart and looks upon the social system as it were from the outside" (*WJ*, 75). And as he traced it in *Desire of the Nations*, this honoring of the individual was, in fact, one of the legacies of the *gospel*'s impact on politics in the West—not just a "natural" insight or the outcome of some inherent right but the effect of an "evangelical" impact. And yet it is just this "transcendence" of the individual that *late* liberalism has effaced. "The liberal tradition used to defer to a point of transcendence in the individual, something which social identity could not account for, something which gave the individual an independent point of view upon society" (*WJ*, 75). But this "individual" was never presumed to be asocial, a being "from nowhere":

> By instructing the individual that conscience had precedence over every social demand, the liberal tradition did not throw him back upon the chances of an untutored imagination. It presumed that conscience had a source beyond both society and individual, that it was more than an echo of social claims, more than a projection of individual dreams. It presumed this because of the monotheistic faith that lay at the heart of its logic. Until the early years of the twentieth century Augustine's controversial thesis, that there can be no "right" in a society that does not acknowledge the right of God, appeared to be the incontrovertible bedrock of liberal society. (*WJ*, 76)[26]

But because this faith in the transcendent has eroded, so too has the transcendence of the individual. Late liberalism, governed by what Charles Taylor would call "exclusive humanism," is on O'Donovan's terms "polytheistic": "A polytheistic society negotiates multiple claims with no cohesion but what it can impose on them, so that, in effect, it enforces its own sovereignty. Late-liberalism, one may say, in taking up the banner of 'pluralism,' has made itself self-consciously polytheistic" (*WJ*, 76).[27]

This is also why late liberalism struggles with a coherent sense of authority. We can see that, based on O'Donovan's account of freedom, authority is a good to be exercised *for the sake of* freedom, not a threat *to* freedom. As such, authority "turns upon the non-reciprocal relation of subjects to rulers" (*WJ*, 127). But nonreciprocality is the great stumbling block of late modern liberalism. The "contract" myth is "an attempt to justify the non-reciprocal relation by deriving it from reciprocality"—I'm really just obeying myself! This is why, "when civilization thinks of political authority as one of its own artifacts, it conceives it in terms of institutions rather than events, and then,

---

26. One might then compare Nicholas Wolterstorff's attempt to *return* liberal society to this assumption in *Justice*.

27. A related point, later on: "There could undoubtedly be worse tyrannies than that of the regnant liberal secularism, so sensitively averse to overt physical suffering. That much must always be said in its favor. But what cannot be said for it is that it fosters freedom" (*WJ*, 237).

equally naturally, begins to resent being asked to defer to institutions of its own making. That is why 'authority' has little place in late-modernity" (*WJ*, 128). And yet we continue to encounter it. O'Donovan offers an alternative *phenomenology* of authority—and the experience of being found under obligation.

Similarly, in *Desire of the Nations* O'Donovan emphasized "acknowledgment" as a key feature of authority (*DN*, 47). In Israel this found expression in *worship*, which is why, as he noted, political allegiances can so easily slide into idolatries: to recognize authority is a kind of low-water mark of a sort of worship. This feature of "acknowledgment" is explored in *Ways of Judgment* in terms of the "recognition" of authority (chap. 8) and how this is worked out in the dynamics of "representation" in the West (chap. 9). The relation between a people and its authorities hangs on the question of representation and hence legitimation (chap. 10). O'Donovan's account here is deeply Augustinian:[28] "To see ourselves as a people is to grasp imaginatively a common good that unifies our overlapping and interlocking practical communications, and so to see ourselves as a single agency, the largest collective agency we can practically conceive." Such a people also "dissolves when it is no longer possible to think of these elements as acting, in some sense, together and for one another" (*WJ*, 150). O'Donovan makes *territory* an essential feature here, a necessary but not a sufficient condition for peoplehood: "To see ourselves as a people is a work of moral imagination. . . . Only when former Mercians, Wessexmen, and, later, Normans called themselves English *without thinking*, could such a thing as the English people be spoken of untendentiously" (*WJ*, 151, emphasis added).

Peoplehood precedes government: this is the conviction behind constitutionalism (*WJ*, 154–56). "Politics arises only in the vis-à-vis of government to people and people to government. But they are not equal and opposite subjects: a government exists to preserve and secure its people, not vice versa, and the condition for its doing so is that it is 'ours,' i.e., that it 'represents' the people" (*WJ*, 157). "The question, Who bears the authority of the tradition? is equivalent to the question, Who represents the community?" (*WJ*, 160).[29] One of O'Donovan's most interesting insights in this account is his emphasis on the *affective* dynamics of representation, "entirely absent from official theories

28. Presaged in his Stob Lectures; see Oliver O'Donovan, *Common Objects of Love: Moral Reflection and the Shaping of Community* (Grand Rapids: Eerdmans, 2002).

29. In *Desire of the Nations*, O'Donovan claims that such a "notion of representation in the Western political tradition is grounded on the relation of redeemed humanity to Christ, the representative of all humanity in his death and glorification" (157)—another one of the "craters" of the gospel in the Western political landscape.

of representation in the modern West" (*WJ*, 163). His observations on this point might be particularly timely, noting once again that our political action is less driven by rational evidence and more drawn out of us by a dynamics of attraction and aversion.[30] "The mysterious alchemy of the affections elicits recognition, a people sees itself in the face of an individual thrown forward for the occasion, and representation occurs" (*WJ*, 164).[31]

The decisive test of any political theology—especially one focused on *judgment* as the essence of the political—is "whether and how clearly it can articulate this counter-political moment in the New Testament proclamation of the cross, with its moral implication: 'Judge not, that you be not judged!' (Matt. 7:1)" (*WJ*, 233). Here O'Donovan echoes themes he broached in *Desire of the Nations*: another one of the gospel's "craters" in the Western political landscape is the *limiting* of judgment (and government) and the incorporation of mercy *in* judgment. In this sense, political theology is a "corrective." Christendom, then, in light of Jesus's command to "judge not," was something of a missional experiment that tried to absorb such an injunction in the work of governing. Rulers were sent out from the *church*, "the community that 'judges not,' but bears witness to a final judgment" (*WJ*, 240). This is why the church, the "paradigm society," is "the locus of social renewal and recovery" (*WJ*, 241): *not* because the church swallows government but because disciples of Jesus, formed in her bosom, are the ones sent to judge in secular governing.[32]

> The society that refrains from judging is not a society *without* judgment, persisting in primal innocence before the knowledge of wrong. Not-judging is not detachment from judgment, nor a bewildering shrug of the shoulders in the face of imponderable demands. On the contrary, it is a society that has felt the need for judgment, has cried to God for judgment, and has seen it revealed in

30. This could now be profitably read alongside Jonathan Chait, *The Righteous Mind: Why Good People Are Divided by Politics and Religion* (New York: Random House, 2012).

31. But note also his later account of the cross in this respect: "The cross challenges the *aesthetic* basis of representative rules and authorities. The ugliest of sights . . . [has] become the object of profoundest attraction. . . . As a visible emblem the cross has drawn men, women, and children into a universal community of attention, overreaching the bounds of their national, tribal, and family identities. . . . The *sweet cross* (*dulce lignum*) has outshone the glamor of attraction that binds us to our political leaders; it has shown their appeal to be shallow and moody, by calling out the deepest springs of our loyalty and love. In the cross God has pronounced his 'Ichabod!' upon the limelight of human importance" (*WJ*, 232).

32. I find these brief reflections on the church more illuminating than his direct engagement with the church in chap. 15 of *Ways of Judgment*, which includes none of the richness of his analysis of the liturgy and sacraments in *Desire of the Nations*. Here his discussion of the church is more clericalist than it was there. (And his critique of the "Aristotelian turn in Protestant theology"—vis-à-vis "practices" [*WJ*, 266]—seems to miss the link to his own discussion of the importance of imagination and affectivity earlier in *Ways of Judgment*.)

Christ; and believing what it has seen, it has judged for itself. A society that refrains from judgment does so because it has the judgment of God to defer to. Living under God's judgment, then, and embracing it as the law of its life, it is free not to judge, since all human judgment is merely interim, waiting for the judgment that is to come. (WJ, 238)

Note that this incursion of mercy into judgment is an explicitly "evangelical" effect, not a (merely) "creational" conclusion: it follows from the specifics of the Christ-event, not because of insight into "natural law" or the "created order." As O'Donovan argues in *Resurrection and Moral Order*, it is a stance that follows from the resurrection (and ascension) of Christ.[33] It is a legacy of Christendom. Overall, O'Donovan takes a "long view" of the relationship between the church and secular government: "An effective church with an effective ministry, in holding out the word of life, than which there is no other human good within the world or outside it, will render assistance to the political functions in society by forwarding the social good which they exist to defend. But that is to take the very longest view of the relationship" (WJ, 292).

In some ways we live among the ruins of this legacy: the foundations of early modern liberalism are still there, under the rubble; on top of them we have created the flimsy, flashy construction of the late modern self and identity politics. We can't let this deformative individual*ism* obscure the good, healthy, biblical affirmation of the individual that emerged in Christendom. "To judge of oneself is the very heart of faith in God. And with this act the individual emerges decisively as the primary agent" (WJ, 294). But in modernity we see the emergence of another *kind* of individual, the "modern" individual. Actually, there are *two* kinds of "modern" individuals. There is the myth of the pre-social, atomistic individual of Descartes, Locke, and Hobbes. This sort of modern individual is rightly criticized (WJ, 297). "But there is another kind of individual to be met with in modernity . . . a subject who *achieved* individuality . . . [who] cannot be dismissed so easily. For we can detect a strong resemblance, and in the case of a Christian writer like Kierkegaard more than a resemblance, to the Christian 'soul'" (WJ, 297–98). *This* modern individual, as a reflective being, is one who bears the marks of the gospel's impact.

33. See especially O'Donovan's prologue to the second edition of *Resurrection and Moral Order*, in which he summarizes the "evangelical principle": that "what is true about the world" is "constituted by what God has done for his world and for humankind in Jesus Christ"—which is coupled with the "Easter principle": that "the act of God which liberates our action is focused on the resurrection of Jesus from the dead, which restored and fulfilled the intelligible order of creation" (ix).

But the inheritance is selective: "Modernity is known by its reflectivity, yet this is not the reflectivity that Christianity shaped. It is not formed by hopeful attention to the inner dialogue with God, but by the incessant and disappointing struggle to get to the core of things, to occupy a position of strategic command. Kierkegaard understood this very well: reflection, he thought, had turned into 'reflective stagnation,' and it was the essential form of despair" (*WJ*, 309). (Paging David Foster Wallace!) In modernity we get something like monastic introspection and a retreat to interiority. But the interior castle is empty; there is no encounter with God to be found there, so the result is despair (*WJ*, 310). As a result, we come to *over*-expect from society:

> For as long as the absoluteness of the Christian revelation was taken for granted, the lofty superiority of the subject from society hardly seemed to matter, since for conscience's sake, or for the will of God, the individual would perform everything and more that society expected of him. He was serviceable to society's political organs, too. Habits of self-direction and self-judgment relieved government of the weight of its ordinary burdens of passing judgment; but more importantly, the subjective capacity to conceive and respond to the will of God as a sufficient reason for doing right and a sufficient justification for suffering pain, relieved society of another burden, which it could never bear and was never meant to, that of justifying right action and patient suffering. (*WJ*, 311)

This "conscientious" modern individual is a selective inheritance, inheriting the burdens of the introspective Christian soul without the word of grace. "The conscientious individual as conceived by modernity is a distorted version of something genuinely redemptive, the evangelical summons to be judge of ourselves" (*WJ*, 312). To receive the injunction "Judge of yourself!" without the good news of the gospel—of God's *judgment* in Christ—is to spiral into self-conscious despair. So again, the church serves society by embodying what it looks like to receive and live within this good news (*WJ*, 319).

"To be alert to the signs of the times," O'Donovan admonishes, "is a Gospel requirement" (*DN*, 273). "For each age, no doubt, this task is differently determined, though it will have formal features common to it in all ages. It will include discerning the signs of promise which alert us to the appearance of Christ's future coming; and it will include discerning the form of Antichrist, the warning of ultimate conflict" (*DN*, 273). There can *be* "signs of promise" precisely because the gospel and the body of Christ have made a dent on history, shaping, changing, and rechanneling some of our political practices, institutions, and hopes. Not even the political is immune to the incursions of the Spirit who blows where he will. But to inhabit the *saeculum* is to realize this "conversion" of the political is always incomplete and ongoing. That is why we need to be equally on guard looking for signs of the beast, especially when he roams about as an angel of light, robed in enlightenment and democratic righteousness. "When," for example, "believers find themselves confronted with an order that, implicitly or explicitly, offers itself as the sufficient and necessary condition of human welfare, they will recognize the beast" (*DN*, 274).

This discernment—looking for signs of promise *and* forms of Antichrist—is what animates the intellectual history of liberalism in this chapter. On the one hand we can see how liberalism is the fruit of an evangelical reform of the political landscape; on the other hand we see liberalism's incompleteness, its continued and new idolatries, its resistance to the reality and challenge of the King's resurrection. Thus the story O'Donovan tells is "how modernity is the child of Christianity, and at the same time how it has left its father's house and followed the way of the prodigal" (*DN*, 275). Even the prodigal remains a son. We shouldn't be bolting the door against him but looking for ways to welcome him back. Or at the very least, we should see the family resemblances of a brother.

Picturing the Law in *Les Misérables*: Two Cheers for Javert

Whenever I watch *Les Misérables*, I end up falling for the villain. So let me play the role of devil's advocate and offer a few words in praise of Javert as a way to articulate the good of judgment, even if we are also admonished to "judge not." At stake here is a Christian affirmation of the good of the law (and a corresponding aversion to "revolutionary" thinking).

For those unfamiliar with the story, Javert is a prison guard and later an inspector, or policeman, tasked with keeping the peace by maintaining law and order. He is the nemesis of the story's protagonist, Jean Valjean, who has been imprisoned by the law that Javert upholds. And Javert has been pursuing him since his release and failure to obey the rules for his parole. In Hooper's film version, the story is an ongoing dance between these two characters.

Let's first resist the temptation to read this as an allegory of salvation, with personifications of Grace and Law in Valjean and Javert, respectively. When we do that, it seems clear that any Christian would of course side with Valjean, mourning the tragic fact that Javert has no room in his worldview for grace or forgiveness. But I don't think the story is best read as an allegory, though it certainly invites us to consider the dynamics of grace and forgiveness in the life of Jean Valjean. If you insist on reading the film in this way, don't treat it as an allegory of salvation; read it as hagiography—one of the "lives of the saints" that tracks the sanctification of Valjean.

But I want to look at the story through the lenses of political theology and consider the place and evaluation of law in the world that Victor Hugo (and Tom Hooper) have created. On this score, it seems to me that the story is in danger of demonizing law *as such*. Granted, we feel the disproportionality between Valjean's crime (stealing bread to feed a hungry nephew) and his punishment (nineteen years of hard labor). Our inner Robin Hood is easily provoked by such a tale. Javert's dogged pursuit of a petty thief seems maniacal. And the fact that he can neither grant nor receive mercy has tragic consequences. Unfortunately he does all of this under the banner of "the law." So in the end Javert's villainy is tied to the fact that he is an agent of the state.

My worry is that a number of people come away from the film with a negative reaction to law as such. That's an easy sell in an age of libertarian self-expression, and it explains why there seems to be overwhelming sympathy for the revolutionaries as well. To side with Valjean is to side with "the people," and to side with "the people" is to be *for* revolution and opposed to Javert. And before you know it—and without thinking about it—you end up thinking negatively about law per se. I think Christians will be especially prone to this if we lack a robust theology of creation that should undergird a fundamentally positive account of law.

But the Reformed public philosophy I'm working from is animated by a tradition that once proudly described itself, following Herman Dooyeweerd, as *de wijsbegeerte der wetsidee*—the philosophy of the law-idea.[34] This wasn't about legalism. Instead, it was a philosophy that recognized that norms and "laws" are inscribed in God's creation for our good. This is the basis for a philosophy of cultural caretaking that affirms the development of cultural norms, laws, and policies as aspects of a good creation—gifts for flourishing and the common good. In some ways Javert has devoted himself to just this work.

Affirming the creaturely goodness of law is also why we shouldn't get too excited about the revolutionary impulse of the youth in *Les Misérables*. The same Reformed philosophical tradition is also identified with Abraham Kuyper's "Anti-Revolutionary Party" for the same reasons.[35] Because of that, once again I find myself unduly sympathetic when Javert, on the eve of the barricades, warns that "one more day to revolution / we will nip it in the bud / we'll be ready for these schoolboys / they will wet themselves with blood." Too many lawless reigns of terror have followed in the wake

34. For a succinct outline of this, see Herman Dooyeweerd, *A Christian Theory of Social Institutions*, trans. Magnus Verbrugge, ed. John Witte Jr. (La Jolla, CA: Herman Dooyeweerd Foundation, 1986). For overall commentary on Dooyeweerd's social philosophy, don't miss Jonathan Chaplin, *Herman Dooyeweerd: Christian Philosopher of State and Civil Society* (Notre Dame, IN: University of Notre Dame Press, 2011).

35. For a contemporary retrieval of this aspect of the Kuyperian tradition, see the Fall 2016 issue of *Comment* magazine ("Join the Anti-Revolutionary Party").

of revolutions. In the face of postrevolutionary lawlessness, it's not surprising to find people reconsidering the Javerts of the world.

The problem, of course, is that Javert can't seem to distinguish between the good of law and good laws. He doesn't seem to have any room for critical distance in his devotion to law and thus ends up uncritically affirming what are unjust laws. (This is a crucial distinction well rehearsed in Martin Luther King Jr.'s "Letter from Birmingham City Jail.") As a result, contemporary viewers of the film, who have been trained by a host of cultural forces to value individual expression and be suspicious of institutions, end up coming away with a negative view of law as such. By showing us the impact of the gospel on the rule of law, O'Donovan shows us how the exercise of law has been invaded by mercy. But perhaps most importantly, this invites us to continue the work of reform so that our policing, law courts, and correctional facilities can imagine a rule of law that is haunted by the mercy of God. While we don't want to demonize Javert, we also don't want to be him. Even Javert needs mercy so that, by grace, he might become merciful.

The Law of Christ and the Laws of the Land

O'Donovan's is just one voice in a chorus of research that demonstrates the way the gospel has made an impact on the political landscape of the West—and not only in modernity. As Peter Leithart has shown, contrary to the contemporary theological penchant to demonize "Constantinianism" as the very byword of depravity and political capitulation of the church, already in Constantine's reign we can see the first craters of the gospel's impact on Western political life. To take one jarring example that was felt in civil society: "There was no arena in Constantinople."[36] To appreciate the political and religious significance of this, we need to recall that "the [gladiatorial] shows were as basic to Rome as sacrifice." Indeed, they were effectively the continuation of human sacrifice by other means. "Rome *was* the arena, and the arena was Rome. What would the empire be without it?"[37] Constantine ran the risk of finding out because, as one who had come to embrace the Son who sacrificed himself to end sacrifice, the emperor issued an edict that curtailed the role—both civil and religious—of such spectacles.

We shouldn't underestimate the extent to which this was a gospel-ed reform of Western politics, precisely because it was a kind of *liturgical* reform, a revision of the rites of the empire. "By eliminating one of the main public

---

36. Peter Leithart, *Defending Constantine: The Twilight of an Empire and the Dawn of Christendom* (Downers Grove, IL: IVP Academic, 2010), 197.
37. Ibid., 196.

venues for the display and inculcation of *Romanitas* he began to chip away at the pagan civilization that had preceded him. It is too much to say that Constantine's legislation 'Christianized' public entertainments, but he clearly de-Romanized them. Rome had been baptized; now it needed to begin the slow work of Christian *paideia*," the empire's "Christian education," we might say.[38] Rather than supposedly leading to a compromised collusion between the empire and the church that lazy critics assume when they bandy about the word *Christendom*, in fact "the conversion of the empire did not bond empire and church inseparably together. It had . . . the opposite effect. It *loosened* the bonds that many Romans felt to the empire, even as it *strengthened* their bonds to another city, another kingdom, one that spilled far over the limits of the empire. Baptized Rome found that it could join with baptized *barbaria*, since Jesus had broken down the dividing wall."[39] This "baptism" of Rome, Leithart later adds, did not translate it into the kingdom of God. "Baptism sets a new trajectory, initiates a new beginning, but every beginning is the beginning of something. Through Constantine, Rome was baptized into a world without animal sacrifice and officially recognized the true sacrificial city, the one community that *does* offer a foretaste of the final kingdom. Christian Rome was in its infancy, but that was hardly surprising. All baptisms are infant baptisms."[40]

So the political order begins to show the signs of gospel impact early on. As we've already sketched with O'Donovan, this trajectory of politics' Christian *paideia* culminates, in many ways, *not* in medieval kingdoms or Venetian city republics but in the emergence of early modern liberalism.[41] This account is reinforced from multiple angles. The legal scholar John Witte, for instance, has documented how early-modern Calvinism was "one of the driving engines of Western constitutionalism."[42] Nicholas Wolterstorff has provided a parallel genealogy of the prized rights discourse of liberalism as grounded in the specific religious heritage of Israel, Judaism, and Christianity, arguing that the

38. Ibid., 204.

39. Ibid., 292.

40. Ibid., 341. And if liberalism was the realization of a Christian political legacy that slowly prioritized the rights of the marginalized, we might see the beginning of this story in Constantine, whose "legislation is frequently driven by a concern to protect the rights of the forgotten little people of the empire from the venality of officials, the burdens of landlords, the petty manipulations of the wealthy and powerful" (208).

41. In case you missed it, this means that the two bogeymen of the Yoder/Hauerwas catalog of threats—"Constantinianism" and "liberalism"—are not the Babylons we need to flee; to the contrary, both bear signs of the earthly city being bent toward the city of God.

42. John Witte, *The Reformation of Rights: Law, Religion, and Human Rights in Early Modern Calvinism* (Cambridge: Cambridge University Press, 2007), xi.

only sufficient, normative ground for human rights is not a merely "natural" property inherent to human beings but rather the revelational insights that human beings are *loved* by God.[43] More recently, political scientist Robert Woodberry has documented how the specifically Christian convictions of "conversionary Protestants" (roughly, evangelicals) are predictive of liberal, democratic values and institutions across a wide array of global contexts. "Western modernity," he observes, "is profoundly shaped by religious factors, and although many aspects of this 'modernity' have been replicated in countries around the world, religion shaped what spread, where it spread, how it spread, and how it adapted to new contexts."[44] Protestant missions created the conditions in which the institutions and habits of liberal democracy and civil society would flourish: "Conversionary Protestants (CPs) were a crucial catalyst initiating the development and spread of religious liberty, mass education, mass printing, newspapers, voluntary organizations, most major colonial reforms, and the codification of legal protections for nonwhites in the nineteenth and early twentieth centuries. These innovations fostered conditions that made stable representative democracy more likely."[45] It would be both irresponsible history and ill-formed ecclesiology to assume that liberalism is essentially antithetical to Christian formation, or that liberal democracy is a regime from which Christians should only flee. While discernment certainly requires that we be on the lookout for Antichrist, it also requires that we be looking for signs of promise, the olive branches signaling that the disastrous flood waters of disordered political life are receding because the light of the Son has begun to dry the ground of the contested territory that is creation.

This is why discernment is a dance of the Spirit, requiring us to be nimble and centered, open and on guard at the same time. Political theology is not, then, some misguided supplementary pursuit merely for young leftish idealists or soothsayers on the right who want to comfort princes. A political theology is entailed by the gospel. Douglas Farrow succinctly captures this in his bracing book *Desiring a Better Country*:

> Christianity is a very political religion. It aims at a polis, and not just any polis, but one whose builder and maker is God. In a certain sense, then, it is a politi-

43. Wolterstorff offers a genealogy of rights from Jewish and Christian traditions and then normatively argues for a theistic grounding of rights and demonstrates the inadequacy of a "secular grounding" (*Justice*, 323–61).

44. Robert D. Woodberry, "The Missionary Roots of Liberal Democracy," *American Political Science Review* 106, no. 2 (2012): 244.

45. Ibid., 244–45. Woodberry's project presses political scientists to call into question their own secularistic and naturalistic biases in order to recognize the *evidence* for this religious, and specifically Christian (and even more specifically Protestant), factor for global democracy.

cally subversive religion, for it has turned its back on the city that is built by men and populated with gods, in favour of that city that is built by God and populated with men. And it encourages others to do likewise. Yet its subversion is not of the kind that the rulers of men, or their court philosophers, commonly suppose. While it has not hesitated to offer stinging critiques of man-made cities, cultures, and empires, pointing out their more demonic dimensions, it has also taken a deep interest in those same cities and cultures.[46]

Like Oliver O'Donovan, Farrow observes how the history of our Western democracies bears this out: as much as we try to tell ourselves that we live in the Common Era rather than the Year of our Lord, the numbers tell the story of a dent made in history by the incarnation, death, resurrection, and ascension of a King. Indeed, Farrow's title is emblazoned on Canada's coat of arms. His comment on this artifact exhibits the fine line he (rightly) walks: "In Canada we have taken as a motto *desiderantes meliorem patriam*. This sounds the note of transfiguration, drawn from Hebrews 11, a text that refers to those who put their hope in the heavenly city of which God himself is the builder. And, of course, the main motto on our coat of arms, *a mari usque ad mare*,[47] is taken from Psalm 72, where it contains a messianic reference to the one whose dominion shall be over the whole world and whose kingdom shall have no end." But he doesn't invoke these relics of Christendom to underwrite any sort of theocratic project. "No one in their right mind," Farrow wryly remarks,

confuses Canada with the kingdom. Yet those who seek a better country by announcing a kingdom not of this world may also seek a better country in this world, in the *saeculum*, as our mottos suggest. They will do so . . . not by demanding establishment for the Church or by insisting that the state translate the teaching of the Church into the law of the land, so as to enforce conformity, but by inviting the city of man to organize itself in a way reflective of, or at least open to, the truth about human sociality revealed in the city of God.[48]

That is to hope for the Christian *paideia* of the state and our political institutions. And a genealogy of liberalism shows the signs that the state has learned something from the church.

46. Douglas Farrow, *Desiring a Better Country: Forays in Political Theology* (Montreal: McGill-Queen's University Press, 2015), ix.

47. In the Authorized Version (KJV): "He shall have dominion also from sea to sea, and from the river unto the ends of the earth" (Ps. 72:8).

48. Farrow, *Desiring a Better Country*, 99.

Democratic Liberalism as Christian Penance

However, this is not only a story of the church as master apprenticing the recalcitrant state. As Ephraim Radner has pointed out, there is also a sense in which the emergence of liberal constitutionalism[49] was a providential chastisement of the failures of the church to live as the alternative *polis* it is called to be. "Christians invented the liberal state, and they did so out of the stones of their own ecclesiological and spiritual struggles and commitments—that is, I would argue, in part a necessary propitiatory sacrifice in the face of their own sins. That this invention has, in some egregious cases, proven a curse is only to say that 'no one can ransom their own soul' (cf. Ps. 49:7–9), even through the reformulation of social and ecclesial life."[50]

Radner's argument starts with a jarring consideration of the ways Christianity has not only prevented but also contributed to violence, which raises questions of how the church should be (and is) related to the state.[51] For those of us in North America (and many other liberal democracies), this becomes a question of how the church should relate to the liberal state. On this front, Radner wades into familiar waters, contesting the Hauerwasian or "neo-Anabaptist" line (as James Davison Hunter calls it) that tends to vilify liberalism. Radner says his goal is "to claim this political space of the Church anew and take it back, as it were, from those who would drive the Church from the sphere of social ordering—often referred to as 'the State'—in order (as they suppose) to save the Church."[52]

For Radner, the Western church has gotten exactly the state it deserves.[53] Given the realities of fragmentation, "the politics of the Christian Church's division and unity must finally include, and not reject, the politics of the mod-

49. Ephraim Radner, *A Brutal Unity: The Spiritual Politics of the Christian Church* (Waco: Baylor University Press, 2012). Radner uses "the 'liberal state' as a shorthand tag for a set of constitutional practices that have been promoted and engaged in various ways, and even on the basis of different motives" (21).

50. Ibid., 49. Radner's argument is also genealogical, but without any triumphalism: "The very close and fertile genetic connections between conciliar ecclesial polity with its debated categories, and the rise of modern (and more secular) constitutionalism . . . [that is,] the line of development at least from pneumatic to procedural providentialism in the church—my own argument here—to the constitutionalism of the young 'liberal' state of England seems undeniable" (286–87).

51. I take up this aspect of his argument in more detail in chap. 6 below (Radner focuses on the case of Rwanda).

52. In case you missed it, that was a clear allusion to Hauerwas, who, oddly, is nowhere cited in the book.

53. Cf. O'Donovan's reminder of "a point made constantly by Gregory the Great, the prime mover of the evangelization of the English: a society gets the form of government from God that it deserves" (*DN*, 271).

ern and now predominantly liberal state." In fact, the church has something
to learn from the liberal state: "Christian ecclesiology should not fear looking
at these secular 'civil' alternatives to the Church but also should positively
learn from them as perhaps examples of things the Church has simply been
unable to fulfill herself. . . . The lesson for the Church, at any rate, is this: let
us look at our shadow in the secular world, and, as one who has forgotten her
identity somehow and for some reason, gain a glimpse of our better self."[54]
The lesson we are inclined to resist is probably the one we most need to learn.
Radner's challenge here runs counter to certain trends of late and is, for just
that reason, jarring and suggestive. In the wake of MacIntyre, Hauerwas,
and others, many have assumed it was the liberal state that taught us to be
something other than Christian. Assimilation of Christianity into the vague
civil religion of the state has been a significant problem in the United States
(less so elsewhere). So Radner's proposal here might sound like part of the
problem rather than part of the solution.

But he is aware of the dangers too. The result is a complex ambivalence.
In looking at a case like Rwanda, Radner concludes that "the Church herself
had a moral responsibility to form individuals capable of ordering a liberal
state. Had she done so, this would have not only served a corporate good but
also saved the Church from the suicidal scandal of her sins." Thus he asks a
question that is almost heretical in contemporary political theology today:
"Dare the Christian church accept the role for itself as a 'servant' of the state
in such a way?" He answers in the affirmative: *for the sake of the common
good*, "churches must reorient their practice more fully, not less so, to the
needs of a stable and accountable liberal democracy." At the same time, he
recognizes the challenge: "Christians in the West are realizing how difficult
this is, at least if they wish to keep the integrity of their gospel intact."[55]

Pursuing the common good with gospel integrity is exactly the challenge.
Radner emphasizes the church's responsibility to foster the former (Christian
concern for civil society) precisely because so much political theology today
is fixated on the latter (maintaining the church's integrity). But Radner's
provocative corrective could probably use some correction itself. He is right
to call the church to social responsibility, pressing us to recognize that our
witness is relative to our unity in Christ. But does the church's concern for
the common good and civil society necessarily translate into being a servant
of *liberal democracy*? Radner praises the modern state for reducing violence
and fostering civility. But he doesn't spend much time considering how the

54. Radner, *Brutal Unity*, 381n52.
55. Ibid., 53, 55.

modern liberal state has also privatized (and thus marginalized) religious faith. Nor does he adequately address the "autonomism" that seems inherent to liberalism as we now experience it—defining freedom in only negative terms, encouraging an atomistic individualism, thereby fragmenting the common good in its own (liberal) way. (Such a nuanced, critical take is what we do get in O'Donovan's distinction between "early" and "late" liberalism.)

Those are serious concerns. But before getting to them, Radner rightly presses us to recognize that pursuing the common good with gospel integrity requires *both* a healthy state *and* an ecclesial anchor. For some of us, that will mean rethinking our tendency to vilify "the state" and its procedures. For others of us, it will mean revaluing the centrality of the church as our political center—a body politic whose worship includes the regular confession of her sins while at the same time laboring for kingdom come, concerned about our country while at the same time desiring a better one (Heb. 11:16).

The "Secular" State as Gift

The history of Western liberal democracy is one filled with craters from the impact of the gospel. That means some of its habits, practices, and institutions (and not just the theories and ideas) are the fruit of a tree whose roots extend into the soil of Christianity (and Israel).[56] So there can be no simple antithesis between the church and "the liberal state." Instead, we need careful discernment, centered critique, and selective affirmation. This shouldn't be confused with a simple affirmation, as if contemporary liberalism were the realization of the kingdom of God.

But what this genealogy shows us is evidence of the state being enrolled in the *paideia* of Christian conversion, as Leithart put it. That conversion is never perfect; sanctification is never perfect. But we can certainly recognize growth, change, "progress." A high point of such political sanctification of the state is when society recognizes the limits of the state; when rulers recognize their power is already eclipsed and passing away. In other words, the sanctified state is one that recognizes it is penultimate. "The most truly Christian state," O'Donovan reminds us, "understands itself most thoroughly as 'secular.' It makes the confession of Christ's victory and accepts the relegation of its own authority. It echoes the words of John the Baptist: 'He must increase, I must decrease' (John 3:30). . . . The only corresponding service that the church can

56. Recall O'Donovan's careful account of the political legacy of Israel in *Desire of the Nations*, 30–81 (rehearsed in chap. 2 above); cf. Eric Nelson, *The Hebrew Republic: Jewish Sources and the Transformation of European Political Thought* (Cambridge, MA: Harvard University Press, 2010).

render to this authority of the passing world is to help it make that act of self-denying recognition. . . . We may say that the church seeks the 'conversion' of the state, provided that we use that term analogously" (*DN*, 219).

So what do we do when such a state backslides from this realization and commitment? While O'Donovan tracks early liberalism's Christian heritage, that rendition of constitutional liberalism sometimes feels like a distant memory in an era when the state swells to be all in all.[57] In this sense, the "end" of Christendom is not synonymous with disestablishment or merely a decline in religious attendance; "Christendom" ends when the state once again begins to assume it is savior. "I take it as beyond dispute that Christendom has in fact ended," at least "in the minimal sense of the verb," O'Donovan remarks. Why? Because "our contemporaries no longer think that the rulers of the earth owe service to the rule of Christ" (*DN*, 244). Of course, that they don't *think* this does not negate its truth. Christendom has "ended" as a shared epistemic ethos; it hasn't been displaced as a normative ideal.[58] "Since Christendom has, on our account, to do with the submission of rulers, it prepares the way for something beyond itself, the replacement of the rulers by the Christ" (*DN*, 243). Insofar as we continue to pray "Thy kingdom come," the latter has not been fully realized. Therefore rulers are still called to submit; and therefore Christendom has not "ended." "Has it fulfilled itself in the transition from the rule of the kings to the rule of the Christ, or has it simply been eclipsed by the vicissitudes of mission, perhaps to return in another form or, if not to return, to provide a standing reminder of the political frontier which mission must always address?" (*DN*, 243–44). Christendom, for O'Donovan, is not an "era"; rather, "the legacy of Christendom" is a "normative political culture" that "must [continue to] be our guide" (*DN*, 249).

But even if "our contemporaries no longer think that the rulers of the earth owe service to the rule of Christ," a society's backsliding from Christendom still holds opportunity. "Society as a whole, however, is too permeated by [Christendom's] memories and traditions to allow of simple relapse. Having taken on the narrative form of the Christ-event, it cannot become unformed. The possibilities open to society with history and memory of the Gospel proclamation do not include naïve malevolence, but only a formation that

---

57. This is why widespread unbelief could be a root of injustice, in which case challenging unbelief and evangelizing society become key components of the church's *political* witness. If a more just state is one that recognizes it is penultimate in light of the ultimacy of Christ's kingdom, then the recognition of that kingdom has *political* consequences. The just state confesses that a transcendent King is ultimate, whereas in our naturalistic "secular" age, society is more and more inclined to see the state as the *last* ultimacy. For an argument along these lines, see Smith, "Revolution*ism* and Our Secular Age."

58. We will return to this theme in chap. 5 below.

is demonic to the extent that it is not redeemed and redemptive" (*DN*, 251). This is why citizens of the city of God, shaped by and centered in the *polis* that is the *ekklēsia*, are sent from the sanctuary to remind society of who and whose they are. And it's why the habits, practices, and institutions of liberalism provide a societal "memory" that can be leveraged for mission, for justice, and for the common good.

Excursus: Common Grace versus Providence

The upshot of this analysis and genealogy is to encourage a posture of critical, selective affirmation regarding Christian participation in the liberal state, even if we must also be wary of how the institutions of late modern liberalism can sometimes *de*form us. Given the Christian legacy of liberalism, Christians stepping into a liberal public square should have a vague sense of familiarity, like someone walking into a long-lost cousin's home and seeing family photos that are familiar, family routines that were your own, and smelling meals emanating from the kitchen that remind you of home. While the politics of the liberal state is still *earthly city* politics, it is nonetheless a configuration of the earthly city that bears the marks of an encounter with the gospel in deep and significant ways. It is not wholly other to the politics of the *ekklēsia*; to the contrary, it might be more like the church-as-*polis* than we realize. Which is precisely why, with careful discernment, we can cautiously affirm and selectively participate in some of its institutions and rhythms, even if we also labor and hope for its continued "conversion"—which, given the dynamics of late modern liberalism, would be akin to the prodigal returning home. To anathematize "liberalism" per se is to write off the prodigal. Furthermore, such simplistic, almost Manichaean assertions of antithesis are plagued by an idealism that fails to recognize differences between political regimes, effectively forgoing the ability to evaluate specific habits, practices, policies, and institutions. It is a kind of idealism whose judgment is obfuscated precisely because it is unable to make differences and distinctions. As Hegel put it, such idealisms operate in the darkness of a night in which all cows are black.[59] In contrast, we have argued for a posture of evangelical judgment that makes it possible to both evaluate and engage in the less-than-ideal realities of political regimes like liberal democracy.

But note the *way* we have underwritten this kind of selective, intentional participation in liberal democracy: it is through a genealogy of the contin-

---

59. G. W. F. Hegel, *Phenomenology of Spirit*, rev. ed., trans. A. V. Miller (Oxford: Oxford University Press, 1977), 9.

gent history of the West (and now the world) and the effects of a temporal encounter not merely with "natural law" but with the specificity of the
gospel and the lived realities of the church as a community that embodies
an alternative politics. In other words, what O'Donovan, Leithart, Farrow,
and others point to is not a vaguely "natural" set of principles that govern
political life in liberal democracy but rather the specific, determinate effects
of what O'Donovan would call "evangelical" politics—a politics shaped by
the christological distinctiveness of the gospel and the incarnational specificity of the body of Christ.

This is quite different from typical Reformed ways of licensing Christian
participation in the public sphere. Particularly in the Kuyperian tradition,
political participation is encouraged by means of an appeal to "common
grace," an operation whereby God, in a fallen world, nonetheless extends a
"preserving" (vs. "saving") grace that restrains sin, sustains creational laws
and institutions, and creates a "commonness" despite the *ultimate* distinction between the elect and the damned.[60] Common grace is akin to what is
sometimes described as "general" revelation: a kind of low-grade dispensa-
tion of the Spirit that illumines and enables up to a point—"just enough"
to restrain what would be the disastrous effects of total depravity left to its
own devices. So "common grace" is what is invoked to explain why societies
continue to exhibit remarkable stability despite the reality of total depravity
and the ubiquity of the fall.

This, in turn, is what underwrites an affirmation of and participation in
the political life of societies. Because these are sustained by common grace,
we can be confident that God is at work within them and hence join that
work.[61] Because God is at work in political liberalism, the argument goes,
who are we to demur from joining in what God is doing there? Who are we
to tear asunder what God has joined together?

My concern with this sort of "licensing" of Christian participation in
liberal democracy is twofold. First, it just doesn't tell us very much beyond
"It's OK; go ahead; be political." There is not much counsel beyond permission and encouragement. This is because the invocation of common grace

60. For a classic statement, see Abraham Kuyper, *Lectures on Calvinism* (Grand Rapids:
Eerdmans, 1943), 123–26. More fulsomely, see the new translation of Kuyper's multivolume
opus on the theme, *Common Grace: God's Gifts for a Fallen World*, ed. Jordan J. Ballor and
Stephen J. Grabill, trans. Nelson D. Kloosterman and Ed M. van der Maas (Bellingham, WA:
Lexham Press, 2016). For further explication, see Richard Mouw, *He Shines in All That's Fair:
Culture and Common Grace* (Grand Rapids: Eerdmans, 2001).
61. Cf., e.g., Vincent Bacote, *The Spirit in Public Theology: Appropriating the Legacy of
Abraham Kuyper* (Grand Rapids: Baker Academic, 2005), and William A. Dyrness, *Poetic
Theology: God and the Poetics of Everyday Life* (Grand Rapids: Eerdmans, 2011).

as a warrant for cultural participation and political collaboration is largely abstract, ahistorical, and idealist, with little attention either to the contingencies and vicissitudes of history per se or, especially, to the unique scandal of particularly that is the history of the church's impact on the political cultures of the West and the wider world. Second, and more importantly, this common-grace license treats as "natural" and "creational" what is in fact evangelical and ecclesial. Talk of common grace abounds where a theology of *providence* is lacking. Common grace invokes a deus ex machina operation to account for cultural realities that are, upon closer analysis (per above), the historical legacy of *special* grace, the remnants of the specifically evangelical influence of Christology, ecclesiology, and the gospel.[62] One of the reforms of Reformed public theology I'm encouraging in the wake of O'Donovan is an appreciation for the specifics of history and the cultivation of a determinately "evangelical" political theology, one nourished by the specificity of the gospel, the insights of special revelation, and the political legacy of the church, all as contributions to the *common* good of pluralist societies.

Against Idealism: Social Reform as If History Matters

Political theology is rooted in a theology of history: we've seen this since Augustine's *City of God*. Any nuanced account of how the church is to relate to the political authorities of this passing-away world depends on an attentive, fine-grained reading of the signs of the times in a particular place and era. "To be alert to the signs of the times is a Gospel requirement, laid upon us as upon Jesus' first hearers," O'Donovan reminds us. "This is not an invitation to uncritical apocalyptic enthusiasm. Always *the context of history* is relevant to the discernment: 'the end is not yet . . . this is but the beginnings of the birthpangs' (Mark 13:7f.)" (*DN*, 273, emphasis added). While the gospel includes a transcultural calling to be the people of God, what it looks like to embody that is essentially contextual. Indeed, even though there are enduring biblical principles that govern faithful political life across the *saeculum*, the *saeculum* is not one thing. There are always and only local instantiations, regional expressions, temporal renditions. Given the gospel's impact across

---

62. In short, Hegel > Kuyper. Here I have in mind not Hegel the metaphysician we find in *Phenomenology of Spirit* but Hegel the historicist we see in *Elements of the Philosophy of Right* (ed. Allen W. Wood, trans. H. B. Nisbet [Cambridge: Cambridge University Press, 1991])—the Hegel who is attuned to the way *Sittlichkeit* emerges over time. For a reading of Hegel along these lines, see Robert B. Brandom, *Tales of the Mighty Dead: Historical Essays in the Metaphysics of Intentionality* (Cambridge, MA: Harvard University Press, 2002). This is also the Hegel that figures into Stout's project in *Democracy and Tradition*.

time, the powers that be have been called to conversion in the meantime and have, at critical junctions, answered the call. The *saeculum* isn't flat.[63] So the challenges and opportunities morph with time, which means that Christians who are going to be "faithfully present"[64] to the society into which they're sent need to be attentive students of history, readers of the zeitgeist, ethnographers of their present. What faithful presence looked like in 410 is different from what it was in 1610 and 2016. The same policy proposal could be faithful in one age and unfaithful in the next, a creative way to bend society toward shalom in one context and a distorted, unjust strategy in another. This is why sophisticated Christian cultural analysis and social engagement must be rooted in a deeply *historical* posture, a sense of our embeddedness in time, and a healthy attention to the specifics of the moment in which we find ourselves.

Consider, for example, the kind of political debate we have in Western societies, especially the United States, about the "size" of government. Why do we find ourselves in a world in which so many seem to have concluded that only government will save us, while others feel that government is the great behemoth devouring growth? What brought us to this point? And why do we tend to talk past one another on these matters? To answer these questions is to be attentive to history.[65]

If, in light of the erosion of civil society and the failure of other institutions to care for the vulnerable, someone pins their hopes on the power of government to right wrongs and foster flourishing, then any challenge to government monopoly will look like a de facto grab for special interests (especially class interests). So if conservatives argue for "limiting" government, or make appeals to nongovernmental solutions to societal problems, this is *heard* as an abdication of duty, a retreat from responsibility. If you've concluded that only the state can save us, then any agenda to limit the state will seem heartless and selfish.

Of course, a host of unexamined assumptions are behind these fears and worries—assumptions about who should make decisions that impinge on the common good and where we should expect to find the resources for the flourishing of all. But the assumptions are just that: unarticulated (and often unexamined) presuppositions about which thoughtful, compassionate people can disagree. If we resort to common, albeit ham-fisted, nomenclature, we might describe "progressives" as those who have decided that only government

63. In chap. 6 I will argue that this is why ecclesiology needs ethnography.
64. See James Davison Hunter, *To Change the World: The Irony, Tragedy, and Possibility of Christianity in the Late Modern World* (New York: Oxford University Press, 2010), 225–37.
65. Yuval Levin's *The Fractured Republic: Renewing America's Social Contract in the Age of Individualism* (New York: Basic Books, 2016) is an excellent example of historically attuned sociopolitical analysis (*and* prescription).

can truly care for "public" good: government is what we all have in common, and therefore government is the caretaker of the common good. Those who believe that public interest and the common good are often better served by "private" communities and nongovernmental institutions are usually described as "conservatives."

But this means that if you're a "progressive," conservatism sounds like it is synonymous with injustice, which is one of the reasons that some of the policy proposals championed by Christians (and Christian think tanks) are misunderstood. This is because Christian social thought has long emphasized the significance of civil society—the spheres and layers and "little platoons" of human social life beyond government that foster flourishing, care for the vulnerable, and contribute to the common good. In my own Reformed tradition, indebted to Abraham Kuyper, we talk about this in terms of "sphere sovereignty": a healthy society comprises a plurality of spheres that together—and in sync—contribute to the common good.[66] It is not just government (or "the state") that fosters care and concern; the church, commerce, schools, and families also have important roles to play in equipping society to be what it is called to be.

In the Catholic tradition, this is articulated in terms of "subsidiarity" and has been one of the most durable principles of Christian social thought over the past century. Like Kuyper's emphasis on a pluralism of spheres, subsidiarity emphasizes that the common good is best served by empowering and trusting every "layer" of society to carry out its function. First articulated by Pope Leo XIII in his 1891 encyclical, *Rerum Novarum*, the principle is succinctly captured in John Paul II's centenary reaffirmation in *Centesimus Annus*: "A community of a higher order should not interfere in the internal life of a community of a lower order, depriving the latter of its functions, but rather should support it in case of need and help to co-ordinate its activity with the activities of the rest of society, always with a view to the common good." This is why policy proposals informed by Christian social thought often seek to challenge government monopolies and push back on a state that has overreached its jurisdiction (either by traipsing into the responsibilities of another sphere or by reaching into more intimate layers of society, such as the home or school). But they also push back on the tendency of the market to monopolize our lives, turning us and everything else into commodities to be bought and sold. Society is best served when both the state and the

---

66. See my explanation of sphere sovereignty in James K. A. Smith, "The Reformed (Transformationist) View," in *Five Views on the Church and Politics*, ed. Amy E. Black (Grand Rapids: Zondervan, 2015), 148–57.

market support and unleash the resources of these other spheres and "little platoons."[67]

For example, one of the reasons Christian policies often champion the cause of school choice and true pluralism in education, challenging the state's monopoly on schooling, is based on evidence showing that the *common* good is better served by the state making room for a diverse array of educational institutions and approaches. In terms of subsidiarity, schooling is the sort of social good that is best tended by smaller "societies" *within* society where parents—and the rest of us—are more intimately invested in the lives of children in our community. Schooling is a local project, not a federal one (the benighted hopes of "common core" notwithstanding). When we recognize this, parents win, children win, and—as the 2014 Cardus Education Survey demonstrates—the public wins too: so-called private schools are a *public* good.[68]

But now imagine how all of this sounds if you believe that "government" is synonymous with "public" and that the "common" good is synonymous with the "public" good: to challenge the state's monopoly and to encourage nonstate communities will sound like a strategy for excusing ourselves from loving our neighbor and seeking permission to set up enclaves that benefit "me and mine." Indeed, if you treat "public," "government," and "the common good" as basically synonymous, then anything "private"—anything outside of the state—is going to be seen as selfish and unjust. (This is why, as Ben Domenech recently put it, "progressives want everything locally grown except government.")[69] Ultimately, I think this sort of reaction is misguided and stems from a tendency to confuse what's "common" with the purview of "the state." In other words, such reactions have a narrow, reductionistic understanding of how to steward the common good.[70] The allergy to nonstate institutions and communities (which we almost misdescribe as simply "private") is, in fact, to the detriment of the common good.

However, there is a legitimate worry and concern that we need to hear in such reactions. For example, on the basis of the principles of sphere sovereignty and subsidiarity, we would encourage the state to make room for microsocieties

67. For a succinct, helpful articulation of this, see Gideon Strauss, "A Market Society? Yes! A Market Economy? No!," *Comment* 23, no. 1 (Fall 2005): 6–7.

68. Ray Pennings et al., *Cardus Education Survey 2014: Private Schools for the Public Good* (Hamilton, ON: Cardus, 2014), https://www.cardus.ca/store/4291/.

69. Ben Domenech, "Progressives Want Everything Grown Locally Except Government," *Federalist*, August 22, 2014, http://thefederalist.com/2014/08/22/progressives-want-everything-locally-grown-except-government/.

70. For a relevant discussion, see James K. A. Smith, "God's Preferential Option for Public Schools? Some Questions," *Convivium*, October 14, 2013, https://www.convivium.ca/articles/gods-preferential-option-for-public-schools-some-questions.

within society to educate children, including the little platoons of faith communities who have thick visions of the good that sustain education in virtue. We would also argue that all children would benefit if educational decisions were unhooked from distant federal puppeteers and entrusted to flourishing local communities of practice.

But then what about those children who don't live in such microsocieties? What about those children who live in the ruins of modernity, unhooked from thick communities of practice, for whom the state is their *only* society? If, according to the wisdom of subsidiarity, we managed to wrest education from the tentacles of provinces, states, and federal meddling in order to entrust it to societies of parents more directly invested in their communities, then what about those children whose parents are uninterested in such investment or unable to participate because of a host of barriers and challenges? Isn't the state their last line of defense? A merely antistate, "small government" agenda is entirely inadequate, as Yuval Levin points out in his important book *The Fractured Republic*. Indeed, such an abstract, reductionistic approach only throws us back onto the vulnerability of individualism in an era when mediating institutions have been eroded. "If we do turn over more responsibility to the institutions of our civil society and local government," as Levin recommends, "we will need to do so with the recognition that these institutions have been weakened in recent decades, for all the reasons we've seen. It would be a mistake to imagine that they stand waiting, ready and strong, just beneath our liberal welfare state, so that we need only roll back that state and they will step up."[71] These institutions haven't just been overshadowed or suppressed; they've been dissolved. "The mediating institutions do not just need to be unleashed—they need to be revived, reinforced, and empowered."[72] Abstract, ideological proposals inattentive to the context of history will only foment injustice.

We need to beware of policy proposals that are "principled" but fail to attend to history. Society is never a blank slate. We always already find ourselves in some historically determined moment. Our "here and now" is always the product of a "there and then." While good policy should be informed by enduring, even timeless wisdom, it is always policy *for* a particular people at a particular moment with a particular history.

So even if the enduring wisdom of sphere sovereignty and subsidiarity gives us helpful resources to imagine how a good, just, flourishing society should be organized, we need to recognize that getting there *from here* will pose

71. Levin, *Fractured Republic*, 144.
72. Ibid., 144–45.

particular challenges. This might mean we can't proceed in a straight line. For example, even if educational policy informed by principles of subsidiarity is right on the money (and I think it is), subsidiarity presumes layers of social well-being and communal health at multiple levels of society. But what if the pretensions of the state over the past century—which we rightly protest—have eviscerated just the sorts of little platoons needed for a "subsidiary" society to flourish? Then simply reorganizing society according to subsidiarity will effectively abandon swaths of society to their own devices without adequate resources. And that not only *looks* unjust; it *is* unjust.

In 2011 Rowan Williams, then archbishop of Canterbury, pointed out something similar in the midst of British discussions about "The Big Society" and calls for devolution and decentralization: "The uncomfortable truth is that, while grass-roots initiatives and local mutualism are to be found flourishing in a great many places, they have been weakened by several decades of cultural fragmentation. The old syndicalist and co-operative traditions cannot be reinvented overnight and, in some areas, they have to be invented for the first time."[73] While some of us like to point to the historic vision of Ruskin or Leo XIII, we have to concede that history has continued on a course in the meantime. And things have changed: while the welfare state continued to live off the borrowed capital of little platoons for a long time, the dual machinations of an overreaching state and a creeping marketization of everything have eroded those historic communities. Curtailing the state's monopolies in order to devolve power to smaller communities only works if smaller communities actually exist.

The puzzling irony, then, is that now, when we call for limiting the state's monopolies to make room for other spheres of social flourishing, we have to recognize that, for many, the state is all they've got. That's not an argument for continuing to prop up the behemoth, but it is the reason why policies that encourage "private" endeavors sound like—and can sometimes be cover for—the pursuit of enclaved special interests that abandon the common good. (It's one of the reasons I worry the language of subsidiarity could fall into the hands of libertarians.)

Those who rightly seek to foster civil society outside government, and who do so for the sake of justice and common good, need to concurrently address how to care for all those who, severed from any meaningful little platoons, are effectively wards of the state. And, in fact, many advocates of subsidiarity are

73. Rowan Williams, "The Government Needs to Know How Afraid People Are," *New Statesman*, June 9, 2011, http://www.newstatesman.com/uk-politics/2011/06/long-term-government-democracy. My thanks to Brian Dijkema for pointing me to this piece.

aware of this. As Pope John Paul II noted in *Centesimus Annus*, the vagaries of history sometimes mean we'll find ourselves in an emergency situation where we have to make up for the microsocieties that are no longer there: "In exceptional circumstances the State can also exercise *a substitute function*, when social sectors or business systems are too weak or are just getting under way, and are not equal to the task at hand. Such supplementary interventions, which are justified by urgent reasons touching the common good, must be as brief as possible, so as to avoid removing permanently from society and business systems the functions which are properly theirs, and so as to avoid enlarging excessively the sphere of State intervention to the detriment of both economic and civil freedom."[74]

The goal, of course, is to encourage, nourish, and support flourishing microsocieties within society. There is, without question, an opportunity for the church to enfold and care for those for whom the state is, effectively, their only "parish" and for whom public schools are their only sanctuary. We can do so even as we encourage healthy Jewish and Muslim "little platoons" educating children for their—and the common—good. But there remain significant questions about whether something like our default humanism and its secular myths are enough to really sustain the civil society we need.

Reform can be enacted only within the messiness of history. So challenging the monopoly of the state should not be confused with burning it to the ground. And calling for the state to make room for flourishing communities to educate children in accordance with their visions might not be mutually exclusive with seeing a limited, if lamentable, role for state schools in the meantime. We are where we are, and we got here for a reason: envisioning and hoping for something better includes taking seriously those at risk in this "meantime."

74. Pope John Paul II, *Centesimus Annus* (1991), available at www.vatican.va.

4

The Limits and Possibility of Pluralism

REFORMING REFORMED PUBLIC THEOLOGY

The Challenge of Pluralism

Kuyperians were pluralists before pluralism was cool. In the Netherlands the tradition has long argued for a pluralist society, with a multiplication of institutions and spheres to ward off the hegemony of the sprawling state. In North America, Neocalvinism has been inherited precisely as a way to ward off Christian hegemony within the state, a way to exorcise theocratic demons from the Religious Right, an antidote to "Christendom."[1] Thus Neocalvinist interventions in US politics often counsel the "embrace" of pluralism.[2] Neocalvinism, you might say, was ahead of its time and should have new resonance and uptake in the fraught pluralization of the democratic West. Neocalvinists might be tempted to think: "Now is our time!"

While I don't want to deflate enthusiasm for Neocalvinism, I do intend to deflate some of our enthusiasm for how we talk about pluralism. My argument in this chapter is a bit iconoclastic, part of my exercise in reforming Reformed public theology. My concern is a blind spot in some influential Neocalvinist accounts of pluralism and political life that stems from a wider, more systemic tendency within Neocalvinism to devalue and displace the significance of the institutional church, site of Word and sacrament. If it seems odd to invoke

---

1. A term rather irresponsibly bandied about along with the epithet "Constantinian."
2. I wonder if our European sisters and brothers think we see such embrace of pluralism as a luxury in a society that is still, in many ways, very homogenous.

the institutional church to talk about pluralism and political life, I suggest this is more a tic of Neocalvinism than a problem with my proposal per se.

I want to argue that these Neocalvinist accounts of pluralism are missing precisely what we need in order to grapple with pluralism today: an appreciation for the virtues and dispositions that are required to live in pluralistic societies and are inculcated through formation in liturgical communities. While we have articulated theories of pluralism, what society also needs are incubators of virtues like patience, longsuffering, and, above all, love.[3] We have offered Christian philosophies of pluralism when what a pluralistic society *needs* is the Spirit-ed virtue incubator that is the church (along with families and schools and guilds that extend this work). But I will be an equal-opportunity offender insofar as I will also argue that the liberal state lacks the formative resources it needs to engender citizens who have the know-how to live well in pluralistic societies, which is precisely why liberal democracies should not only "make room" for traditional religious communities but, in fact, *depend* on them. As we reach the other side of the great liberal democratic experiment, perhaps we'll find that what liberalism needs is not just Christian *theories* but the formative communities of the church.

The challenge of pluralism is the challenge of forging a life in common in neighborhoods, communities, territories, and states that are populated by citizens with divergent worldviews, different ultimate beliefs about the good, and different practices and rituals that they understand to constitute a life well lived. In short, the challenge of pluralism is how to forge common life in the midst of what I'm going to call "confessional" diversity, or what John Inazu simply calls "deep differences."[4] This "common life" need not be a *uniform* life and certainly doesn't require any kind of *national* uniformity. By "forging a life in common" I simply mean the human endeavor of seeking to live in some kind of harmony and peace with our neighbors—the ability to collaborate on necessities of human life in the shared territory of creation. This endeavor is articulated well in Augustine's *City of God*:

> While this Heavenly City . . . is on pilgrimage in this world, she calls out citizens from all nations and so collects a society of aliens speaking all languages. She takes no account of any difference in customs, law, and institutions, by which earthly peace is achieved and preserved . . . , provided that no hindrance is presented thereby to the religion which teaches that the one supreme and true

3. Cf. Eric Gregory's important intervention in *Politics and the Order of Love: An Augustinian Ethic of Democratic Citizenship* (Chicago: University of Chicago Press, 2008).

4. John Inazu, *Confident Pluralism: Surviving and Thriving through Deep Difference* (Chicago: University of Chicago Press, 2016).

God is to be worshipped. Thus even the Heavenly City in her pilgrimage here on earth makes use of the earthly peace and defends and seeks the compromise between human wills in respect of provisions relevant to the mortal nature of man, so far as may be permitted without detriment to true religion and piety.[5]

Citizens of the heavenly city are called to live alongside citizens of the earthly city in the time of the *saeculum*, even being catalysts to help forge and sustain the *compromise* that is inherent to political life (the art of the possible, as they say).[6]

Place is a condition of this, and such "life together" will always be located and bounded. As Oliver O'Donovan rightly points out, the concreteness of particular societies is linked to place: "Place is the social communication of space. A saying of Gregory the Great preserved in Bede declares, 'Things should not be loved for the sake of places, but places for the sake of good things.' Places are the precondition for social communication in material and intellectual goods."[7] This shared territory could include collaboration through our local neighborhood association, a public library in our city, health care policy in our state or province, economic legislation at federal levels, and a million things in between. In this sense the challenge of pluralism is not merely governmental or political; it is part of the human endeavor of solidarity for all sorts of needs and goods. In Inazu's terms, we are trying to figure out "how to live together in society," drawing upon "certain shared resources and common aspirations" in order to attain "some modest unity in our diversity."[8] Contrary to Rousseau, we might put this even more starkly: the challenge of pluralism is how to "live at peace with those we regard as damned."[9]

Many responses to such deep diversity and contestation about the good life seek to overcome it by imposing a hegemonic consensus. There are religious versions of this (either historically or globally, including Christian and Muslim versions) but also secular versions of such intolerant consensus that seem to characterize the newly emergent progressive intolerance that religious communities sense today. These are "responses" to pluralism only insofar as they see a de facto reality and seek to normatively quash it.

However, if pluralism can be threatened by hegemonic consensus that imposes a common life, it can also be threatened by an apathy, cynicism, and

5. Augustine, *City of God*, trans. Henry Bettenson (London: Penguin, 1984), 19.17.
6. For further reflection on the call to compromise, see James K. A. Smith, "Faithful Compromise," *Comment* 32, no. 1 (Spring 2014): 2–4.
7. Oliver O'Donovan, *The Ways of Judgment* (Grand Rapids: Eerdmans, 2005), 255.
8. Inazu, *Confident Pluralism*, 7.
9. Jean Jacques Rousseau, *Social Contract and Discourses*, trans. G. D. H. Cole (New York: Dutton, 1913), 4.8.34, http://www.bartleby.com/168/408.html.

atomistic egoism that simply abandons any interest in solidarity. O'Donovan describes the broad communal impulse of society in terms of communication. "To 'communicate,'" he says, "is to hold something in common, to make it a common possession, to treat it as 'ours,' rather than 'yours' or 'mine.'"[10] While we have long counted on a social impulse that is a creational structure, we might have overestimated its preservation. All sorts of cultural forces seem to have unleashed an individualism and egoism that has eroded habits of solidarity to the point that the very "communication" that undergirds society is in danger of being shredded by tribalisms of class, race, and, most significantly, self-interest, reducing our concern to the tribe of one—me. In this sense, the diversity of a pluralistic society would be a complex mix of commonality and difference: in a society where atomistic individualism is a widely *shared* "social imaginary," the pervasiveness of this imaginary also divides us into islands of self-interest. Society becomes an archipelago of egoists.[11]

So we have a twofold challenge to the social task of forging life in common: the deep, confessional diversity that shapes how we think about a life well lived and the norms for a good society; and the corrosive, antisocial forces—often fostered by the pseudo-community of the market and the state—that incline us toward Randian self-interest and self-preservation. Atlas shrugs while the ties that bind fray to breaking.

Accounting for Pluralism

In the face of these forces, the Reformed tradition of social thought nourished by Kuyper, Bavinck, and Dooyeweerd has persistently articulated a robust vision for societal health. In this respect, what has been called (Kuyperian) "principled pluralism"[12] (PP) has often been fighting on two fronts. On the

10. O'Donovan, *Ways of Judgment*, 242.

11. In a recent essay, Jonathan Rauch has described this as "chaos syndrome": "Chaos syndrome is a chronic decline in the political system's capacity for self-organization. It begins with the weakening of the institutions and brokers—political parties, career politicians, and congressional leaders and committees—that have historically held politicians accountable to one another and prevented everyone in the system from pursuing naked self-interest all the time. As these intermediaries' influence fades, politicians, activists, and voters all become more individualistic and unaccountable. The system atomizes. Chaos becomes the new normal—both in campaigns and in the government itself" (Rauch, "How American Politics Went Insane," *Atlantic*, July/August 2016, https://www.theatlantic.com/magazine/archive/2016/07/how-american-politics-went-insane/485570/).

12. For a recent, succinct statement of this, see Stephen V. Monsma and Stanley W. Carlson-Thies, *Free to Serve: Protecting the Religious Freedom of Faith-Based Organizations* (Grand Rapids: Brazos, 2015), 96–101. See also James K. A. Smith, "The Reformed (Transformationist)

one hand, it has functioned as an internal critique of Christian hegemony over public life and the political sphere in particular. Invoking sphere sovereignty (especially when coupled with an appropriate eschatology), PP criticizes Christian attempts to simply silence or deny directional diversity. This is Neocalvinism's anti-Constantinian, antiestablishment, (supposedly) anti-Christendom move.[13] (It is perhaps ironic that in the United States, where there has never been an established church, Protestant evangelicals who have appropriated Kuyper have often been most enthusiastic about his doctrine of sphere sovereignty as a theological rationale to underwrite the separation of church and state.)[14]

On the other hand, PP also pushes back on the myth of any feigned secular "neutrality" in the political sphere or any hegemonic liberal denial of directional diversity (and finds allies in such a critique from nonreligious voices like Jeffrey Stout and William Connolly).[15] It argues that democratic, pluralistic societies need to make room for religious voices and religious communities in the wider web of civil society as a matter of societal health.

This is part of a broader Neocalvinist articulation of a pluralistic social philosophy. Philosophers and theorists such as Herman Dooyeweerd, Richard Mouw, Sander Griffioen, James Skillen, and Jonathan Chaplin have all articulated, under slightly different nomenclatures, a taxonomy of difference and plurality that we encounter in modern, globalized societies. Let me take Jonathan Chaplin's "map" of societal plurality as representative, particularly since he sees himself refining and updating the prior work of the others I've just mentioned. Chaplin notes three kinds of societal plurality:

1. *Structural* plurality (what Mouw and Griffioen call "associational" plurality) "refers to the plurality of qualitatively distinct, functionally specific associations, institutions or communities populating a modern society."[16] In other words, in a healthy society we will find an array of

---

View," in *Five Views on the Church and Politics*, ed. Amy E. Black (Grand Rapids: Zondervan, 2015), 139–62.

13. Cf. Kristen Deede Johnson's persistent cautions about Christianity "taking over" in *Theology, Political Theory, and Pluralism: Beyond Tolerance and Difference* (Cambridge: Cambridge University Press, 2007), 184, 198, 215, 224, 235, 253–54. I will return to Johnson's cautions below.

14. See, e.g., John Bolt, *A Free Church, a Holy Nation: Abraham Kuyper's Public Theology* (Grand Rapids: Eerdmans, 2001).

15. See Jeffrey Stout, *Democracy and Tradition* (Princeton: Princeton University Press, 2004), and William E. Connolly, *Why I Am Not a Secularist* (Minneapolis: University of Minnesota Press, 1999).

16. Jonathan Chaplin, "Rejecting Neutrality, Respecting Diversity: From 'Liberal Pluralism' to 'Christian Pluralism,'" *Christian Scholar's Review* 35, no. 2 (2006): 146.

institutions, associations, and communities—schools, art guilds, labor
unions, families, churches, mosques, bowling leagues, and so forth—
that make up what political scientists describe as "civil society."[17] This
plurality of social structures is rooted in a *creational* calling. Families
and schools and businesses aren't just "good ideas" that we came up
with; they are forged in response to something that creation itself calls
for.[18] Thus Chaplin emphasizes that "structural plurality has ontological primacy, since it arises from the most fundamental and enduring
imperatives of our created social nature, giving rise to what might be
called the social analogue of 'creational kinds.'"[19]

2. *Cultural* plurality (what Mouw and Griffioen call "contextual" plurality) refers to the diverse expressions realized in human culture across
history and around the globe. The realization of ontological structures
like families and businesses takes on different vibes, flavors, and looks,
depending on cultural context. These different expressions can be "equally
expressive of the potential for human diversity rooted in divinely created
potentials." The divine calls folded into creation can be unfurled with a different flair in Indonesia or Indiana. "The plurality of particular cultures,"
Chaplin notes, "each opening up a different facet of God's gifts of social
intercourse, communal organization, linguistic and artistic expression,
intellectual and technical exploration and so on, is not something that
should be resisted by Christians but rather joyfully celebrated."[20]

3. *Directional* plurality names "the plurality of religions, worldviews or
other fundamental spiritual orientations" that animate people and communities in diverse societies.[21] This form of plurality is "directional"
insofar as these spiritual orientations and fundamental conceptions of

---

17. In *Herman Dooyeweerd: Christian Philosopher of State and Civil Society* (Notre Dame,
IN: University of Notre Dame Press, 2011), Chaplin thus locates this account in a family of
political theories devoted to "normative institutional pluralism."

18. James Olthuis argues that this gift/call dynamic is inscribed in the very nature of creation,
such that calls *are* gifts. See Olthuis, "Be(com)ing: Humankind as Gift and Call," *Philosophia
Reformata* 58 (1993): 153–72.

19. Chaplin, "Rejecting Neutrality," 146–47.

20. Ibid., 147. There are serious questions about race as an instance of plurality. While on
the one hand it should be seen through the lens of cultural plurality, and hence celebrated as a
prismatic realization of good creational differences, on the other hand race is clearly overlaid
with all sorts of matters of public (in)justice; and in those societies where identity politics has
taken hold, race also functions as its own worldview or "direction," perhaps especially for those
who imagine themselves "color blind" (i.e., dominant whites). See Willie James Jennings, *The
Christian Imagination: Theology and the Origins of Race* (New Haven: Yale University Press,
2010). We will return to this in chap. 6 below.

21. Chaplin, "Rejecting Neutrality," 147.

the good direct and govern what we pursue, what we value, and how we act in society—which is precisely why it is *this* plurality that poses our most fundamental challenge, since it strikes at the very possibility of imagining ourselves having a common life together. We might call this "confessional" plurality. This, as you should expect, is the most challenging form of pluralism for living in common since this sort of pluralism means we disagree about the very shape of the good life.

Mouw and Griffioen and Chaplin rightly note that each of these can have descriptive and normative expressions. We might think of this as the difference between descriptive recognition of de facto pluralities and a normative call to preserve or foster such plural*ities* as plural*isms*.[22] This distinction adds some nuance and complexity to exhortations for us to "embrace pluralism" or "celebrate diversity." With this taxonomy, what we get is "two cheers" for pluralism: a normative "celebration" of pluralism with respect to structural and cultural plurality, while directional/confessional plurality is descriptively recognized and constructively addressed but not normatively celebrated. "While structural and cultural plurality are divine gifts to be celebrated," Chaplin remarks, "this clearly cannot be said of directional plurality. Deep differences of spiritual direction cannot, from a Christian viewpoint, be regarded as anything other than the bitter fruits of the Fall."[23]

Nonetheless, this does not simply entail Christian opposition to directional plurality but rather entails a constructive program for its negotiation. It is precisely at this juncture that Chaplin and other Neocalvinists locate the unique responsibility of *one* of those diverse societal structures—the state. So I want to briefly consider Chaplin's notion of a "Christian diversity state" as a constructive Christian response to the reality of directional plurality, one that refuses to celebrate directional plurality but also stops short of trying to eliminate it; indeed, it is a proposal for the state to *make room* for directional diversity as a matter of public justice.

Chaplin's "Christian Diversity State"

Since Chaplin's proposal for a Christian diversity state is quite obviously rooted in a broadly Dooyeweerdian social theory, we might look at his explication

22. See James H. Olthuis, "Exclusions and Inclusions: Dilemmas of Differences," in *Towards an Ethics of Community: Negotiations of Difference in a Pluralist Society*, ed. James Olthuis (Waterloo, ON: Wilfrid Laurier University Press, 2000), 1–10.
23. Chaplin, "Rejecting Neutrality," 148.

of Dooyeweerd as relevant context and background. In his remarkable and singular book *Herman Dooyeweerd: Christian Philosopher of State and Civil Society*, Chaplin locates "Christian pluralism" in a family of theories that advocate "normative pluralism." Such theories all share two claims:

1. "that a healthy, just, free, and stable civil society requires a multiplicity of relatively independent and qualitatively distinct associations, communities, institutions and other social bodies, through which individual human capacities or interests can be realized and apart from which the fabric of social unity will wear thin";[24] and
2. "that the principle function of the state is to actively facilitate this realization by protecting or promoting the responsible independence of, and interaction between, these bodies."[25]

This accords a delimited (though not necessarily minimal)[26] role for the state as the social structure that is responsible for fostering a healthy society that makes room for nonstate social structures to flourish and relate well to one another (classic sphere sovereignty, in some ways). Chaplin calls this "public justice": "Public justice, then, requires the state to acknowledge the legitimate rights, duties, and competences of persons and structures and to create the necessary legal protection for them to realize them. . . . The state is to create a network of just interrelationships between the various social structures and persons within the territory."[27]

So what does this entail with respect to the state's role in the face of *directional* plurality? As the arbiter and meta-relater of society's diverse institu-

---

24. Chaplin, *Herman Dooyeweerd*, 16. Chaplin adds an important contrastive proviso: "Unlike Aristotelians, republicans, nationalists, or collectivists of all stripes, [normative pluralists] deny that membership in the *polis* is either morally prior to or more ennobling than membership in other communities or associations." However, these seem to accept the long Aristotelian assumption that there is always and only *one polis* governing any particular territory, whereas the MacIntyrean point seems to be that there are or can be competing *poleis* within a defined territory.

25. Ibid. Here, too, an illuminating, contrastive qualifier: "Unlike bureaucratic centralizers, they deny that the state has the capacity or the competence to manage and direct the whole of society, and unlike minimal statists, they deny that just and cohesive relations between social institutions arise spontaneously apart from active political coordination." Cf. "political enkapsis," which denies "that the state has any original competence in nonpolitical structures while also affirming the competence of the state to regulate externally any nonpolitical structure insofar as its activities have public consequences" (222).

26. See ibid., 228–29, on "the public interest."

27. Ibid., 225. Note: "The state is not responsible for the *internal* legal domain of a social structure; it may not impose compulsory dieting on persons or families, or set prices for private industries." But doesn't it? What if the state administers health care?

tions and communities, is the state merely a neutral referee, confessionally agnostic? In the name of Christian pluralism, does sphere sovereignty end up being another way to mere liberalism?

Chaplin insists not. In a constructive proposal of his own, Chaplin explicitly rejects the notion that the state could be "neutral," rejecting the "neutralist paradigm" that has been criticized by others (and not only religious theorists). Riffing on William Galston's notion of the confessedly *liberal* "diversity state," Chaplin offers a distinctly Christian account of how and why the state ought to make room for directional diversity. A Christian diversity state would encourage a robust civil society (associational pluralism), would celebrate cultural diversity (contextual pluralism), and would recognize and take seriously the reality of directional plurality. As Chaplin summarizes:

> [A] Christian diversity state would be attentive to all three types, recognizing structural and cultural plurality as rooted in and deriving their own normative design from the inclinations of created order, and acknowledging directional plurality (itself a result of the fall) as deserving of just adjudication. But, . . . and crucially, it would embrace all these things on the basis of a clear understanding of the normative content and limits of the purpose of the state *itself*. . . . A Christian diversity state, then, would not merely seek to promote a neutral state which Christians happened to be able to endorse. . . . It would offer much more than a pluralist or communitarian gloss on individualistic liberal neutralism, but would aspire towards an authentically Christian model of a directionally tolerant constitutional democracy.[28]

This model is tied to an understanding of the purpose and *telos* of the state as arbiter of public justice. Thus, contrary to "establishment" models, the Christian diversity state doesn't endorse a direction *qua state*; but contrary to liberal models, neither does it pretend to be neutral, nor does it make directional pluralism a *goal*. The Christian diversity state is animated by *Christian* convictions for being impartial.[29] So it is not directionally neutral, but because it would be animated by a Christian direction, it would have substantive reasons to "respect diversity."

This is an especially unique and capacious *Christian* responsibility for the state in comparison to burgeoning political movements and parties in Europe and the United States that, while claiming a "Christian" mantle, evaluate almost all diversity—especially cultural and directional—as differences to be quashed, eliminated, barred, and prevented. I want to underscore my deep

28. Chaplin, "Rejecting Neutrality," 168–69.
29. Ibid., 173.

sympathy with Chaplin's vision for a state that recognizes "what time it is"—that is, a state that recognizes that we remain in the *saeculum*, that the eschaton has not arrived, that we cannot institute kingdom come, and that the elimination of directional diversity is not the state's job.[30] Nonetheless, precisely because I am sympathetic with Chaplin's Neocalvinist articulation, I want to push back on aspects of his proposal.

Naturalizing the State: Sphere Sovereignty as Macroliberalism?

What has long bothered me about the way sphere sovereignty functions in public theology is its tendency to yield what, at the end of the day, seems like a kind of macroliberalism—what, following Michael Sandel, we might call "a procedural republic."[31] Principled pluralism rightly calls into question the myth of neutrality that so often underwrites secularism, and it decries the laissez-faire individualism that undergirds liberalism. Thus Neocalvinist public philosophy has long argued for a directional diversity in the state that makes room for Christians to not only sustain churches and other Christian institutions in civil society but also speak in the arenas of politics with substantively Christian voices.[32] But it is a *principled* pluralism because it simultaneously argues that *all* confessions and directional orientations should have the same opportunity and access. And so it ends up making a *meta*-argument for what I'm calling a kind of *macro*liberalism wherein a "just" society is one in which different confessional communities are free to pursue *their* visions of the good.

In Chaplin's proposal, this becomes a principled argument for an impartial state since the state is that one institution charged with being the arbiter between different confessional communities. Chaplin argues on the basis of a distinction that is, I think, problematic. Criticizing those who favor "establishment" models of the Christian state (such as Andrew Walker and Oliver O'Donovan), he says they "fail to make a vital distinction between *directional* truth—the ultimate truth about our existence—and *political* truth—the truth about the shape of a normative political order."[33] This distinction becomes the

30. As O'Donovan points out, "The most truly Christian state understands itself most thoroughly as 'secular.'" Oliver O'Donovan, *The Desire of the Nations: Rediscovering the Roots of Political Theology* (Cambridge: Cambridge University Press, 1996), 219.

31. Douglas Farrow cites the term in *Desiring a Better Country: Forays in Political Theology* (Montreal: McGill-Queen's University Press, 2015), 53.

32. See the important discussion in Robert Audi and Nicholas Wolterstorff, *Religion in the Public Square: The Place of Religious Convictions in Political Debate* (Lanham, MD: Rowman & Littlefield, 1997).

33. Chaplin, "Rejecting Neutrality," 166.

basis for his vision of an impartial state that can function as a "just" arbiter: "Insisting on the distinction between religious and political truth-claims is not to embrace a *neutral* state, only a *limited* state. It is to identify correctly the boundaries of the different structural spheres—ecclesial and political—in which distinct . . . kinds of truth claims are appropriately authoritative."[34]

This is an odd sort of distinction for a Neocalvinist to make. For what "truth" isn't suffused with directional commitments? What "truth" isn't normed by God's ordinances for creation? What "truth" isn't taken up in the cosmic scope of Christ's redemption? Is not political life a sphere of creaturely reality over which Christ claims lordship? And therefore isn't the state also answerable to that lordship in its gospel-ed specificity?

And yet Chaplin's distinction between "directional" and "political" truth only functions in his argument if "political" truth is somehow circumscribed to something less than directional insight. Functionally, it seems to me, "political" truth seems to be sequestered to the penultimate and operates in ways akin to "natural law." At the very least, it seems to suggest that the *directional* resources of revelation are inappropriate in the "political" sphere. Hence the macro-liberalization of the state leads (quite naturally?) to a *naturalization* of the state and politics, effectively accepting the epistemic standards of secularization.[35] Too much Neocalvinist political thought generates sophisticated theological acrobatics for treating the political as a "natural" sphere and seems to be embarrassed by any suggestion otherwise. It's as if principled pluralism becomes a theological rationale for assuring liberal democrats that we're willing to play along with their functionally naturalized, secularized political game. Give us a seat at the table. We won't be a bother. We won't be so gauche as to invoke Jesus. We understand the rules: we promise to only invoke "political" truth.

For those Neocalvinists who have adopted this minimalist—one might even say timid—posture, it can be jarring to read our forebears. Kuyper's and Bavinck's remarks in parliament or the States General will be disconcerting, even embarrassing.[36] Most jarring, I think, will be the analyses and diagnostic

---

34. Ibid., 166–67.

35. I have argued elsewhere that natural law approaches end up doing the same. See James K. A. Smith, *Introducing Radical Orthodoxy: Mapping a Post-Secular Theology* (Grand Rapids: Baker Academic, 2005), 50–54.

36. Consider, for example, Herman Bavinck's remarkable essay that contrasts the politics of Rousseau and Calvin, "On Inequality," in *Essays on Science, Religion, and Society*, ed. John Bolt, trans. Harry Boonstra and Gerrit Sheeres (Grand Rapids: Baker Academic, 2008), 145–63. While Rousseau, he notes, "quietly withdrew into seclusion without moving a finger to reform society," Calvin "derived from the same will of God, which he had come to know in Christ as a will of grace, the motive for strong, energetic, and far-reaching actions" (158). But not only was Calvin's *motive* distinctly "evangelical" (i.e., gospel-ed); so

of Guillaume Groen van Prinsterer. I daresay that Kuyperian advocates of principled pluralism today would cringe at Groen van Prinsterer's forthright critique of *unbelief*. We have accepted naturalism and disenchantment as the price of admission. We have gone from being the people of the Anti-Revolutionary Party to accepting the Revolution's terms of engagement. We have sequestered "political" truth from transcendent claims. "Common grace" becomes cover for a practical atheism.[37] So in the name of "public justice" we scale back what counts as "political truth" in ways that effectively rule out the specificity of what we know by special revelation. But more specifically, because of an outsized desire to *not* "take over," we shrink to a kind of minimalism in our public engagement that just asks either for "a seat at the table" or for room in the corner of society to follow what we understand to be lives well lived.

If we are convinced (convicted) that in Christ and his Word we know something about *how to be human*, then shouldn't we seek to bend social practices and policy in that direction *for the good of our neighbors*? We cannot and ought not to instantiate the kingdom, of course. But neither is society impervious to the gospel.[38] If, as Chaplin points out, the state will "necessarily reflect the preponderant influence of one or more particular directionally-oriented political perspectives,"[39] why shouldn't we hope that might be a *Christian* direction? Or if, per Kristen Deede Johnson, "political theory is nothing if not an exercise of imagination," and if "indeed the success or popularity of a political theory could be said to depend upon the extent to which it offers a picture of political society and life that is more attractive and persuasive than that of the *status quo*,"[40] then why not imagine the possibility that a *Christian* political theory or social imaginary could be persuasive for a society? It was once. There's nothing *in principle* to rule it out again. Why should we settle for a minimum

---

too was the source of norms of societal reform. "If we steadfastly believe the *will* of God is the cause of all things, then our reverence for that same will, which has been revealed in Scripture as the rule for our lives, must compel us to promote its dominion everywhere and as far as our influence reaches" (158). Thus Bavinck concludes that "the example of Geneva proves that Calvin's religious philosophy of life, when applied, also contains a promise for today's society": "When we believe in a higher order of things, the holy and gracious will of God, which comes to us not only through the facts of history, but also through the testimony of his Word, then we have found a norm with which to measure the present and change it" (161–62). Note Bavinck's invocation of *special* revelation as a source of norms for societal reform more broadly. (Thus later in the same collection he articulates a critique of natural law [269].)

37. Inverting this, we should note, is not equivalent to quashing pluralism.
38. See Peter Leithart, *Against Christianity* (Moscow, ID: Canon Press, 2002), 137–38.
39. Chaplin, "Rejecting Neutrality," 159.
40. Johnson, *Theology, Political Theory, and Pluralism*, 22.

we think is "winnable"?[41] The flourishing of our neighbors and the vulnerable among us might depend on it. Such a robust vision and hope would not be a defense measure of securing our "rights" but rather a missional concern to see our neighbors—including those with different directional orientations and confessions—live with the grain of the universe, for their own good.[42]

We do well to reacquaint ourselves with the unapologetic forthrightness of Groen van Prinsterer in tracing the political ills of society to unbelief (even if there are other factors). "*Atheism* in religion and *radicalism* in politics," he points out, "are not only *not* the exaggeration, misuse or distortion, but in fact the consistent and faithful application of a principle which sets aside the God of Revelation in favour of the supremacy of reason."[43] At the heart of this Revolutionary standpoint (direction) is the sovereignty of man, independent of the sovereignty of God.[44] So how likely is such a society to listen to prattle about "sphere sovereignty" if the society's foundation is a disenchanted immanence in which man is the last sovereign standing? Indeed, "the Revolution doctrine is the Religion, as it were, of unbelief."[45]

41. "What have we done," Groen van Prinsterer asks, "and what are we doing? Nothing. We eliminate ourselves. We render ourselves insignificant. Because we do not aspire to anything higher, we are a coterie in the church and conformists or outcasts in the state" (G. Groen van Prinsterer, "Unbelief and Revolution: A Series of Historical Lectures" [1847], in Harry Van Dyke, *Groen van Prinsterer's "Lectures on Unbelief and Revolution"* [Jordan Station, ON: Wedge Publishing Foundation, 1989], 424n17 [citing Van Dyke's marginal page numbers to the Dutch edition]).

42. As Joan Lockwood O'Donovan notes, far from being a worry for other religious communities, an unapologetically Christian orientation of the state can actually turn out to be the best way to secure minority religious rights. Considering the specific case of Anglican church establishment in England, she notes:

The capacity of the Anglican establishment to accommodate religious plurality in the public realm, while protecting the independence of non-Anglican communities, has been appreciated across the English religious spectrum, with the result that current appraisals of the legitimacy and appropriateness of establishment, while undoubtedly mixed, are not divided along denominational and religious lines. . . . Within non-Christian religious communities in Britain, there has been considerable support for a continuing Anglican church establishment that gives representation to minority religious voices, while increasingly sharing public space with them. Notable authorities and personages from the Jewish, Muslim, Hindu and Sikh communities have favoured the constitutional "umbrella" of the Church of England as the most historically truthful, politically effective, and even theologically acceptable, manner of relating religious minorities to public governance in Britain, tempering claims of civil equality with those of national historical identity and religious tradition. ("The Liberal Legacy of English Church Establishment: A Theological Contribution to the Legal Accommodation of Religious Plurality in Europe," *Journal of Law, Philosophy and Culture* 6 [2011]: 22)

43. Groen van Prinsterer, "Unbelief and Revolution," in Van Dyke, *Groen van Prinsterer*, 183.

44. Ibid., 185.

45. Ibid., 192. Van Prinsterer also anticipates why unbelief will become so intolerant of belief: "To deny the truth is also of necessity to despise and to hate actively—not just philosophically, but militantly—everything that is adjudged false and therefore evil. And the

Perhaps we've let sphere sovereignty be co-opted by the Revolution. Sphere sovereignty with respect to the state should not naturalize it; nor does recognizing the limits of the state reduce it to immanence. Distinguishing the state from the church doesn't nullify the state's creaturely calling, nor does it insulate it from the claims and insights of *special* revelation. What if unbelief is, in fact, the most significant barrier to justice in politics? What if the acceptance of a disenchanted world has encased us in a claustrophobic "immanent frame" that also cuts us off from the sources we need in order to live well together in the midst of directional plurality? Then limiting ourselves to a "political" truth that is sequestered from revelational insight is not the path to justice but instead a reinforcement of the root problem. What if only theism can actually underwrite toleration?[46]

Practicing Pluralism: Reforming Reformed Social Thought

Thus far I've argued that, while Neocalvinist public philosophy has articulated a helpful, nuanced account of social plurality and rightly desires a society and state that can manage directional diversity without merely stamping out difference, there are reasons to worry that the Neocalvinist solutions have, of late, ceded too much to secularism and liberalism. To this let me add a second substantive concern.

Neocalvinism's advocacy for pluralism has largely been architectonic; that is, principled pluralism mostly offers an alternative *account*, a different *theory* or "perspective"—one that reframes public life so that Christians can see why they should abandon culture warrior "takeover" bids and so that liberals will see why they ought to refuse the same. While this sort of theoretical, architectonic concern about principles and procedures is surely right, it is inadequate insofar as the challenge of "forging common life in the midst of directional diversity" requires not only theoretical scaffolding but also *dispositions* and

---

Gospel and Christian belief are certainly false and evil from the viewpoint of the unbelieving philosophy. Once denied, revealed truths are nefarious superstitions, the worst of the impediments blocking the road to enlightenment and self-perfection. Wherever the lie triumphs, it must hate every element of the truth that still remains. Even deism, however diluted, is an offense to an atheist. In his estimation, whoever believes in a God, of whatever description, is a bigoted proponent of childish and harmful ideas" (198–99). After citing Burke, van Prinsterer surmises that "the defining feature of the Revolution is its hatred of the Gospel, its anti-Christian nature" (199).

46. There might be an argument to spin here that is akin to Nicholas Wolterstorff's genealogy of rights in *Justice: Rights and Wrongs* (Princeton: Princeton University Press, 2008), wherein cogent rights-talk needs to avail itself of the moral sources of a distinct theism that affirms every person is loved by God.

> ### To Think About: The Future of Christianity in Updike's Manhattan
>
> It is fashionable today to lament the loss of Christianity's cultural privilege and power in the West. We are regularly confronted with data that documents the demise of denominations, declines in church attendance, the rise of the "nones," and various other realities of post-Christian society. There's no denying these realities. What is more contestable is the extrapolation from such data, the prognostications that assume the future is always and only a straight line, in which case the public influence of Christianity is expected to diminish to zero.
>
> We might want to be more cautious about such predictions. The rise of Christianity looked pretty unlikely under Diocletian too. Why should we think its return is impossible?
>
> I'm reminded of a jarring observation in an early short story by John Updike, published in 1961: "The churches of Greenwich Village had this second-century quality. In Manhattan, Christianity is so feeble its future seems before it."[a]
>
> Who knows? Why not?
>
> a. John Updike, "Packed Dirt, Churchgoing, a Dying Cat, a Traded Car," in *The Early Stories: 1953–1975* (New York: Random House, 2003), 105.

habits—yea, *virtues*—of citizens who live and act in common within society. A healthy, pluralistic society requires more than simply policing sphere boundaries and getting law and policy right (though it certainly includes that); it also requires attention to the *formation* of agents and actors within those parameters who inhabit both the specific sphere of the state and the other social structures that make up civil society.[47] Indeed, the formation of dispositions—as "know-how"—may be primary since it is not likely that policy will be endorsed without citizens having affective sympathy with the goods articulated in such policies.[48] In short, any account of "good" citizenship in a pluralistic society needs to be rooted in a sufficiently holistic anthropology that is attentive not only to the systems of a just-yet-diverse society but also to the formation of citizens with the requisite habits and virtues.

Unsurprisingly, this virtue focus has been largely absent from Reformed accounts of pluralism and politics, symptomatic of wider trends.[49] (To be

47. Directional plurality is not *only* a challenge in the political sphere; it can also manifest itself in the spheres of education, commerce, and even the family.

48. The utter implausibility of religious freedom to a rising generation of secularized liberals would be a case in point. Arguments for such policies are met with either blank, uncomprehending stares or cynical dismissals of them as power plays.

49. Those trends would include at least two aspects. The first is a kind of default "intellectualism" that yields a rather stunted picture of human agents as primarily deliberative and governed by rational concerns. (I have articulated a critique of this rationalist anthropology in James K. A. Smith, *Imagining the Kingdom: How Worship Works*, Cultural Liturgies 2

fair, it has also been largely absent from liberal accounts of the same.) This is where legal scholar John Inazu's argument in *Confident Pluralism* makes an important new contribution to our discussion of pluralism and the public good. While Inazu attends to important systemic concerns about constitutional law and precedent (part 1 of his book), he also rightly recognizes that forging a common life in the midst of deep directional diversity requires specific *dispositions* of tolerance, humility, and patience.[50] Insofar as virtues are (good) habits, and habits are internal dispositions that are inscribed by imitation and practice, these virtues of good citizenship can be acquired only by *formation* through immersion in social practices (as defined, say, by MacIntyre). But at least Inazu's proposal is attentive to the necessity of formation in ways that, to date, Neocalvinist proposals have not been. This appreciation for the importance of formation raises two lines of inquiry.

First, it raises real challenges for the prospects of such virtue formation in a postreligious, "secularized" society. In short, liberalism needs to face some difficult questions: Where does a generic, "secular" liberalism provide such communities of practice—a space for citizens to acquire the dispositions of tolerance, humility, and patience? Where in a stratified, segmented society do citizens have the opportunity to "practice" encounter with and tolerance of difference? What story would orient them and motivate them to be patient? Who is going to teach them to be humble and give them a reason why? Does a liberal pluralist society have what it *needs* to be what it *wants* to be?[51]

[Grand Rapids: Baker Academic, 2013]. But one could also look to developments in behavioral economics [Richard Thaler, Cass Sunstein, et al.] for alternative resources to make a similar point.) Second, and in part because of this default rationalism, Reformed ethics has tended to privilege deontology over virtue accounts. I have argued elsewhere that this is an unfortunate and unnecessary emphasis; see *You Are What You Love: The Spiritual Power of Habit* (Grand Rapids: Brazos, 2016).

50. See *Confident Pluralism*, part 2, "Civic Practices" (83–124). Inazu's project is characterized by some ambiguity in this regard. Recognizing the challenge for a liberal society to inculcate virtues (since liberalism precludes identifying a substantive *telos* that is the precondition for virtue), Inazu describes these as "aspirations." But the change of nomenclature doesn't change the nature of what tolerance, patience, and humility *are*, especially since he recognizes them as "dispositions." We are on the terrain of virtue here.

51. Cf. Jeffrey Stout's observation at the beginning of *Blessed Are the Organized: Grassroots Democracy in America* (Princeton: Princeton University Press, 2010), 9: "Skillful and virtuous citizens of any social class acquire their skills and virtues under specifiable conditions, as members of groups that gather people of good will, provide them with information, and cultivate their dispositions to behave well. The evidence that makes democracy seem like a foolish wager is best understood as evidence of how poorly organized, poorly trained people behave. The members of any social class, if poorly organized and poorly trained, are likely to behave irresponsibly and ineffectively."

As James Davison Hunter has commented, "There have never been 'generic' values."[52] The issue is a kind of "sources of the self"[53] concern: Does a secularized, post-Christian, increasingly antireligious society have the sources (formative communities) to engender the dispositions/virtues needed for "a modest unity" and a tolerant pluralism? In *The Fractured Republic*, Yuval Levin makes this point with a Tocquevillian accent: in many ways the ideal of a pluralistic liberal society has lived off the borrowed (formative) capital of "illiberal" (mostly religious) communities—including the family—as incubators for the dispositions of good citizenship. But insofar as both liberalism and capitalism[54] tend to devour and erode just these institutions and communities, they end up being a parasite that, starved by its own hunger, consumes the host and thus engenders its own demise. This raises serious questions about the viability of pluralism *from the left*, which has of late exhibited neither patience nor tolerance nor humility. While Christian political theologians continue to fret about the perceived threat of a Constantinian "takeover," in fact the most potent forces of hegemony and homogeneity have been progressives who are all too confident that they know the truth and thus disinclined to be tolerant of those who disagree, or to wait for them to catch up with "the right side of history." Thus pluralism is looking less and less like a *liberal* ideal. What if it is, in fact, religious[55] communities that are best able to articulate *why* we ought to be tolerant and that have the resources to cultivate tolerant citizens?

This leads to a second line of inquiry once our consideration of pluralism starts to take into consideration the necessity of virtue formation: we can also ask whether Christian communities have been (or can be) incubators of such dispositions/virtues, and if so, how. A first exercise might be to align Inazu's aspirational virtues (tolerance, humility, patience) with the rhythms and rituals of historic Christian worship and consider how/whether/why

52. James Davison Hunter, *The Death of Character: Moral Education in an Age without Good or Evil* (New York: Basic Books, 2000), 215.

53. As developed by Charles Taylor in *Sources of the Self* (Cambridge: Cambridge University Press, 1989). For a helpful elucidation of Taylor's "method" here that puts him in conversation with Alvin Plantinga's Reformed epistemology, see Deane-Peter Baker, *Tayloring Reformed Epistemology: Charles Taylor, Alvin Plantinga, and the* de jure *Challenge to Christian Belief* (Grand Rapids: Eerdmans, 2007).

54. "Capitalism depends upon some very demanding cultural preconditions and yet frequently undermines those very preconditions, so that its very preservation demands some limits on its freedom to shape society in its image" (Yuval Levin, *The Fractured Republic: Renewing America's Social Contract in the Age of Individualism* [New York: Basic Books, 2016], 103). This sort of pushback on the market should characterize a Neocalvinist social philosophy, since it is not only the state that can transgress its sphere.

55. I use the term advisedly, since I don't want to presume that *only* Christian communities can do this.

these emerge from the imaginary carried in liturgical practices. For example, we might consider how the Christian practice of confession engenders an epistemic humility that should characterize our public posture when we are "sent" from the sanctuary; or we might consider how the implicit eschatology of the Eucharist should engender, over time, a deep patience (and hope) that should temper any activist, Pelagian penchant to "take over"; or we might consider how through congregational prayers even our enemies come into the purview of our concern by being brought before God in prayer; or we might consider how the lectionary is its own sort of epistemic discipline that confronts us with the whole counsel of God and thus won't let us ignore widows, orphans, and immigrants; and so on.[56]

Now, I readily admit that such an exercise must have a self-critical moment that asks: *Does* Christian worship do this? If not, why not? Is it partly because Christian worship has been co-opted by other stories/liturgies, other dynamics? Here is where I see the importance of both the "ecclesiology and ethnography" discussion (Christian Scharen and others) and the work of Willie Jennings on how the social imaginary of "whiteness" has been collapsed with Christianity.[57] The (albeit partial) renewal of good citizenship, then, would also depend on the renewal and reformation of the church.

Recognizing (and documenting) how Christian worship forms citizens *for* pluralism might be a way to counter the "religion-is-poison" narrative by out-narration, showing that it is in fact Christianity (and perhaps religious communities more broadly) that does the work of forming citizens for common life and the public good.[58] The irony would be that Christianity would remind society how to be (classically) liberal. That's not meant to instrumentalize Christian formation as if that's the point, but rather to recognize a kind of by-product that flows from the fact that the gospel is how we learn to be human and the church is where we learn what a *polis* should look like. Thus

56. For a timely and constructive discussion of this, see Matthew Kaemingk, *Christian Hospitality and Muslim Immigration in an Age of Fear* (Grand Rapids: Eerdmans, 2017), esp. chap. 8.

57. These questions are the focus of chap. 6 below.

58. This, I think, is one of Jeffrey Stout's conclusions—to his own surprise!—in *Blessed Are the Organized*. Whereas in *Democracy and Tradition* he worried that Christians like MacIntyre, Hauerwas, and Milbank were encouraging Christians to exile themselves from democratic politics, in *Blessed Are the Organized* he recognizes the role religious congregations play in the grassroots democracy he extols. Commenting on the role of religious communities in the Industrial Areas Foundation (IAF), the confederation of community organizations founded by Saul Alinsky, Stout observes: "The number of synagogues, mosques, schools, and labor unions involved in IAF is growing, and organizers hope to hasten this trend. Still, if one subtracted the churches from IAF and other similar organizing networks, then grassroots democracy in the United States would come to very little" (*Blessed Are the Organized*, 4–5).

the sort of "influence" we desire is not merely on the order of political truth
but entails opening up the political to the transcendent, directional truth of
the gospel, including the revelation of a risen, ascended King.

A key passage in Johnson's *Theology, Political Theory, and Pluralism* is
relevant here, and worth citing in full in order to comment:

> Claims . . . that participation in the Heavenly City offers the only way for sinful
> differences to be reconciled and God-given differences to be celebrated, that
> participation in God provides the only means by which unity and diversity can
> be brought together in harmony, do not lead on to a political picture in which
> the ontology of Christianity takes over the political realm. Christianity does
> uniquely offer resolution to the problems that plague our political societies,
> problems that have led us to try to address the dilemmas left unresolved by both
> modern and post-Nietzschean attempts to create pluralist societies marked by
> tolerance and/or deep embrace of difference. But this resolution will not be
> fully visible this side of the eschaton, nor, with its understanding of sin and the
> *libido dominandi*, does it expect that any earthly city could [fully?] reflect the
> realities of the Heavenly City. It hopes, of course, that citizens of the earthly city
> will become citizens of the Heavenly City, finding through participating in the
> Triune God the community, the peace, the justice, and the love that many had
> hoped to find in the earthly city. It cares for the earthly city and its members,
> offering, at least ideally, service that is not marred by lust for glory and power,
> in joint pursuit of goods which the Heavenly City shares with the earthly city
> while it is on its pilgrimage. And it influences how citizens view and contribute
> to earthly justice and peace through its understanding of heavenly justice and
> peace. But . . . it does not seek the [complete?] realization of its picture of rec-
> onciliation, or any picture of complete restoration, in the earthly city. Indeed,
> its role in reminding the earthly city to limit its ambitions and be realistic about
> its aspirations is a crucial one.[59]

Here Johnson walks the fine line I am commending to Neocalvinism. In particular, I commend the way that evangelization is woven into the political
hopes of this account in the *hope* "that citizens of the earthly city will become
citizens of the Heavenly City." We Neocalvinists are sometimes embarrassed
to talk like that, and that is a problem. I would also note, however, that precisely because Johnson is right on this point, she should temper her persistent
worries about "takeover" in the rest of the book. While there are legitimate
concerns about an institutional confusion whereby the state becomes subservient to the church, we can nonetheless hope—as she herself affirms—that
our vision will *influence* society widely, even capture the imagination of a

59. Johnson, *Theology, Political Theory and Pluralism*, 184–85.

nation. We must be careful not to unwittingly buy into the "autonomism" of liberalism that effectively makes any sort of "influence" an unjust imposition on individual autonomy.

In this respect, there might also be a legitimate place for a Groen van Prinsterer–like critique of the way that unbelief engenders social configurations that *by nature* end up absolutizing one "direction" in ways that are intolerant, arrogant, and impatient.[60] In that sense, an affirmation of transcendence *might* (might!) be a condition for the dispositions that liberalism wants and that a "confident pluralism" needs—which would mean that challenging the default naturalism and secularism of society and the state would be precisely the way to call it toward being a better democratic, pluralistic society.

Finally, this would also reframe the *political* relevance of the church in ways that Neocalvinism has failed to articulate, not as a sphere-trumping institution that would reign over society but as a habit-forming *polis* in which we gather to be shaped and (re)formed by the Spirit in ways that make us good neighbors, even to our enemies.[61]

60. Cf. Joseph Bottum, *An Anxious Age: The Post-Protestant Ethic and the Spirit of America* (New York: Image, 2014).

61. I make a similar point in my discussion of Eric Gregory's *Politics and the Order of Love* in "Formation, Grace, and Pneumatology: Or, Where's the Spirit in Gregory's Augustine?," *Journal of Religious Ethics* 39 (2011): 556–69.

5

Redeeming Christendom

OR, WHAT'S WRONG WITH NATURAL LAW?

A *liturgical* political theology is a *missional* political theology. While it envisions and hopes for an evangelical influence on politics and public life, its strategy is centered in the politics of the *ekklēsia* with a ripple effect from those sent from worship into the world. If it hopes for a "conversion" of the political—or what Leithart described as a Christian *paideia* for the various kingdoms in which we find ourselves—this is only because it hopes for a cascading influence of the Spirit that reverberates from the advance of the gospel itself. As Oliver O'Donovan puts it, this is to observe a "missionary order": "society first, government after. The truth in that order is that Christ has conquered the rulers from below, drawing out their subjects from under their authority."[1]

This means—and is the reason why—the shape of Christian political witness is not merely a nostalgic appeal to "creation norms" or a minimalist appeal to "natural law" that is accessible by "natural reason"; rather, it is nourished by the christological specificity of the gospel and the model of Christ the King and his relationship to his body. The institutions of the *polis* are exposed to the transformative power of the gospel itself and can be envisioned otherwise. Indeed, we have rehearsed the ways that liberal democracy bears the stamp of the gospel's imprint even in our "post-Christian" age.

1. Oliver O'Donovan, *The Desire of the Nations: Rediscovering the Roots of Political Theology* (Cambridge: Cambridge University Press, 1996), 193 (hereafter cited in text as *DN*).

While we have tended to settle for what seems natural or feasible or, worse yet, "winnable," the missional heritage of the church's public witness hoped for (and witnessed) much more.

Perhaps this is why Augustine's description of the happy ruler in *City of God* is jarring to our ears, accustomed as they are to such diminished expectations, even embarrassed by such forthrightly Christian criteria. Try to hear this again with an ear attuned to the Scriptures:

> We Christians call rulers happy if they rule with justice; if amid the voices of exalted praise and the reverent salutations of excessive humility, they are not inflated with pride, but remember that they are but men; if they put their power at the service of God's majesty, to extend his worship far and wide; if they fear God, love him and worship him; if, more than their earthly kingdom, they love that realm where they do not fear to share the kingship; if they are slow to punish, but ready to pardon; . . . and if they do all this not for a burning desire for empty glory, but for the love of eternal blessedness; and if they do not fail to offer to their true God, as a sacrifice for their sins, the oblation of humility, compassion, and prayer. It is Christian emperors of this kind whom we call happy; happy in hope, during this present life, and to be happy in reality hereafter, when what we wait for will have come to pass.[2]

Our imaginations have been sufficiently disciplined by the assumptions of liberalism to be uncomfortable about and embarrassed by such forthrightly Christian hopes for temporal government. What, then, to make of Augustine's encomium for the emperor Theodosius, who "was more glad to be a member of that Church than to be ruler of the world"?[3] Augustine celebrates not primarily the emperor's power or accomplishments but rather his Christlike humility:

> Nothing could be more wonderful than the religious humility he showed after the grievous crime committed by the people of Thessalonica. On the intercession of the bishops he had promised a pardon; but then the clamour of certain of his close supporters drove him to avenge the crime. But he was constrained by the discipline of the Church to do penance in such a fashion that the people of Thessalonica, as they prayed for him, wept at seeing the imperial highness thus prostrate, with an emotion stronger than their fears of the emperor's wrath at their offense.[4]

2. Augustine, *City of God*, trans. Henry Bettenson (London: Penguin, 1984), 5.24.

3. Ibid., 5.26.

4. Ibid. Across his reflections on political life—not only in *City of God* but also in letters and sermons—Augustine persistently points to humility and mercy as markers of a Christian politics. So when we speak of "gospel-ed specificity" in politics, it is less about laws and rules and more about dispositions and character that contribute to *how* we determine policy and

Much that traffics under the banner of "Christian" political theology and public engagement has little to do with the cross and resurrection of Jesus Christ. Instead, what we get from allegedly "Christian" public theologies are appeals to creation order and natural law, norms restricted to general revelation and the dictates of "reason." But where does reason dictate penance? And where does the natural law commend forgiveness and mercy? Did creation order ever drive us to our knees in a passionate prayer of confession? Yet are not such practices and virtues germane to the image-bearing task of governing?[5]

This scene from *City of God* suggests a more integral link between the church and the state without simply conflating or identifying them. It suggests that the practices of the church as *polis* are germane to the political goods of even the earthly city, that the liturgy of the body of Christ shapes those worshipers who are then sent to take up the vocation of earthly rule. This suggests a Christian political theology that is rooted in the substance of the gospel and the specific practices of the cruciform community that is the church. The public task of the church is not just to remind the world of what it (allegedly) already knows (by "natural" reason) but to proclaim what it couldn't otherwise know—and to do so as a *public* service for the sake of the common good. In short, Augustine hints at what Oliver O'Donovan develops more robustly: a properly *evangelical* political theology in contrast to the political deisms currently on offer.

My goal in this chapter is to sketch the lineaments of O'Donovan's provocative and incisive articulation of an integrally Christian, properly evangelical, and rightly *ecclesial* political theology—yet undertaken with a rigorous awareness of democratic liberalism and refusing any nostalgia. In doing so, we will take notice of how and why he rejects the moral minimalism of a "natural law" project as a sub-Christian expression of political theology.

Rethinking Nature and Grace, Creation and Resurrection

A Christian political theology always already assumes a theology of culture that in turn assumes a theology of creation. And any *Christian* theology of creation has to articulate an understanding of the relationship between the order of creation and the order of redemption—how we should understand the relationship

---

law. The traits of an "ecclesial" politics are cruciform: charity, sacrifice, humility, peace, and attention to the vulnerable. These are not generally reflective of the way of life that is allegedly dictated by natural law; they are not dispositions that are "rational" by usual measures.

5. Cf. Andy Crouch's description of leadership that "descends to the dead" in *Strong and Weak: Embracing a Life of Love, Risk, and True Flourishing* (Downers Grove, IL: InterVarsity, 2016), 143–62.

between nature and grace. O'Donovan's political proposals are nourished by a holistic model at this most fundamental level. As he puts it in the opening of *Resurrection and Moral Order*, "The foundations of Christian ethics must be evangelical foundations; or, to put it more simply, Christian ethics must arise from the gospel of Jesus Christ. Otherwise it could not be *Christian* ethics."[6] Any properly Christian ethics, he emphasizes, "depends upon the resurrection of Jesus Christ from the dead" (*RMO*, 13). (How many paradigms of supposedly "Christian" political theology operate as if this never happened?)

However, this gospel specificity is *not* a way to paint ourselves into a sectarian corner of cultural irrelevance. Because the resurrection of Jesus is the reaffirmation of creation—"the confirmation of the world-order which God has made" (*RMO*, 14)—in the incarnation and resurrection of Jesus "the whole created order is taken up into the fate of this particular representative man at this particular moment of history, on whose one fate turns the redemption of all." The resurrection is "the sign that God has stood by his created order" (*RMO*, 15). So there is no tension or choice to be made between an "ethics of the kingdom" and an "ethics of creation." "This way of posing the alternatives is not acceptable," O'Donovan comments,

> for the very act of God which ushers in his kingdom is the resurrection of Christ from the dead, the reaffirmation of creation. A kingdom ethics which was set up in opposition to creation could not possibly be interested in the same eschatological kingdom as that which the New Testament proclaims. At its root there would have to be a hidden dualism which interpreted the progress of history to its completion not as a fulfilment, but as a denial of its beginnings. A creation ethics, on the other hand, which was set up in opposition to the kingdom, could not possibly be evangelical ethics, since it would fail to take note of the good news that God had acted to bring all that he had made to its fulfilment. (*RMO*, 15)

With natural theology, O'Donovan affirms the objective moral order that inheres in creation (*RMO*, 17). But taking seriously humanity's fallenness

---

6. Oliver O'Donovan, *Resurrection and Moral Order: An Outline for Evangelical Ethics*, 2nd ed. (Grand Rapids: Eerdmans, 1994), 11 (hereafter cited in text as *RMO*). He explicitly challenges those "forms of belief in natural law or in the opposition of law and gospel" that "make a virtue of denying that 'Christian ethics' in the strict sense can exist." When we do so, he points out, we effectively conclude that ethics is "not open to special illumination from the gospel." I hear this as resonant with the Christian specificity Alvin Plantinga called for in his "Advice to Christian Philosophers" (*Faith and Philosophy* 1 [1984]: 253–71), which exhorted a program of reflection that unapologetically starts from "what we know *as Christians*." Cf. Plantinga, "The Reformed Objection to Natural Theology," *Proceedings of the American Catholic Philosophical Association* 15 (1980): 49–62.

(per Rom. 1) undercuts the *epistemic* confidence on which natural theology programs depend: "In speaking of man's fallenness, we point not only to his persistent rejection of the created order, but also to an inescapable confusion in his perceptions of it. This does not permit us to follow the Stoic recipe for 'life in accord with nature' without a measure of epistemological guardedness" (*RMO*, 19). We can rightly affirm

> that man's rebellion has not succeeded in destroying the natural order to which he belongs; but that is something which we could not say with theological authority except on the basis of God's revelation in the resurrection of Jesus Christ. We say that this, that or the other cultural demand or prohibition . . . reflects the created order faithfully, but that too is something which we can know only by taking our place within the revelation of that order afforded us in Christ. It is not, as the sceptics and relativists remind us, self-evident what is nature and what is convention. . . . The *epistemological* programme for an ethic that is "natural," in the sense that its contents are simply known to all, has to face dauntingly high barriers. But we are not to conclude from this that there is no *ontological* ground for an "ethic of nature," no objective order to which moral life can respond. We may only conclude that any certainty we may have about the order which God has made depends upon God's own disclosure of himself and of his works. (*RMO*, 19)

I think this gives us a way to be frank about *why* natural law programs fail to actually persuade in public debate:[7] because what we rightly see as "rational" and "natural" itself depends on illumination and epistemic virtues[8] that are *not* universally available to those who have become "futile in their thinking"

7. I'm thinking, for example, of the failure of Girgis, Anderson, and George's *What Is Marriage?* to garner any "rational" converts, serving largely only to shore up the confidence of a choir who already agreed with them. See Sherif Girgis, Ryan T. Anderson, and Robert P. George, *What Is Marriage? Man and Woman: A Defense* (New York: Encounter Books, 2012).

8. This is linked to O'Donovan's account of knowledge as "participatory": "Knowledge is the characteristically *human* way of participating in the cosmic order. Man takes his place, which is the place of 'dominion,' by knowing the created beings around him in a way that they do not know him" (*RMO*, 81). "To know," then, "is to fill a quite specific place in the order of things, the place allotted to mankind. But that means the exercise of knowledge is tied up with the faithful performance of man's task in the world, and that this knowing will stand or fall with his *worship* of God and his obedience to the moral law" (*RMO*, 81, emphasis added). This is, in a sense, the core conviction of the Cultural Liturgies project: the liturgical conditions of rightly ordered perception. This is why "true knowledge of the moral order is knowledge 'in Christ'" (*RMO*, 85). This is *exclusive* knowledge whose subject is *inclusive*—the whole of creation (*RMO*, 85). "Knowledge of the natural order is moral knowledge, and as such it is co-ordinated with obedience. There can be no true knowledge of that order without loving acceptance of it and conformity to it, for it is known by participation" (*RMO*, 87). And that participation is the *practice* of in-Christ-ness we call Christian worship.

(Rom. 1:21 ESV). As Francesca Murphy notes in one example, we need to realize that rightly discerning the lineaments of "nature" actually requires faith. Commenting on the societal understanding of marriage, she notes: "A teaching that was once part of the common sense of society has now become an item of faith, and rather an esoteric faith. Only those with biblical principles, including those Catholics who use natural law, seem to be able to see the need to restrict marriage to heterosexual couples. The rational arguments we offer fall on deaf ears. We may as well be citing Scripture."[9] O'Donovan makes a similar point, twenty years earlier, about divorce. It sometimes seems as if natural law strategies are minimalist approaches that are shooting for what could be "winnable" in public debate. Taking up the example of public debate about divorce law, O'Donovan stingingly observes that, on the basis of this approach, it would seem that "when the church contributes to public debate on matters of concern to secular society at large, it should forget that it is the church of Jesus Christ and should address society on terms common to all participants" (RMO, 20). Such an approach, O'Donovan observes, can only be understood "as a rather cynical counsel for rhetorical effectiveness: if the church wants to be heard, let it speak only words that it knows will be welcome to its hearers! We can certainly not appeal to the doctrine of Natural Law to stand between us and the moral disaster to which such a policy must undoubtedly lead" (RMO, 21).

Murphy at least exhibits theological honesty on this point: once one recognizes that supposedly "winnable" but minimalist natural-law appeals aren't winning, then why settle for the minimalism? Appeals to nature depend on the illumination of special revelation. But this does *not* mean the norms only apply to the Christian community; they remain norms for a flourishing humanity. Thus she counsels arguing for her view on this matter from an unapologetically Christian starting point: "I think the traditional view of marriage has indeed become a matter of faith and we have to keep on arguing for it to be on the law books, until and even after every state has ratified same-sex marriage."[10] Recognizing the revelational conditions for insight into human nature does not preclude public proclamation.

Because creation is reaffirmed in Christ's resurrection, and because "nature" is only known "in Christ," any Christian account of even our "this-worldly" life has to be unapologetically *evangelical*, rooted in what we know in—and because of—the gospel. This must include our *political* theology,

9. Francesca Aran Murphy's contribution to "The Church and Civil Marriage," a symposium in *First Things*, April 2014, https://www.firstthings.com/article/2014/04/the-church-and-civil-marriage.
10. Ibid.

even though our political theology involves an account of how to live with those who are not "in Christ." In our construction of a Christian political theology—and in our public and political witness—we ought not to operate as if we are working in the dark with everyone else, without revelation and illumination. Contravening King Lear, O'Donovan emphasizes: "God has no spies. He has prophets, and he commissions them to speak about society in words which rebuke the inauthentic speech of false prophets" (*DN*, 11). This is why Christian political theology is at once evangelical and scandalously historical. "True prophets," he continues, "cannot speak *only* of the errors of false prophets. Their judgment consists precisely in what they have to say of God's purposes of renewal, his mercy towards even such weak and frangible societies as Israel and Judah, unstable communities on which the fate of souls depends. Christian theology must assume the prophet's task, and, accepting history as the matrix in which politics and ethics take form, affirm that it is the history of God's action, not sheer contingency but purpose" (*DN*, 11–12). This is exactly O'Donovan's exercise in *Desire of the Nations*: to read Israel's history both as "a history of redemption" and as *our* history—the pedigree of democratic liberalism. This is to read Israel's history "as the story of how certain principles of social and political life were vindicated by the action of God in the judgment and restoration of the people" (*DN*, 29).[11]

"Nothing in modern democracy has changed the fact that political existence depends upon structures of command and obedience" (*DN*, 18). Thus at the heart of a Christian political theology is discerning the nature of authority, which in Scripture is bound up with the reign of God (*DN*, 19). But once again, O'Donovan emphasizes the continuity with creation here: "The history of divine rule safeguards and redeems the goods of creation. . . . When we speak of divine rule, we speak of the fulfillment promised to all things worldly and human" (*DN*, 19). This is why the Christian political vision is its own sort of humanism: Jesus is the image of God that humanity was always made to be, and hence he is the exemplar of and for humanity. His resurrection is the realization, not the trumping, of humanity. "The moment of the resurrection does not appear like an isolated meteor from the sky but as the climax of a history of divine rule" (*DN*, 20). This is why a coherent and prophetic

---

11. "The difference between this approach and that of the 'Whig history,'" he continues, "is that the theological coherence is allowed to rise from within the history and is not imposed upon it from the existing norms of our own historical period. It is not assumed that God's purpose was to make ancient Israel as like modern Europe and America as could possibly be done within the constraints of time and material. Yet we must not let go of the theological assertion that God had a purpose with Israel" (*DN*, 29). Israel is the hermeneutic lens of O'Donovan's project: "Through this unique political entity God made known his purposes in the world" (*DN*, 27).

Christian political theology cannot operate under the guise of methodological naturalism, pretending the revelation of God in Christ is somehow irrelevant for our so-called penultimate political life. His life and revelation are the only way we could possibly understand how political life should be rightly ordered. Thus "political theology must go beyond such general conceptions, and take on the character of a proclamatory history, attesting the claim that Yhwh reigns. Its subject is God's rule demonstrated and vindicated, the salvation that he has wrought in Israel and the nations. Unless it speak in that way it can only advance a theological type of political theory, not an evangelical political theology, a 'Law,' in the theological sense, rather than a 'Gospel'" (*DN*, 81).

This means that political theology is scandalously rooted in the specificity and particularity of God's self-revelation in Christ and the equally particular history of his covenant with his people Israel and the new covenant people that is the church. The body of Christ is that *polis* in which we participate in Christ, in which our perception is sanctified by the Spirit so that we might be able to discern the reign of God and thus be equipped for public proclamation that submission to Yahweh's reign is the way humanity is liberated.

Rethinking the "Secular," Redeeming Christendom

But what could this possibly mean for our relationship to neighbors who don't know Christ, for a political order that refuses divine reign? How is this unapologetically "evangelical" project not license for sectarian irrelevance and walling ourselves up in the echo chamber of our Christian enclave? What possible purchase could such forthrightly theological and revelational claims have on a public square that is designed to be "secular"?

O'Donovan has already provided parts of his answer. First, what we know through the specificity of the gospel and biblical revelation is still knowledge *of* creation and human nature per se. So it is insight into the *common* good. Second, as we've shown in chapter 3, a crucial task of evangelical political theology is patient historical, genealogical work that points out the debts our current supposedly "secular" order owes to the specificity of Israel and Christ. "Like the surface of a planet pocked with craters by the bombardment it receives from space, the governments of the passing age show the impact of Christ's dawning glory" (*DN*, 212).

Above all, such a political theology refuses to let the political remain sequestered from the specificity of the gospel's impact. Our political institutions, habits, and practices are contingent cultural configurations that are included in the *ta panta* that Christ redeems (Col. 1). So the political is not insulated from the impact of the Christ-event and the specific witness of the church in history—including the political habits learned in the *polis* that is the church. Such a "political theology shaped by the Christ-event," O'Donovan points out, must first "criticize existing notions of political good and necessity, not only classical republican notions but imperial and theocratic notions, too, in the light of what God has done for the human race and the human soul. . . . Ideas of what government is must be corrected in the light of that imperious government which the Spirit wields through the conscience of each worshipper" (*DN*, 122–23).

This gospel mystery—that the King of the universe knows the number of hairs on *your* head—unleashes its own political revolution: no individual can be a mere cog in a collectivist machine if the Spirit of the Creator King rules the conscience of individuals. This is all rooted in a core conviction of the gospel: that Christ *now* reigns, that "the kingly rule of Christ is God's own rule exercised over the whole world. It is visible in the life of the church . . . *but not only there*" (*DN*, 146, emphasis added). Everything is *now* in subjection to Christ (Heb. 2:5–8); he has *already* disarmed the principalities and powers (Col. 2:15). But we live in the "not-yet" where this is not universally recognized. It is this *time*—between cross and kingdom come, between ascension and parousia, between the universal *scope* of his lordship and its universal *recognition*—it is this time or season that is "the secular," the *saeculum*, the *age* in which we find ourselves. "Within the framework of these two assertions," O'Donovan observes, "there opens up an account of secular authority which presumes neither that the Christ-event never occurred nor that the sovereignty of Christ is now transparent and uncontested" (*DN*, 146). Earthly rulers remain in place, but their authority is a kind of lame-duck authority. Or rather, their authority is not ultimate: they are now answerable to the King of kings. "Secular authorities are no longer in the fullest sense mediators of the rule of God. They mediate his judgments only" (*DN*, 151). It's not that "secular" authorities have full authority over a limited jurisdiction; they have only delegated authority *for a time* (the *saeculum*).

Something of this dynamic is illustrated in a scene from the film *Lord of the Rings: Return of the King*. Arriving in Minas Tirith, Gandalf approaches the one sitting on the throne with a kind of subversive respect: "Hail Denethor, son of Ecthelion, Lord and Steward of Gondor." Denethor, Gandalf reminds him, is a *steward* of the throne but not its rightful king. The fact is not lost on Denethor, who perceives Gandalf's presence as a threat to his power and dominion. "Do you think the eyes of the white tower are blind?" Denethor asks. "I have seen more than you know. With your left hand you would use me as a shield against Mordor. And with the right you seek to supplant me.

I know who rides with Theoden of Rohan. Oh yes, the word has reached my ears of this Aragorn son of Arathorn. And I tell you now, I will not bow to this Ranger from the North, last of a ragged house, long bereft of lordship." The steward of Gondor understands very clearly whom Gandalf represents: he is an ambassador of the rightful king (Aragorn). And as such, Gandalf represents a king who threatens Denethor's demand for allegiance. Thus Gandalf will never be a docile subject of Denethor; rather, he is a subversive. And his departing words remind Denethor of just this fact: "Authority is not given you to deny the return of the king, *Steward*." The result, as O'Donovan puts it, is a humbling of earthly rulers and "desacralisation" of politics by the gospel (*DN*, 151). The penultimacy of the "secular" is now reasserted in a different mode. As we noted above, "The most truly Christian state under- stands itself most thoroughly as 'secular'" (*DN*, 219).

So we don't shuttle between the jurisdictions of two kingdoms; we live in the seasons of contested rule, where the principalities and powers continue to grasp after an authority that has been taken from them. The church is now the site for seeing what Christ's kingly rule looks like; and it will be *from* the church that the authorities—the "stewards"—of this world might come to recognize their own penultimacy. Thus O'Donovan takes up an analysis of "the true character of the church as a political society" (*DN*, 159). It is when we fail to appreciate this—if we "cease to understand the church as a society ruled by 'another king' (Acts 17:7)"—that the church "becomes accommodated to existing political societies as a system of religious practice that can flourish within them, a kind of service-agency . . . which puts itself at the disposal of a multitude of rulers" (*DN*, 162). Instead, the church should be the political center of gravity that shapes how we relate to the authorities of this passing age.

On the one hand, that means relativizing the "secular" authorities. But on the other hand, it also means the church's mission can make a dent there too. In the church's proclamation and her embodiment of a *polis* in which Christ reigns, "the nations and rulers of the world [are] confronted with the rule of God" (*DN*, 193). It is the very mission of the church that takes it into the imperial palace, into the executive mansion, into halls of the capitol. "The church addressed *society*," O'Donovan notes, "and it addressed *rulers*. Its success with the first was the basis of its great confidence in confronting the second. . . . Christ conquered the rulers from below, by drawing their subjects out from under their authority" (*DN*, 193). Far from the caricatures trotted out under the critique of "Constantinianism,"[12] the "Christendom" project

---

12. O'Donovan points out that most of the examples of "Christendom" held up for cri- tique are, in fact, examples of something else—a church that has lost its *missional*, evangelical

> ### To Think About: Learning to Live in the *Saeculum* at Gate A12
>
> The *saeculum* in which we find ourselves is a long "between," an extended overlap of realities that are both now and not-yet. To live in the *saeculum* is to move in a world over which both the cross and coming kingdom cast long shadows. The kingdom has dawned, but the former administration won't leave the building. And in the meantime, we are not so secretly hoping these recalcitrant rulers might become captivated by the dawning kingdom and become agents of it while we're waiting. In any case, as citizens of the city of God, we experience the territory of creation as a contested "between" space precisely because of the *time* or epoch in which we find ourselves.
>
> This odd suspension between two regimes, two polities, hit home for me one day while I was flying home from Toronto. As at a number of international airports in Canada, travelers flying to the United States from Toronto go through US customs and passport control. After checking in, we pass into an odd space that is governed by US authorities. The pre-clearance hall is even adorned with iconic images of the United States: Mount Rushmore, the Capitol building, Arches National Park in Utah, a New England village whose Puritan church dominates its tiny skyline. We proceed to the counter and are processed by US border patrol agents, and after being processed, we are effectively in "US space." We use US dollars like we're in the States. When I'm sitting at gate A12 at Pearson airport in Toronto, if you pinged my phone it would show up on the north side of Toronto, but in another sense I am allegedly already in the United States. And yet if an altercation were to happen, the RCMP or Ontario Provincial Police would supervise the investigation. If someone were injured or experienced a heart attack, the Canadian St. John's ambulance would show up. We're in a "between" space of overlapping authorities.

was fundamentally a *missional* endeavor in which the regnant authorities recognized the lordship of Christ, recognized they were simply stewards for a coming King (*DN*, 195). More specifically, it was a vision of government and society that was captivated not by mere recognition of "natural"[13] laws but by

---

center and that forgot how to pray, "Thy kingdom *come*." Once the church forgot this was still the *saeculum*—once it fell into the trap of thinking the kingdom had arrived in its configuration of society—the result was a "negative collusion": "the pretence that there was now no further challenge to be issued to the rulers in the name of the ruling Christ" (*DN*, 213). (O'Donovan notes the same happens as one of the "quietist implications of Luther's doctrine of two governments"—the state is insulated from evangelical obedience, exempt from Christ's reign, in which case the status quo is reinforced [*DN*, 213].) O'Donovan's name for this collusion and eschatological forgetting is blunt: this isn't "Christendom," he argues; this is "Antichrist" (*DN*, 214). This is why any true Christendom has to always be ready for martyrdom even as it must also be "prepared to welcome the homage of the kings when it is offered to the Lord of the martyrs" (*DN*, 215).

13. See O'Donovan's critique of the "Salamanca school" (which serves as a ready stand-in for contemporary two-kingdoms and natural-law approaches) as abandoning a distinctly "evangelical basis for civil rule and justice" (*DN*, 209–10). Recall also in this context his critique

a distinctly *gospel*-ed imagination—by submission to Christ, by modeling the forgiveness and mercy and compassion of Jesus, by reflecting more broadly political realities first practiced in the church. Thus O'Donovan brings us back again to Theodosius: "In censuring him the church took up the task of judging judges, and began the slow work of *reforming the criteria of earthly justice*" (*DN*, 201, emphasis added)—a work to which we liberal democrats remain heirs!

Christendom, then, is a missional endeavor that refuses to let political society remain protected from the lordship of Christ while also recognizing the eschatological distance between the now and the not-yet. From the center of the church as a political society, Christendom bears witness to how society should be otherwise in a way that imagines the possibility of conversion—not only of souls but of our social imaginaries. This is a vision of political witness and engagement that proclaims the political significance not just of "nature" or "creation" but of the gospel as that revelation that truly shows us how to be human and what the world is called to be in the resurrection of Jesus. Thus Christendom bears witness from the specificity of the gospel.

This boldness and scandalous specificity is ultimately an act of love. Here we might connect O'Donovan's discussion of Christendom with an earlier question in *Resurrection and Moral Order*. What does it mean to love my neighbor? he asks. "In the first place, we are to love the neighbor *because the neighbor is ordered to the love of God*" (*RMO*, 228).[14]

> True neighbourliness requires the recognition of the supreme good simply in order that we may see the neighbour for what he is. But that means that our pursuit of the neighbour's welfare has to take seriously the thought that he, like ourselves, is a being whose end is in God. To "love" him without respecting this

---

of the First Amendment in the US Constitution (*DN*, 244–46): "By denying any church established status in principle, the framers of the First Amendment gave away more than they knew. They effectively declared that political authorities were incapable of *evangelical* obedience. . . . Excluding government from evangelical obedience has had repercussions for the way society itself is conceived" (*DN*, 246, emphasis added).

14. In this respect, O'Donovan echoes Augustine in *City of God*:
> Now God, our master, teaches two chief precepts, love of God and love of neighbor; and in them man finds three objects for his love: God, himself, and his neighbor; and a man who loves God is not wrong in loving himself. It follows, therefore, that he will be concerned also that his neighbor should love God, since he is told to love his neighbor as himself; and the same is true of his concern for his wife, his children, for the members of his household, and for all other men, so far as is possible. And, for the same end, he will wish his neighbor to be concerned for him, if he happens to need that concern. For this reason he will be at peace, as far as lies in him, with all men, in that peace among men, that ordered harmony; and the basis of this order is the observance of two rules: first, to do no harm to anyone, and, secondly, to help everyone whenever possible. (19.14)

fundamental truth about him would be an exercise in fantasy. Saint Augustine used to say that our first duty to the neighbour was to "seize him for God." This does not mean, as some critics would pretend to warn us, that every gesture or act of love towards the neighbour will have a religious goal or an "ulterior motive." It means simply that there is, in our love for the neighbour, a recognition of his high calling and destiny to fellowship with God and a desire to further that destiny in the context of concern for his welfare. (*RMO*, 229)

If we truly love our neighbors, we will bear witness to the fullness to which they are called. If we truly desire their welfare, we should proclaim the thickness of moral obligations that God commands as the gifts to channel us into flourishing, and labor in hope that these might become the laws of the land, though with appropriate levels of expectation. This would be political action that recognizes that humanity's natural end is supernatural, that the fullness of human being is elucidated in the gospel, not the minimalism of "nature."

Indeed, once we understand that the "Christendom project" is this sort of *missional* endeavor that hopes and aims to expose governments and systems to the transformative power of the gospel, then we can see how something as prophetic as the civil rights movement was a kind of twentieth-century Christendom project, as is the Christian community development movement that grew out of it. Bearing witness from the specificity of the gospel's injunction to *love*, informed by the specifically christological exemplar of nonviolence, fostered by the practices of the Christian church, the civil rights movement in its animating impetus was an endeavor that refused to imagine that society was impervious to the rule of Christ but instead imagined that it could become "a beloved community." As Charles Marsh comments in his remarkable history of the civil rights movement, "the beloved community" they sought should "finally be described as a gift of the kingdom of God introduced into history by the church, and thus it exists within the provenance of Christ's mystery in the world."[15] John Lewis, then chairman of the Student Nonviolent Coordinating Committee (and now longtime congressman), said the civil rights movement was animated by "nothing less than the Christian concept of the Kingdom of God on earth."[16]

In the civil rights movement, one sees not only the centrality of a theological vision but also a center of gravity rooted in the ecclesial practices of the body of Christ, yielding "a portrait of the Christian faith as a set of social

15. Charles Marsh, *The Beloved Community: How Faith Shapes Social Justice, from the Civil Rights Movement to Today* (New York: Basic Books, 2005), 207.
16. Ibid., 3.

disciplines shaped by gratitude, forgiveness and reconciliation."[17] Through his
embedded experience in the Montgomery bus boycotts, Reverend King came to
see the limits of Niebuhr's abstract public theologizing. "Abstractions cannot
empower acts of compassion and sacrifice," Marsh summarizes, "or sustain
the courage to speak against the day. Niebuhr's much-heralded Christian realism was about working out ethical problems within the framework of options
provided by Western liberalism. It was not about having a dream."[18] That
dream was the kingdom of God, and King learned it at church. But it wasn't
just *for* the church: it was a vision of what the world was called to be. For
King, the realization of this was not some merely evolutionary development
but rather a divine gift. "God remains from beginning to end the ultimate
agent of human liberation, not only in America but throughout all the nations and in creation. The fading of the 'old order' and the emergence of a
'new age' is not written into the genetic code as its manifest destiny; rather,
beloved community depends on a theological, one might say ecclesiological,
event. In other words, the brotherhood and sisterhood of humankind radiates
out from the fellowship of the faithful."[19] Like O'Donovan's account of the
missional endeavor of Christendom (and akin to Kuyper's vision of the church
as institute "radiating" throughout society via the organic church), King's vision for justice is one centered in the *ekklēsia*, but an *ekklēsia* for the world.[20]

It was in the church, nourished by the Word made flesh, their imaginations fueled by the gospel, that the witnesses and martyrs of the civil rights
movement learned to long for a better country (Heb. 11:16) but also imagined
that *this* country could look more like it. That, and nothing less, is the hope
of Christendom.

17. Ibid., 5.
18. Ibid., 41. Marsh goes on to observe: "The boycott year had renewed the mission of
the church. The boycott showed the world a church whose power stemmed from its deliberate
discipline, whose moral authority was the hard-earned result of its suffering and willing to
love the enemy—religious passions, it should be noted, that Niebuhr's thin ecclesiology could
never embrace" (47).
19. Ibid., 50.
20. This is why there is nothing inherently "conservative" about the Christendom project;
to the contrary, there are ways in which it *must* be disruptive of the status quo. O'Donovan, in
fact, is consistently critical of an ideological "conservatism." In *DN*, commenting on Romans
13:1–7, all too often described as "conservative" or invoked as such, O'Donovan points out:
"St. Paul's famous paragraph about the authorities arises naturally from his claim for Israel.
Christ's victory, after all, is the same victory that was promised to Israel over the nations, the
victory of a God-filled and humanized social order over bestial and God-denying empires, a
victory won for Israel on behalf of all humankind. As Israel is claimed for faith, then, so the
authorities are claimed for obedience to Israel, chastened and reduced to the familiar functions
that were once assigned to Israel's judges" (*DN*, 147).

6

Contested Formations

OUR "GODFATHER" PROBLEM

If Christianity is . . . an alternative form of cultural joining and interaction, then Christian communities and their theologians will have to reckon with their legacy of ecclesial failure.

Willie James Jennings, *The Christian Imagination*

Picturing Competing Formations in *The Godfather*

"I believe in America." These are the first words of Mario Puzo and Francis Ford Coppola's *The Godfather*. A supplicant Amerigo Bonasera has come to the office of Vito Corleone as part of a Sicilian ritual. On the day of his daughter's wedding, the Godfather is doling out favors in a spirit of largesse, a benevolent patriarch showering blessings on the community. Bonasera has come looking for nothing less than "justice" for his daughter, who has been beaten and disfigured. "I believe in America," Bonasera confesses. "America has made my fortune." But American justice has let him down. The perpetrators receive a suspended sentence and walk free. And so he comes to the Godfather: "For justice," Bonasera tells his wife, "we must go to Don Corleone." After expressing disappointment that Bonasera sees this as merely an economic rather than a familial exchange, the Godfather grants his wish. Bonasera can count on justice, which, as becomes clear, is reduced to the *lex talionis*.

Already foreshadowed in this first scene is the complex overlap and intertwining of religion and violence, capital and capitulation, ritual and retaliation. On the one hand, the entire world of the film is framed by the rituals of the church—from the opening wedding rite to the baptismal rite at its climax. Indeed, the very title and dynamics of *The Godfather* hearken back to the baptismal liturgy. The world of "business" in the film is conducted by "families," and no one is more of a "family man" than Don Corleone. ("Do you spend time with your family?" he asks his godson, Johnny Fontaine. "Because no one can be a man who doesn't spend time with his family.") Because the families are bathed and constituted by the rituals of the church, the blending of bloodlines by liturgical practices forges bonds that are charged with ultimacy. "Corleone is Johnny's grandfather," Tom Hagen, the adopted son, observes. "To the Italian people that is a very religious, sacred, close relationship." In a way, you'd almost be tempted to say this is a world held together by the bonds of love.

On the other hand, the business conducted by these families is the very antithesis of peace and makes a mockery of the very rites they participate in. The bonds of love turn out to be merely a kind of in-group consolidation against enemies. The business bleeds into all-out war, and their work becomes synonymous with illicit trade, intimidation, exploitation, and violence. No one would mistake their "business" for the kind of economic life described in Catholic social teaching.

It is this aspect of the Godfather's world that the youngest son, Michael (played by Al Pacino), is determined to escape. When his girlfriend Kay first meets the family, Michael insists: "That's my family, Kay. It's not me." To resist the family business, he also has to resist the family's bonds and rites. And so he's an aloof presence at the opening wedding festival, hovering on the margins. But that changes when his father, the Godfather, is attacked and almost killed. This triggers something in Michael, an angry loyalty that snaps tight the bonds of family and pulls him in. "I'm with you now," he whispers to his father in a hospital bed, kissing his hand. "I'm with you now." He joins the family business and so spirals into the world of violence and retaliation, power and domination.

This trajectory culminates when Connie, Michael's sister, asks Michael to be her child's godfather at the same time that he assumes responsibility for the family business.[1] The narrative arc comes full circle. Once again we are at the intersection of the church and the family as Michael assumes the role of godfather in the baptismal liturgy. But here too, at the climax of the film, the dissonance between their ritual participation and the nature of the "family business" is starkly portrayed through one of the master sequences of film editing. In a dizzying array, we cut back and forth from the hushed rites inside the church to a series of brutal assassinations ordered by Michael

---

1. Interestingly, Don Corleone does seem to have hoped that Michael would *not* inherit the family "business" but would have become a senator or a governor. Like so many immigrant parents, he hoped that Michael would be more properly assimilated to the "America" of the opening line. At the end of his life, he laments to Michael that this dream wasn't realized: "There just wasn't enough time," he mourns. "We'll get there, Pop," Michael replies.

Corleone. Coppola is ruthless in this sequence, bringing us face-to-face with violence while also immersing us in the theological thickness and specificity of the baptismal rite. As we witness the horrible violence of the family business, we witness a solemn confession of the gospel.

The priest breathes on the child, symbolizing the renewal of the Holy Spirit, and then salts the baby's mouth, ears, hands in the name of the Father, and the Son, and the Holy Ghost while the camera transports us to a scene of grisly execution.

The priest poses the Credo to Michael, who is standing as the child's godfather.

"Michael, do you believe in God, the Father Almighty, Maker of heaven and earth?"

"I do," Michael replies.

"Do you believe in Jesus Christ his only Son, our Lord?"

"I do," Michael insists.

"Do you believe in the Holy Ghost, the holy catholic church?"

"I do," he responds.

But the hits keep coming: enemy after enemy falls prey to his assassination commands while we are taken back inside the church to see Michael participate in the exorcism.

"Michael Francis, do you renounce Satan?" the priest asks.

"I do renounce him," Michael affirms, while his henchmen carry out his diabolical commands.

"And all his works?"

"I do renounce him."

"And all his pomps?"

"I do renounce him," is the continued reply.

The entire sequence ends with a benediction: "Go in peace, and may the Lord be with you. Amen." But all the while the pomps and works and wiles of the evil one are carried out in the name of the family's "business," capital sins committed in the name of capital and "justice."

The Godfather amounts to a visual parable of a challenge and critique that dogs the Cultural Liturgies project: while I extol the formative power of historic Christian worship practices, it would seem that there can be—and *are*—people who have spent entire lifetimes immersed in the rites of historic Christian worship who nonetheless emerge from them not only unformed but perhaps even malformed.[2] Or, to put it otherwise: clearly, regular participation in the church's "orthodox" liturgy is not enough to prevent such "worshipers"

2. My thanks to Rev. Steve Bezner for some correspondence on this point that has helped me to appreciate what's at stake in this question.

from leaving the sanctuary to become (sometimes enthusiastic) participants in all sorts of unjust systems, structures, and behaviors. Like the people of Judah critiqued by the prophet Jeremiah, we can "come through these gates to worship the Lord," announce our allegiance, and superstitiously claim protection ("This is the temple of the LORD!"), but spend the rest of the week burning incense to the gods of mammon, prostrating ourselves to the idols of power and domination, baking cakes for the queen of heaven (Jer. 7:1–26).

Let's call this "the Godfather problem": you can liturgically renounce the works of the devil and carry them out at the same time. Liturgical participation is no guarantee of formation in the virtues or the acquisition of the fruits of the Spirit. Liturgy is not a silver bullet that guarantees holiness; nor is there any guarantee that mere worship attendance is a sufficient condition to make the people of God a "contrast" society. To say that there is would be to lapse into a kind of liturgical determinism that assumes a simplistic view of formation and a kind of "purity" about the church that is misplaced.[3]

Does the Godfather problem undercut the core argument of the Cultural Liturgies project? I don't think so. But it is a fundamental challenge that needs to be accounted for—a challenge I've noted from the beginning of the project.[4] If liturgy forms us by conforming us to the image of Christ (Rom. 8:29), then why are Christians so often conformed to the world (per Rom. 12:2)? Answering that question is the focus of this chapter.

Concurrent Formation and the Dynamics of Deformation: Case Studies

In many ways, though the Cultural Liturgies project is focused on the primacy of liturgical formation in Christian discipleship, this was largely prompted by the reality of our cultural assimilation. How are we to make sense of the

3. It might seem that we are simply dealing with the phenomenon of hypocrisy: that the Michael Corleones of the world are doing one thing "for show" while *really* caring about something else. But it's more complicated than that, and I'm not convinced that the elements of hypocrisy are adequate to account for this phenomenon. (If you asked Michael Corleone whether he *believed* what he said in the baptismal rite, what would he say?) See Adam B. Seligman, Robert P. Weller, Michael J. Puett, and Bennett Simon, *Ritual and Its Consequences: An Essay on the Limits of Sincerity* (New York: Oxford University Press, 2008), and Seligman, "Ritual and Sincerity: Certitude and the Other," *Philosophy and Social Criticism* 36 (2010): 9–39. See also John Witvliet, "'Planting and Harvesting' Godly Sincerity: Pastoral Wisdom in the Practice of Public Worship," *Evangelical Quarterly* 87, no. 4 (October 2015): 291–309.

4. See James K. A. Smith, *Desiring the Kingdom: Worship, Worldview, and Cultural Formation*, Cultural Liturgies 1 (Grand Rapids: Baker Academic, 2009), 208n115. This chapter is fulfilling the promissory note planted there. The final section (186–89) of *Imagining the Kingdom: How Worship Works*, Cultural Liturgies 2 (Grand Rapids: Baker Academic, 2013), is also relevant.

fact that Christians can have a wealth of knowledge *about* Christianity and yet live as practical naturalists, giving themselves over to ways of life that are, in some respects, the very antithesis of shalom? If the core goal of my project has been to argue that our loves are rightly ordered through the "habitation of the Spirit" that is Christian worship, this is in no small part a response to the way we are co-opted by rival stories and visions of the good life. In short, the emphasis on *counter*-formation in worship is a fire-meets-fire response to the *deformation* of our loves that manifests itself as conformity to "the world." That conformity, I've argued, is *not* usually the result of having been convinced by ideas but rather the result of our hearts and longings (and hence action) being conscripted by rival liturgies.[5] So if we have emphasized the significance of liturgical formation, that is not because Christian worship is sui generis or some deus ex machina intervention into our lives. Rather, it is because we are liturgical creatures who are always already being shaped by *some* liturgies. In other words, "liturgy" is as much an account of the problem (of assimilation) as it is a solution.

And, in fact, it's important to appreciate the complexity of being-in-the-world and recognize that we are always already subject to multiple communities of practice, caught up in multiple (and rival) liturgies that enact competing visions of the good life. There is no "purity" for liturgical creatures in the *saeculum*; I am never caught up in just one tradition or liturgical community. Even if we prioritize the church's worship as the primary site of the Spirit's sanctifying transformation, we are never only subject to the church's worship, nor is the church's worship a "pure" instantiation of the kingdom. I am subject to competing apprenticeships of the heart. I am concurrently enrolled in competing pedagogies of desire. And the church—both as a sacramental institution and as a people—is caught up in a web of liturgies that constitute "the world." So the emphasis on liturgical (re)formation is rooted in a creational anthropology that recognizes humans are liturgical animals, creatures of habit whose loves are (de)formed by *some* liturgy. "Everybody worships," as David Foster Wallace reminded us.[6]

But this emphasis on liturgical formation of rightly ordered love is often met with a pointed question: Aren't there all kinds of Michael Corleones in the world, people who have spent a lifetime "practicing" a ritualized Christian faith with what seems to be little evidence of any sanctification? Don't we see all kinds of examples in which Christian liturgical participation has

5. See the phenomenology of temptation in Smith, *Imagining the Kingdom*, 140–42.
6. See his famous 2005 Kenyon College commencement address, published as David Foster Wallace, *This Is Water: Some Thoughts, Delivered on a Significant Occasion, about Living a Compassionate Life* (New York: Little, Brown, 2009), 100.

Concurrent Formations

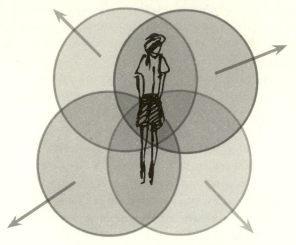

not been reformative and seems to have done nothing to stave off cultural assimilation? Indeed, isn't it disturbing how much and how often such ritual performances of faith can become caught up in the most egregious expressions of injustice? While we've claimed that it is participation in the thick strangeness of historic Christian worship that makes the church a "peculiar people," aren't there all kinds of people who have been immersed in such liturgies who seem exactly like their neighbors—happy consumers pursuing their self-interests, caught up in the same injustices that come with privilege, content to shore up the status quo? So it would seem that liturgy is not the answer to our cultural assimilation.

I want to tackle these questions head-on by first considering a couple of case studies that are, I believe, some of the starkest examples of "the Godfather problem." If there is going to be any "answer" to this challenge, it needs to be articulated on the other side of actually going *through* the problem. So after laying out the force of this challenge in these case studies, I'll then sketch the facets of a complex, nuanced response that, I will argue, requires us to take seriously an emerging conversation between ecclesiology and ethnography.

Case Study 1: Whiteness and the Inadequacy of Liturgy

Akin (and indebted) to the work of Stanley Hauerwas, my argument regarding liturgical formation is broadly "MacIntyrean," inheriting Alasdair MacIntyre's retrieval and renewal of an Aristotelian and Thomistic emphasis on habit, character, and virtue—and hence narrative, tradition, and community. While in chapter 2 I addressed Jeffrey Stout's critique of this framework, perhaps the most stinging critique of this theological project was penned by Willie James Jennings in his magisterial work *The Christian Imagination: Theology and the Origins of Race*.[7] Jennings is also diagnosing Christianity's fundamental and blameworthy assimilation to a dominant culture—in this case the church's long capitulation and contribution to a racialized world fraught with harrowing injustice and inscrutable evil that was, time and again, baptized with "Christian" justification and even blessing. While Christian theology over the past generation has fixated on the effect of the Germanic Enlightenment and the theoretical legacies of modernity,[8] Jennings brings us face-to-face with the material, embodied realities of modernity that find expression in the Iberian conquest and subsequent European colonization. While we have worried whether theology bought into the rationalism of Descartes or the liberalism of Locke, Jennings documents the heinous capitulation of the church to a very different aspect of modernity: the slave trade. The flipside of modernity's rationalization was a capacity to diminish and devalue black bodies, engendering a default racialization that characterizes modern life (particularly in the United States). "Europeans," Jennings argues—and he means European *Christians*—"enacted racial agency as a theologically articulated way of understanding their bodies in relation to new spaces and new people and to their new power over those spaces" (*CI*, 58). Paralleling my earlier discussions of "social imaginaries" in *Desiring the Kingdom* and *Imagining the Kingdom*, Jennings documents the emergence of "whiteness" as an imaginary: "Whiteness from the moment of discovery and consumption was a social and theological way of imagining, an imaginary that evolved into a method of understanding the world" (*CI*, 58).[9]

What good, Jennings asks, did "the tradition" do to prevent such capitulation to injustice? The church-as-*polis* did nothing to prevent the construal of Africans as chattel, commodifying human beings made in the image of God. The seeming magic of "the liturgy" did nothing to prevent or even temper

7. Willie James Jennings, *The Christian Imagination: Theology and the Origins of Race* (New Haven: Yale University Press, 2010) (hereafter cited in text as *CI*).

8. And here I would have to indict the emphases of my own early work in *Introducing Radical Orthodoxy*, *Who's Afraid of Postmodernism?*, and other works that tend to fixate on the theoretical reverberations emerging from German and French universities and equate this with "modernity," too often ignoring the material realities of the European "discovery" of the "New World" that preceded many of these intellectual shifts of the Enlightenment. In short, I concede—yea, confess—that my own theoretical focus has privileged intellectual modernity and too often overlooked those who experienced the all-too-embodied underside of modernity.

9. Recall the discussion of "sanctified perception" in Smith, *Imagining the Kingdom*, 151–66. What Jennings is describing is a cursed, desecrated perception that is inculcated in a similar manner.

this descent into inhumanity. To the contrary, the rituals of church simply enfolded such injustices into the narrative. In the opening of his book, Jennings recounts a heart-rending scene captured for posterity by Gomes Eanes de Azurara (or Zurara). Chronicler for Prince Henry of Portugal in the fifteenth century, Zurara recounts a turning point in the fate and power of the Portuguese Empire: On August 8, 1444, a ship has arrived from Africa bearing "black gold," 235 enslaved Africans who represented the new global power of Portugal. Rather than unloading them under the cover of night, perhaps hiding the shame of this "necessary evil," Infante Henrique choreographed a public spectacle at dawn, one bathed in ritual. "This ritual was deeply Christian," Jennings comments,

> Christian in ways that were obvious to those who looked on that day and in ways that are probably even more obvious to people today. Once the slaves arrived at the field, Prince Henry, following his deepest Christian instincts, ordered a tithe be given to God through the church. Two black boys were given, one to the principal church in Lagos and another to the Franciscan convent on Cape Saint Vincent. This act of praise and thanksgiving to God for allowing Portugal's successful entrance into maritime power also served to justify the royal rhetoric by which Prince Henry claimed his motivation was the salvation of the soul of the heathen. (*CI*, 16)[10]

Indeed, this ritual signals the insidious way the tradition's narrative can enfold injustice and sanctify it by re-narration. So "the Christian story," rather than "sanctifying them in truth," remakes the world to conform to the truth of colonial enslavement.[11] In his chronicle, "Zurara deploys a rhetorical strategy of containment, holding slave suffering inside a Christian story that will be recycled by countless theologians and intellectuals of every colonialist nation.

10. Jennings notes Zurara's penitential prayer in this context: "O, Thou heavenly Father . . . I pray thee that my tears may not wrong my conscience; for it is not their religion but their humanity that maketh mine to weep in pity for their sufferings. And if the brute animals, with their bestial feedings, by a natural instinct understand the suffering of their own kind, what wouldst Thou have my human nature to do on seeing before my eyes that miserable company, and remembering that they too are of the generation of the sons of Adam?" (*CI*, 17). This engenders a new question of theodicy, Jennings argues: "Zurara asks God in this prayer to grant him access to the divine design to help him interpret this clear sign of God-ordained Portuguese preeminence over black flesh. He seeks from God the kind of interpretation that would ease his conscience and make the event unfolding in front of him more morally palatable. His question seeds a problem of theodicy born out of the colonialist question bound to the colonialist project" (*CI*, 18). In other words, the scene engenders a question of theodicy only because Zurara accepts the "right" of the colonialist project.

11. Cf. Stanley Hauerwas, *Sanctify Them in Truth: Holiness Exemplified* (Nashville: Abingdon, 1998).

The *telos* and the denouement of the event will be enacted as an order of salvation, an *ordo salutis*—African captivity leads to African salvation and to black bodies that show the disciplining power of the faith" (*CI*, 20). And the church, rather than being the counter-*polis* of resistance, happily accepts the tithe of black flesh. "This act is carried out inside Christian society, as part of the *communitas fidelium*. This [slave] auction will draw ritual power from Christianity itself while mangling the narratives it evokes, establishing a distorted pattern of displacement" (*CI*, 22).

Thus Jennings directly challenges the sort of "virtue project" articulated by Hauerwas and others (like myself), which places so much confidence in the power of tradition and ecclesial formation to create a counterculture. The idealism of this claim, Jennings argues, conveniently ignores the church's capitulation to the horrors of modernity.[12] "One could fault MacIntyre but more importantly those theologians who have followed his thinking on tradition for not seeing the effects on the Christian tradition triggered by the modernist elements at the beginning of the age of Iberian conquest." We need to "watch how traditioned Christian existence, first that of the Iberians and then that of all Europeans, fundamentally changed as they ascended to hegemony in the New Worlds" (*CI*, 71). Why didn't their tradition, their narrative, and their liturgy prevent this stark failure of holiness and sanctification?[13] Indeed, this is less an assimilation or capitulation to some "external" unjust society and more an internal projection from the church itself: "It would be a mistake to see the church and its ecclesiastics as entering the secular workings of the state in the New World," Jennings cautions, "or to posit ecclesial presence as a second stage in the temporal ordering of the New World. No, the church entered with the conquistadors, establishing camp in and with the conquering camps of the Spanish. The reordering of Indian worlds was born of Christian formation itself" (*CI*, 81).

So the church's liturgy, tradition, and narrative can't be simplistically construed as an antidote to modernity or injustice. To the contrary, the Jesuit José de Acosta Porres "thus fashioned a theological vision for the New World that drew its life from Christian orthodoxy and its power from conquest." His work "reveals in a very stark way the future of theology in the New World,

---

12. My hunch is that Hauerwas would respond by arguing that it wasn't "the church as church" that capitulated in this way but rather a church that had already capitulated to "Constantinianism." We'll address this evasion below.

13. In chap. 2 of *The Christian Imagination*, Jennings focuses on the young Jesuit José de Acosta Porres as a case study. Formed by just the sort of thick, rigorous tradition that MacIntyre extols as lost in modernity, Acosta nonetheless became an apologist for colonialism and a key re-narrator of the Christian tradition, enfolding the colonialist narrative within an ecclesial justification.

that is, a strongly traditioned Christian intellectual posture made to function wholly within a colonialist logic. . . . The inner coherence of traditioned Christian inquiry was grafted onto the inner coherence of colonialism" (*CI*, 83). Drawing on Pierre Bourdieu's account of *habitus*, Jennings points out that Acosta's inculcation into an ecclesial *habitus* did nothing to temper his complicity with colonialism: "When Acosta looked out onto the New World, the Christian habitus in which he had been shaped became the expression of a colonialist logic" (*CI*, 104).[14]

The result was not merely an epiphenomenal sin on top of an intact foundation of holiness—an appendage of injustice tacked onto an otherwise healthy body of Christ.[15] Rather, the result was "the emergence of [a] Christian-colonial way of imagining the world," a racialized worldview that was inseparable from the "Christianity" that journeyed across the Atlantic on ships. Jennings voices the jarring question this chapter aims to answer: "How is it possible for Christians and Christian communities to naturalize cultural fragmentation and operationalize racial vision from within the social logic and theological imagination of Christianity itself?" (*CI*, 208). He answers the question by documenting how, and to what extent, Christianity became inextricably bound up with the twin logics of nationalism and capitalism: creation is reduced to property, and property is there for plundering. In a careful analysis I can't replicate here, Jennings shows how this was connected to the "vernacularization" of Christianity—projects of translation (of the Bible, of liturgy, of hymnody)[16] that "facilitated the dissemination of the idea of a nation and the expression of cultural nationalisms"—which then transformed space where whiteness governs (*CI*, 208–9), "a geographic expansion of identity around the body of the master, the body of whiteness" (*CI*, 241).[17] As Jennings shows, the architecture of the slave owner's home became a wider *social* architecture, creating a distorted social space that was synonymous with the productive, consumptive nation (*CI*, 241–47). "What connected

14. Recall our discussion of Bourdieu and *habitus* in *Imagining the Kingdom*, chap. 2.

15. If anything, a bastardized Christian piety was tacked onto a very different foundation. "Evangelical piety," Jennings remarks, "was not merely an inheritance of a theological past, [but] it was also an innovation of a Protestant/slavery present. That is, it was language being quickly adapted to function *on top of* the more decisive transformation of the multiple peoples of Africa into black slaves, leaving little room to imagine salvation as the transformation of the social order of things" (*CI*, 196).

16. See Jennings's stunning analysis of Isaac Watts's nationalist (and supersessionist) hymnody (*CI*, 210–19) and his harrowing citation of catechisms for slaves (*CI*, 238–39).

17. In this argument Jennings draws on the important work of Elizabeth Fox-Genovese and Eugene D. Genovese, *The Mind of the Master Class: History and Faith in the Southern Slaveholders' Worldview* (Cambridge: Cambridge University Press, 2005).

these spaces was the racial imagination that permeated both the creating and shaping of perception and helped to vivify both spaces" (*CI*, 241). The result is what Charles Taylor would call a "misprision"[18] of Christianity, or what Jennings seems to suggest is a *mis*performance of biblical Christianity that both caused and is the fruit of a malformed body of Christ. Christianity was effectively trumped by these rival logics even when it claimed to be engaged in a "missional" endeavor.

How to account for this profound "ecclesial failure"? What happened? How could the community that heralds the gospel of grace so easily morph into the community that trades in black flesh? Jennings locates this misprision and failed performance in the heart of our project: a distorted habitus that reflects a failed *pedagogy*. "Christianity is a teaching faith," he emphasizes. "It carries in its heart the making of disciples through teaching." However, that doesn't mean that all the "teaching" the church carries out is *Christian* teaching. A formative Christian pedagogy must be carried out "inside its christological horizon and embodiment, inside its *participatio Christi* and its *imitatio Christi*" (*CI*, 106). But this is precisely where the colonialist pedagogies of "New World" Christianity failed so miserably: "The colonialist moment indicates the loss of that horizon," Jennings shows, and its replacement by a "racial optic." The result is an inversion whereby Christian confession and theology are subordinated to a different imaginary, a different logic—that of capital.[19] There is a collusion and elision here that continues to haunt us: "The operation of forming productive workers for the mines, encomiendas, haciendas, the obrajes, and the reducciones merged with the operation of forming theological subjects" (*CI*, 107). "Teaching" here is not merely didactic information transfer. Indeed, what is taught is precisely a *habitus* that is caught through a kind of "pastoral power" (per Foucault) that suffuses this formative dynamic in a wide web of relationships, systems, and institutions. "This is the ground upon which the ideologies of white supremacy will grow: a theologically inverted pedagogical habitus that engenders a colonialist evaluative form that is disseminated through a network of relationships, which together reveal the deep sinews of knowledge and power" (*CI*, 109).

And what was "caught" in this web? Specifically, and fundamentally, a *parody* of the Christian doctrine of creation, a rival story of where we are and who we are that was all the more seductive because it came with a distorted Christian accent. The anthropology yielded by this rival creation story

---

18. Charles Taylor, *A Secular Age* (Cambridge, MA: Harvard University Press, 2007), 643–56.

19. For a stinging, well-documented indictment of the collusion of US economic institutions with slavery, see Edward E. Baptist, *The Half Has Never Been Told: Slavery and the Making of American Capitalism* (New York: Basic Books, 2016).

collapses humanness with whiteness and reduces black bodies to property, all under the guise of a perverted doctrine of creation captive to the logics of colonialism and capitalism.[20] "The profound commodification of bodies that was New World slavery signifies an effect humankind has yet to reckon with fully—a distorted vision of creation" (CI, 43). But again, this "doctrine" of creation was disseminated less as a propositional dogma to be affirmed and more as a subconscious—but nonetheless powerful—social imaginary that was absorbed in the policies and practices of colonial configurations of the world. And as Jennings concludes: "If Christianity is going to untangle itself from these mangled spaces, it must first see them for what they are: a revolt against creation" (CI, 248).[21] This will require "a different social imagination," not just refinement of our theological syllogisms. It requires a *healing* of the Christian imagination that addresses "an abiding mutilation of a Christian vision of creation and our own creatureliness" performed by colonialist innovation. Christians, says Jennings, must "recognize the grotesque nature of a social performance of Christianity that imagines Christian identity floating above land, landscape, animals, place, and space, leaving such realities to the machinations of private property. Such Christian identity can only inevitably lodge itself in the materiality of racial existence" (CI, 292).

This distorted theology of creation arrived with the slave ships. Indeed, as Equiano's subversive narrative suggests, the slave ship *is* "creation" in colo-

20. In my all-too-brief summary here, I am not doing justice to the importance of supersessionism in Jennings's account. The "replacement" of Israel by the church was able to position Christian identity "fully within European (white) identity" precisely because the faith had been placed outside the identities of the Jews. "Here was a process of discerning Christian identity that, because it had jettisoned Israel from its calculus of the formation of Christian life, created a conceptual vacuum that was filled by the European" (CI, 33). "In the age of discovery and conquest supersessionist thinking burrowed deeply inside the logic of evangelism and emerged joined to whiteness in a new, more sophisticated, concealed form. Indeed, supersessionist thinking is the womb in which whiteness will mature" (CI, 36). Note also the discussion of how Equiano's *Interesting Narrative* "draw[s] the black body next to the Jewish body" (CI, 189–90).

21. There seem to be three primary deficiencies of the "Christian" doctrine of creation here that enabled it to be caught up in a distorted colonialist version: (1) It is a doctrine of creation undisciplined by Christology. (2) It is a creation doctrine unhooked from eschatology. Glaringly absent from Pope Nicholas V's notorious bull *Dum diversas* (1452, cited by Jennings [CI, 29]) is any sense of what Graham Ward calls the "eschatological remainder." Instead, the church is the agent of a wholly realized eschatology that unleashes the church to act like the Christ of the book of Revelation—a sure sign of an immanentization of the eschaton. (3) It is a doctrine of creation that is disconnected from—or at least inadequately connected to—salvation, an *arche*-ology apart from soteriology. "At heart," Jennings concludes, "there was an important aspect of the connection between creation and redemption that probably never seemed to take hold in the Christian imagination" (CI, 248). Streams of the Kuyperian tradition are particularly prone to all three of these deficiencies.

nialist theology. The slave ship (re)makes the world. "The slave ship positions itself next to creation, next to the creating act of creation's recapitulation. It is a moment of metaphysical theft, an ambush of the divine *creatio continua*, the continuing creative act" (*CI*, 186).

Equiano's *Interesting Narrative* (1789) steals creation back by deconstructing the heretical version of the slave ship's doctrine of creation. Since the slave ship remakes the world, in a sense when Equiano boards the ship, he is stepping into a new world. "Equiano must make sense of his life no longer in a village configured in ancient space, but on ships configured by global commerce and the calculus of exchange" (*CI*, 188). Left in the hold to despair, Equiano sees the reality before him: "I now saw myself deprived of all chance of returning to my native country, or even the least glimpse of hope of gaining the shore" (*CI*, 188). This "new world" of the ship—the "creation" into which he has been loaded—is governed by market logic. "Unbridled European consumption and production transubstantiated African bodies. Black bodies juxtaposed to such things as East Indian textiles, Swedish bar iron, Italian beads, German linens, Brazilian tobacco flavored with molasses, Irish beef, butter, pork, Jamaican rum, and North American lumber announce ownership. In godlike fashion, merchants and traders transformed African bodies into perishable goods and fragile services" (*CI*, 188).

Equiano directly challenges this perverted "creation" with a scriptural imagination that calls out the heretical rendition, calling it back to orthodox Christianity. Thus his *Narrative* "carries the demand for humanizing relationships as central to the performance of Christian identity, the very identity claimed by his white readers" (*CI*, 189). Lamenting his separation from his sister—so common in the slave auctions governed only by the logic of the market—and despairing at her fate, Equiano utters a lament, a prophetic prayer: "O ye nominal Christians! Might not an African ask you, learned you this from your God? who says unto you, Do unto all men as you would men should do unto you? Is it not enough that we are torn from our country and friends to toil for your luxury and lust of gain? Must every tender feeling be likewise sacrificed to your avarice?" (*CI*, 192).

Equiano—who "read the world scripturally"[22] (*CI*, 194)—is diagnosing the extent to which the white theological imaginary has replaced scriptural lenses with colonialist, capitalist spectacles. The functional worldview of that imaginary is one to which Christianity is subject, not one in which a

22. Jennings describes Equiano working out of "theological holisms that shun sacred/secular dualism" (*CI*, 195). See also Willie James Jennings, "Binding Landscapes: Secularism, Race, and the Spatial Modern," in *Race and Secularism in America*, ed. Jonathan Kahn and Vincent Lloyd (New York: Columbia University Press, 2016), 207–37.

gospel imagination governs. And so Equiano's conversion is also an inversion. Converted on a slave ship named *Hope*, his narrative challenges and overturns the slave-ship creation narrative. "He brought the remade world into the world created by God who saved him" (*CI*, 197). The creation called into existence by Christ, sustained by the ascended Lord, is the creation in which the Word became flesh and endured death on a cross. And that same Jesus meets the broken Equiano on the *Hope*. That encounter and conversion unleash the forces that will upend the perverse bastardization of creation carried on board that same ship. Equiano "assumed a prophetic position as one who spoke from within the Christian tradition, arguing through its internal logics and utilizing its scriptural wisdom. However, what he was not fully aware of was how far down the absurdity reached into Christianity's performance in the new worlds" (*CI*, 183).

This is seen in Equiano's appeal to his baptism. His protest was not just an abstract, dogmatic claim. It was also rooted in liturgy, in the rites of worship. Hastily sold by the captain of one ship, without a chance to say farewell to friends or crew that had befriended him, Equiano tried to argue for freedom with his old and new masters: "I told him my master could not sell me to him nor to any one else . . . I have served him . . . many years, and he has taken all my wages and prize-money, for I only got one sixpence during the war; besides this I have been baptized; and by the laws of the land no man has a right to sell me" (*CI*, 182). Equiano (rightly!) sees the rite of baptism as an ontological change, the basis for equality and an indication of everything that's wrong with commodification of human beings. But then Jennings points out the limits of this appeal: "We also see the symbol of Christianity's fundamental limitation, the inefficacy of baptism in the presence of a racial calculus. As performed in the slaveholding Christian West, baptism enacted no fundamental change in the material conditions of Christian existence" (*CI*, 182). Our liturgies are liable to co-option by trumping imaginaries. And so we feel the force of the question that occupies us in this chapter: Why should we think liturgy is the counter-formative discipline we've suggested?

But also constructively: "What does it mean to form faithful people, given the complex social situations for our theological pedagogies?" (*CI*, 285). While we need to grapple with the ubiquity and ingression of perverted creation heresies carried on slave ships and in marketized distortions of human nature, we must also refuse the temptation to concede these are "natural," just "the way things are." The hope of the gospel is a reimagining of the world *as* the creation that holds together in Christ (Col. 1:15–20), which comes with the hope of imagining our own re-formation in ways that can resist the pedagogies of white supremacies and other injustices woven into the liturgies of Western market societies. With Equiano, we are called to "attempt to imagine belonging and relationship beneath the guiding hand of God through relations that are fundamentally diseased and reflective of the remade world" (*CI*, 186). How to remake the remade world? How to reconfigure the disconfiguration of creation we have inherited? And how to be *faithful* to the word of a resurrected Jew in the midst of modernity's markets? How to sing the Lord's song in a strange land?

🌿 Picturing Liturgical Capture in *The Mission*

In discussions of economics, regulation, and public policy, you are bound to run into the concept of regulatory capture. First articulated by the Nobel laureate George Stigler, regulatory capture describes a situation in which a government agency that is supposed to regulate an industry becomes dominated by the very industry and companies it is supposed to police. So instead of acting in the public interest to protect consumers, the environment, and the common good, the "captured" agency acts in ways that benefit the industry. In a common analogy, it is said that in such cases the gamekeeper turns poacher.

This happens because companies have vested interests in controlling whatever would like to control them. Since regulation could put a cramp on profits, industries are more motivated than a broader consumer public to lobby, persuade, and influence regulatory agencies. And since regulators need the sort of expertise that only people in the industry have, it is often industry experts who become the regulators. In the most thorough form of "deep capture," as Jon Hansen and David Yosifson describe it, the regulator begins to think like the regulated industry.[23] At that point, the capture is complete: it has been internalized.

Perhaps we could analogically describe a situation of "liturgical capture"—one in which the liturgies of the church are captured and dominated by the disordered, rival liturgies they are meant to counter. Given that the rival *polis* has a vested interest in minimizing challenges and resisting the control of other liturgies, the rites of the market and empire can seek to absorb the rites of the church as merely a subservient, qualified expression that can be disciplined by market forces—either by compartmentalizing the religious to the merely "spiritual" or by privatizing the religious to interior, domestic life (both of which amount to the same thing).[24]

23. See Jon D. Hansen and David G. Yosifson, "The Situation," *University of Pennsylvania Law Review* 152 (2003–4): 129.
24. This is William Cavanaugh's diagnosis of Christianity's co-option by the regnant regime in Pinochet's Chile. See *Torture and Eucharist: Theology, Politics, and the Body of Christ* (Oxford: Blackwell, 1998).

This is pictured in maddening, heartbreaking ways in Roland Joffe's award-winning film *The Mission*, starring Jeremy Irons as Father Gabriel and Robert De Niro as Rodrigo Mendoza, the mercenary/slave trader turned Jesuit. Set in 1758 in the blurry border-lands hidden deep in the jungle of Argentina, Brazil, and Paraguay, it opens with the retrospective voice of the cardinal who has been dispatched from Europe to resolve a tension in the colonies. As a result of a treaty between Spain and Portugal, a vast swath of the jungle and its inhabitants—the indigenous Guaraní—have been transferred from Spanish to Portuguese rule. But this isn't merely an administrative transfer between distant colonial powers. There is a very tangible and dire consequence: the Guaraní would now be at the mercy of Portugal's slave trade. Officially, Spain has repudiated slavery, but in fact the Spanish governor, Don Cabeza, is deeply invested in the slave trade. And one of his most important "providers" is the mercenary hunter Rodrigo Mendoza.

Complicating this "industry opportunity" is the presence of Father Gabriel and a community of Jesuits who have risked their lives, and suffered martyrdom, to bring the gospel to the Guaraní. The peaceful placidity of their witness is embodied by the plain-tive notes of Father Gabriel's oboe as he first invites, and encounters, the Indians. With stuttering breaths that betray his fear, Father Gabriel nonetheless comes to them with a new song that the Guaraní will make their own.[25] As the cardinal remarks in his report to the pope, "With an orchestra the Jesuits could have subdued the whole continent." Gabriel's evangelism is aesthetic.

"So it was," the cardinal narrates, "that the Indians of the Guaraní were brought to the everlasting mercy of God . . . and the short-lived mercy of man." For European poli-tics is playing itself out in these distant colonies, and the missions and their inhabitants are pawns that will have to be sacrificed. If the Jesuits refuse to evacuate the missions in South America—thereby exposing the Guaraní to become chattel in Portugal's slave trade—then the Jesuit order will be expelled from Europe. Furthermore, the missions have become industry rivals, generating self-sustaining economies that are the envy of the Portuguese governor, Senhor Hontar. The missions have become too prosperous, he remarks to the cardinal. "You should have achieved a noble failure if you wanted the approval of the state. There's nothing we like better than a noble failure."

But the Indians refuse to leave, and neither will the Jesuits at the mission of San Carlos, facing excommunication as a result. Father Gabriel refuses to abandon his Guaraní sisters and brothers and so remains in solidarity, though taking up a pacifist stance. Rodrigo, who has by this point undergone a radical conversion and become a Jesuit, also refuses to abandon them. But his response is that of the proto-liberation theologian: he is staying to fight, along with other priests.

25. Indeed, the missions will become a source of countless musical instruments played in the cathedrals of Europe. And it will be the beauty of their choral voices that overwhelms the cardinal when he finally visits.

What is nothing short of disgusting is how the politics of the papacy allows itself to be cowed by the politics of the nation-state. This has happened in no small part because the papacy has configured the church as it if *were* a state, another rival alongside Spain and Portugal—which is why the Portuguese see themselves in a power struggle with the church and are asserting their power in return. Similarly, the allegedly "Catholic" governor, Don Cabeza, exhibits a racialized ideology that shows no signs of discipline by a Christian imagination. And so the inevitable happens: the cardinal, ambassador for the papacy, effectively sanctions a military operation that will end with the slaughter of the Guaraní and the Jesuits who remained in solidarity with them. Rodrigo dies with his sword in his hand; Father Gabriel is shot while carrying the Host.[26]

What we witness is an example of liturgical capture: for the powers-that-be, whether from Spain, Portugal, or the papacy, the rites of the church have been co-opted by a rival story. Their performance is bastardized, their enactment compromised because they have been repositioned within a story and mythology that guts their kingdom orientation. When the Spanish and Portuguese authorities assemble their armies for the oncoming slaughter, we hear a prayer that has become an utter parody: *Dominus vobiscum*, "The Lord be with you." So, too, they have become hoodwinked by a market logic. When the cardinal receives the report of the slaughter and asks whether it was really necessary, Don Cabeza's stunted commercial imagination answers in the affirmative: "I did what I had to do given the legitimate purpose which *you* sanctioned." Don Hontar distills the lie of this "tragic" logic: "You had no alternative, your eminence. We must work in the world. The world is thus."

But the cardinal, complicit as he is, also refuses to buy this logic: "No, Senhor Hontar. Thus have we *made* the world. Thus have *I* made it."

Case Study 2: Liturgies of Violence in Rwanda

We are trying to face head-on one of the most trenchant critiques of the Cultural Liturgies project, what we're calling "the Godfather problem": How can we claim that worship uniquely forms a "peculiar people" when there seems to be so much evidence of people who have been immersed in the church's liturgies yet exhibit "worldly" ways? Or why should we imagine the church's worship forms us as a distinct *polis* when Christians immersed in such rituals so often exhibit the same "earthly city" politics as the world? We are submitting ourselves to the reality check of case studies as an antidote to

26. In the visual epilogue of the film, however, in the burned-out remains of the mission, some young Guaraní who survive gather things to begin again. They pass over the swords and pick up the violin. They still want to sing the song Father Gabriel brought to them.

ecclesiological idealism. That includes facing up to cases where the church has not only failed to resist but actually fomented injustice—what Jennings names "ecclesial failure."

In his dense study *A Brutal Unity*, Ephraim Radner puts the church's own ugliness before us and proposes a counterintuitive thesis: if you care about justice and the common good, you should care about the church. Exhibit A in his argument is a very stark one: Rwanda. This case study emerges in the context of Radner's critique of William Cavanaugh's argument in *The Myth of Religious Violence*.[27] Responding to Hitchens-like claims that religion causes violence, Cavanaugh argued that, in fact, it was the politics of statecraft that really generated the so-called Wars of Religion in Europe, for example. In that sense, contrary to liberal and secularist "myths" that blamed such violence on religious belief, Cavanaugh argued that the liberal state generated such violence. And it was just to the extent that Christianity assimilated itself to the liberal nation-state that it became embroiled in such violence. If the church retained its identity as "the church," Christianity wouldn't have been implicated in such violence. You can see a working hypothesis about the relationship between church and state at work behind this argument—a model that we might describe as loosely "Hauerwasian."[28]

Whatever explanatory power Cavanaugh's account might have for a European context, Radner says, the fact is there is just no way to excuse the church from violence in a context like Rwanda.[29] While not a "sole" cause (contra the New Atheist thesis), the fact is that the church—and specifically "intra-Christian competition"—contributed to violence in the Rwandan genocide.[30]

27. William Cavanaugh, *The Myth of Religious Violence: Secular Ideology and the Roots of Modern Conflict* (New York: Oxford University Press, 2009).

28. While no parrot of Hauerwas, Cavanaugh was one of his students.

29. I suspect that Cavanaugh would largely agree with Radner's concerns here, but his apologetic project in *The Myth of Religious Violence* has a different axe to grind.

30. Radner presses us to recognize that intrachurch division has an impact on the church's ability to contribute to the common good more broadly. Intra-Christian competition fragments our social and political witness. If, as various Christians claim, matters like abortion or marriage or climate change or patterns of material consumption are all deeply religious and moral issues of salvific status, the fact that Christians hold diverse views about these things, and also that their very structures of decision making are so disparate and unconnected, means that Christians probably have little leverage within the larger society for any kind of influence on issues that touch these matters. The lesson to be learned is that *catholicity* has implications for Christians' social and cultural witness. In a way, we live in a new moment in this regard: one can see all kinds of collaboration (rather than competition) between Roman Catholics and Protestants, for example, rooted in a deep sense of common catholic confession and a shared concern for the public good. This would seem to counter the religious competition that Radner notes, though he would also press us to be "realistic" and recognize that the realities of Protestant and Roman Catholic division (not

As Radner asks, "Given that Christians did the killing and did so surrounded by their lived Christian symbols and spatial forms and led often by their Christian pastors, in some cases taking Mass quite self-consciously before going out to kill, how are we to understand the nature of their faith?"[31]

Rwanda, in other words, is the countervailing exemplar to the oft-celebrated French village of Le Chambon.[32] The church in Rwanda is not the hero; it is a creator of villains. "We must seek to identify the Church first of all as a killer," Radner argues, "if we are to understand the nature of ecclesial existence properly" (*BU*, 19–20).[33] If some have invoked the formative power of Christian practices to make sense of how a Protestant village in France was moved to undertake the risk of sheltering Jewish neighbors and strangers from the Nazis, what do we make of those same practices functioning as the prelude to genocide? It won't do to simply attribute the violence to nonreligious factors of ethnic identity fomented by postcolonial policy.

> Christianity simply stares one in the face in Rwanda's modern history: the historian must account for its presence, character, and action as a matter of objective understanding. The pervasiveness of Christian forms within Rwandan society—churches everywhere, priests and pastors and the religious integrated into the quotidian as well as elite structures of society at every point—made possible, at least on some basic ordering of public space, the fact that more people were killed during the genocide in church *buildings* than perhaps anywhere else.[34] How and why did the bodies end up *there* and murder happen *there*, such that today the most numerous and chilling memorials to the genocide are churches

---

to mention the institutional splintering of Protestantism) are liabilities for the *public* good. We need to hear this.

31. Ephraim Radner, *A Brutal Unity: The Spiritual Politics of the Church* (Waco: Baylor University Press, 2012), 31 (hereafter cited in text as *BU*).

32. See Craig Dykstra's invocation of this example in *Growing in the Life of Faith: Education and Christian Practices*, 2nd ed. (Louisville: Westminster John Knox, 2005), 56–64, heavily dependent on Philip Hallie, *Lest Innocent Blood Be Shed: The Story of the Village of Le Chambon and How Goodness Happened There* (New York: Harper & Row, 1979).

33. The broadly Hauerwasian foil of his project is clear in the remainder of the same paragraph: "And it is in the political realm that this question arises. To tackle the question, however, I will need to first claim this political space of the Church anew and take it back, as it were, from those who would drive the Church from the sphere of formal social ordering—often referred to as 'the State'—in order (as they suppose) to save the Church. But the Church cannot be so saved by moving her about the pieces of the world, and that is at the center of understanding who the Church is" (*BU*, 20).

34. This is a kind of perverse inversion of Augustine's quasi-apologetic claim in the opening of *City of God*, wherein he points out to the pagan critics of Christianity that in fact the very architectural artifacts of the church—her buildings—were sites of sanctuary, mercy, and protection for them (1.1–3).

filled with the bones and skulls of victims slaughtered among the pews and before the altars? (*BU*, 30–31)

How can we make claims about the formative power of liturgy—the way a visual and sonic environment sanctifies perception and restor(i)es the imagination—when these rites not only did nothing to prevent this genocide but in fact were caught up as contributors to it? At stake here is not just a particular theological agenda but the integrity of the gospel and sacramental nature of the church. Facing up to this question does not preclude appreciation of the complexity and nuance of factors involved. Following Longman, Radner points out the contingent history of interweavings not unlike those diagnosed by Willie Jennings. A long missionary history (that focused on emerging leaders among the Batutsi) is intertwined with the reality of Protestant versus Catholic "religious competition," creating divisions that were exploited by Rwandan ruling forces. Furthermore, the necessary work of translation and contextualization also enshrined and sacralized *some* existing political realities and divisions, often unwittingly. So "when push came to shove, the Church herself had constituted sacred power along constructed and deeply divisive ethnic lines, ones that she bequeathed to the emerging sphere of civil-political governance" (*BU*, 34).[35] In ways parallel to the case of New World slavery, in Rwanda the church was not so much trumped by racial politics as responsible for it. "In the case of Rwanda," Radner concludes, "it is not possible to overestimate the formative and enabling power of these religiously grounded conceptualities and their origins" (*BU*, 37).

> If Christians are responsible for violence, if the conceptions of their motives are given in Christian terms, if these conceptions have been shaped and gathered together in their hostile force through particular decisions made on behalf of Chris-

---

35. This also included the sacralizing of *oppositions*, contributing to a literal "demonization" of rival parties. "'Sacralizing' oppositions," Radner points out,

> proves to be a particularly powerful effect of some Christian translations and a key element in the literal "demonization" of human forces, evident in other African contexts that have been engulfed by violence. . . .
>
> The "dehumanization" of the Batutsis, which most analysts recognize as a demanded psychological basis for the massacres, was not the product of a simple shift in rhetorical reference; rather, it was necessarily informed by a profound reoriented *religious* judgment about human personhood that permitted murderers to discern their victims as "cursed" and "abandoned by God." The work of turning "the Other" into a "nothing," whose brutalized bodies could physically symbolize this transformation, was the product of a long-term remolding of metaphysical perceptions. (*BU*, 35–37)

What's really at work here is not just a didactic metaphysics but an imaginative map of preintellectual perception.

To Think About: Stand There and Take It

Dana Perino, who served as the White House press secretary for a time under George W. Bush, recounts a time when the president visited wounded soldiers and their families at Walter Reed National Military Medical Center near the White House.[a] Perino was moved by the intimacy of the president's time with these families. Expecting resentment and anger, Perino observed almost unanimous gratitude from families who were thankful for the president's attention and concern. In one case, the president oversaw the ceremony for presenting a Purple Heart to a young marine who was intubated and unconscious. After the presentation, "the Marine's little boy tugged on the president's jacket and asked, 'What's a Purple Heart?' The president got down on one knee and pulled the little boy closer to him. He said, 'It's an award for your dad, because he is very brave and courageous, and because he loves his country so much. And I hope you know how much he loves you and your mom, too.'" As the president hugged the boy, medical staff were scurrying because the Marine had woken up. "The president jumped up and rushed over to the side of the bed. He cupped the Marine's face in his hand. They locked eyes, and after a couple of moments the president, without breaking eye contact, said to the military aide, 'Read it again.'"

But not everyone was happy to see the president. One family was devastated by grief and understandably angry at what this war had done to their son. The mother yelled at the president, wanting to know why it was her child and not his who lay in that hospital bed. While her husband tried to calm her, Perino "noticed that the president wasn't in a hurry to leave—he tried offering comfort but then just stood and took it, like he expected and needed to hear the anguish, to try to soak up some of her suffering if he could."

Later, as they returned to the White House on Marine One, only the engine of the helicopter could be heard, Perino recalled. "As the helicopter took off, the president looked at me and said, 'That mama sure was mad at me.' Then he turned to look out the window of the helicopter. 'And I don't blame her a bit.' One tear slipped out the side of his eye and down his face. He didn't wipe it away, and we flew back to the White House."

a. Dana Perino, "Why George W. Bush Stood There and Took the Wrath of a Soldier's Mom," *Chicago Tribune*, August 3, 2016, http://www.chicagotribune.com/news/opinion/commentary/ct-trump-purple-heart-george-bush-perspec-20160803-story.html.

---

tianity's ecclesial vocation, so understood, and if, finally, these decisions and their forms can be shown as bearing the power of violence, it is appropriate . . . to speak of a specifically *Christian* responsibility for violence, one . . . that must fill every onlooking Christian with "anguish" because of its *religious* import. (*BU*, 37–38)

The faithful response here is not to rush to a defense, to an explanation, to deflect the force of this anguish. This anguish is something to be entered, a kind of interrogation room in which we need to dwell, feeling the hot light of the question.

Radner's disturbing question demands an account, if not quite a defense. And Radner provides some resources for diagnosis—not to excuse the church but rather, Nathan-like, to confront it with the depth of the question. In some significant sense, he argues, the propensity for the church to contribute to such unjust social and political realities stems from the lamentable reality of denominational division and "ecclesial competition" (very much against Jesus's prayer in John 17): "A divided Church simply magnifies political contests, that is, the violent contestability of human life in general. It is also incapable of forming resisting—redemptive—communities of a particular character; that is, of forgiveness, reconciliation, and sacrifice" (*BU*, 73–74).[36] In the case of Rwanda, this ecclesial competition tracked back to missionary competition: "The competitive missionary spheres, making use of longstanding antagonistic rhetoric now inflated by local political and social wrestling, ended up by teaching church members distinctions and antipathies that were informed by specifically salvific claims" (*BU*, 70). In terms we've used above, penultimate differences were invested with ultimacy; the language of ultimacy was marshaled as a motivator for penultimate political realities. The line, in short, was blurred. "Divide and conquer" as a missionary strategy became the horrific Tutsi-Hutu divide of the genocide. And it's not just that liturgy didn't prevent this; it seems to have contributed to the horror.

Examples of such tragic "ecclesial failure" could, of course, be multiplied—"German Christianity" under National Socialism; apartheid in the Dutch Reformed Church of South Africa; the treatment of First Nations peoples in Anglican residential schools; and, sadly, many more. How can we account for the inadequacy, even exacerbation, of liturgy in these cases, given the sorts of claims we've been making about liturgical formation? Do these cases disprove such claims?

What if liturgical formation is both the problem *and* the solution? What if these tragic cases both challenge and confirm our thesis?

Analyzing Ecclesial Failure

Brian Bantum's consideration of race suggests the complexity of the challenge. Like Jennings, Bantum rightly points out all the ways the church's worship licensed racialization and racism. Particularly harrowing is the antebellum baptismal rite of confession for slaves recorded by Francis La Jau, an Anglican bishop from colonial South Carolina: "You declare in the Presence of God

---

36. This is why the heart of Radner's book in chaps. 4–6 (to which I am unable to do justice in this context) is focused on strategies for addressing ecclesial division as a matter of *public* good.

and before this Congregation that you do not ask for the holy baptism out of any design to free yourself from the Duty and Obedience you owe to your Master while you live, but merely for the good of Your Soul and to Partake of the Graces and Blessings promised to the Members of the Church of Jesus Christ."[37] Bantum points out the heinous domestication of the baptismal rite at work here: "The presence of God was invoked, not as an entrance into a new kind of community, but in order to concretize one's participation in a racialized community." Rather than signaling the radical reorientation of an upside-down kingdom and initiation into the politics of the city of God, the baptismal moment only reinforces the status quo. Indeed, it becomes "a moment of profound cultural encounter where the meaning of blackness and whiteness are arbitrated through the language of baptism. . . . Here the church, as well as the presence of God, are but tools that fortify a reality far deeper and more profound than God and the church—race."[38] The religious liturgy has been marshaled for the reinforcement of another social imaginary. "Even the explicitly religious has been co-opted by a reality that is understood to be prior and primary," Bantum comments. And that trumping reality is "the telos of white life."[39]

The disturbing insight of Bantum's work highlights how racialized formation is its own kind of perverted discipleship, a social imaginary we absorb not only from "secular" liturgies but from misdirected, co-opted Christian worship as well. Thus he presses us to see race "as a religious modality" and our assimilation to racist imaginaries as a kind of liturgical deformation.

> Racial identity constitutes a form of discipleship that must be theologically accounted for and resisted. That racial performance exists as a social phenomenon is certainly a challenge to Christian discipleship. But to suggest it is a religiously grounded form of being in the world is to infer a theological response that must be more precise in its description of the problem and the way forward. Racial performance is not simply a sinful behavior that must be avoided, but a way of being in the world that is more than difficult to resist, for it is the air we breathe.[40]

This is why the way forward begins with a forthright stock-taking of our deformation, which is itself a prelude to repentance. "To imagine a life in Christ," Bantum counsels, "we must begin to reimagine the shape of our unfaithfulness, our complicity in the economy of race, in order to faithfully

37. Brian Bantum, *Redeeming Mulatto: A Theology of Race and Christian Hybridity* (Waco: Baylor University Press, 2010), 35.
38. Ibid.
39. Ibid., 36.
40. Ibid., 17.

imagine what it might mean to participate in the renunciation of an old life marked by the tragedy and violence of race."[41]

And yet, while Bantum doesn't flinch from diagnosing the depth of our complicity, the answer to such perverted racial discipleship is the counter-formative power of discipleship in Christ. "The possibility of imagining discipleship in a racial world must begin with Jesus. To imagine a life of discipleship, a way of being in the world that disrupts racial logic and formation, the church must begin to look anew at the center of our faith"—Jesus, the mulatto, hybrid God-man.[42] "The possibility of our renunciation of a discipleship inflected by race only becomes possible by entering into the body and life of another."[43] And so, while Bantum points out how the rites of baptism could be co-opted, he also points to baptism as the way we are reborn: "Baptism is entrance into the work of Christ's person. It is the initiation into his body *and his people*. As such, this entrance marks the renunciation of the world's claims upon the baptized as well as the renewal, or rebirth, of the person. It is an entrance that requires a departure from the racial economy of the West and its children. To be baptized is to enter into Christ's mulattic personhood and an economy of negotiation that such a presence is necessarily bound to."[44]

Baptism is not a magical solution. It is the beginning of this "negotiation"; it "draws us into a drama of God's presence in the world," calling us to a "mulatto/a Christian existence" that comprises "the negotiation of identity inherent in our claim to be 'in Christ.'"[45] Liberation from myths of "purity" might be the beginning of wisdom for grappling with questions of deformation and sanctification.

Ecclesiology and Ethnography

Locating the Church

What characterizes the work of Jennings, Radner, and Bantum is a theologically motivated accountability to empirical realities, disciplining the claims of liturgical formation and ecclesial identity with the realities of our compromise and complicity. Thus their work can be seen as part of a wider conversation at the intersection of ecclesiology and ethnography.[46] Unlike other paradigms of

41. Ibid., 16.
42. Ibid., 87–88.
43. Ibid., 89.
44. Ibid., 142. The final chapter of Bantum's book considers prayer as a discipline for the reformation of desire.
45. Ibid., 143, 142.
46. The chapter on Bourdieu in *Imagining the Kingdom* (chap. 2) should be read as part of this conversation as well.

encounter between theology and social science—in which social science is taken to be the neutral arbiter and "objective" assessor of theological claims[47]—the emerging conversation between ecclesiology and ethnography appropriates the methods and practices of social description from a confessedly theological center, and with a primarily theological interest. As John Swinton has remarked, "If the church's task is to bear witness in the ways Hauerwas suggests, then the need to explore the empirical church is of great importance, not for sociological purposes but for theological reasons."[48] There is no witness that isn't empirical; otherwise we're on the road to gnosticism. Insofar as witness is embodied, and the church is Christ's body, all of our ecclesiological claims are de jure "exposed," in a sense, to empirical assessment. Any claim about the formative power of the church's worship is, by nature, falsifiable even if the operations of the Spirit are not subject to merely natural assessment. Nonetheless, "by their fruits you shall know them."

Christian Scharen penned something of a manifesto for theology's need of ethnography just over a decade ago. The catalyst was John Milbank's rather grandiose claims about "the Church" in his landmark work *Theology and Social Theory*.[49] Responding to critiques that his account of the church was too idealized, Milbank conceded that there remained an important role for "judicious narratives of ecclesial happenings which would alone indicate the shape of the Church that we desire."[50] Here Scharen sees an argument for ethnography *as* ecclesiology—not evacuating theology into social science but appreciating the theological import of attending to the embodied shape of actual congregations and parishes.[51] Theologians, he says, need to "be better students of the real."[52]

And herein lies the accountability and challenge. Despite claims about the church as a "contrast society," an "alternative *polis*," an outpost of the

47. Following John Milbank, I've described this as a "correlational" strategy that undercuts theology, engendering what Milbank describes as a "false humility" for theology and ecclesiology. See Smith, *Introducing Radical Orthodoxy*.

48. John Swinton, "'Where Is Your Church?': Moving toward a Hospitable and Sanctified Ethnography," in *Perspectives on Ecclesiology and Ethnography*, ed. Pete Ward (Grand Rapids: Eerdmans, 2012), 74. Swinton's chapter (71–92) serves as a succinct introduction to the ecclesiology and ethnography project. For a more expanded introduction, see Christian Scharen, *Fieldwork in Theology: Exploring the Social Context of God's Work in the World*, The Church and Postmodern Culture (Grand Rapids: Baker Academic, 2015).

49. For a summary of the relevant aspects of Milbank's argument, see Smith, *Introducing Radical Orthodoxy*, chap. 7.

50. John Milbank, "Enclaves, or Where Is the Church?," *New Blackfriars* 73 (1992): 341–52.

51. Christian Scharen, "'Judicious Narratives,' or Ethnography *as* Ecclesiology," *Scottish Journal of Theology* 58 (2005): 125–42. This builds on Scharen's own ethnographic work among congregations in Atlanta, Georgia; see Scharen, *Public Worship and Public Work: Character and Commitment in Local Congregational Life* (Collegeville, MN: Liturgical Press, 2004).

52. Scharen, "'Judicious Narratives,'" 131.

city of God, it turns out that when you simply attend to the exhibited lives of congregations and congregants, "actual church people look rather a lot like everybody else."[53] For Scharen, what's needed is "a means to account directly for cultural pluralism and the complicated, bifurcated social-structural worlds shaped by and shaping Christian people and their communities."[54] Without a sufficiently complex analysis and account, "one may miss the ways real communities of faith are Christian in ways that tightly interrelate with . . . their congregational 'communal identity.' Without this more complex understanding of culture and community, it is difficult to account for the identity 'given' through eucharistic participation, never 'generic' but always particularly incarnate within the life of this or that Christian community."[55] In other words, an idealistic ecclesiology that fails to attend ethnographically to the nitty-gritty sociological realities of competing formation will, ironically, be unable to properly recognize and diagnose the dynamics of the church's assimilation. Simplistic, grand claims about the church as "anti-*world*" will miss the ways churchgoers are shaped by "the world."[56] As Scharen puts it, "Sociologically uninformed dichotomies between the church and the world, because of the simplistic and holistic understanding of culture implied, really harm their own efforts better to lead the church in being the church exactly because their crude cultural lens cannot see exactly the ways in which they are bound up with the world in their very ways of being the church."[57]

53. Ibid., 128. Scharen points to the research in Robin Gill, *Churchgoing and Christian Ethics* (Cambridge: Cambridge University Press, 1999).

54. Scharen, "'Judicious Narratives,'" 129.

55. Ibid.

56. While Scharen rightly criticized simplistic dichotomies of "church" and "world," this seems to sometimes bleed into a more normative blurring of the distinction. In a desire to affirm that "God is at work in the world (too)," he seems to be uncomfortable with the New Testament's own drawing of the line between the church and the world (e.g., 1 John 2:15–17). See my discussion of the ambiguity of "world"-talk in Scripture in *Desiring the Kingdom*, 187–90.

57. Scharen, "'Judicious Narratives,'" 133. Nicholas Healy presses this ethnographic point in his critique of what he calls the "ecclesiocentrism" of Stanley Hauerwas in *Hauerwas: A (Very) Critical Introduction* (Grand Rapids: Eerdmans, 2014), esp. 73–99. In order for Hauerwas's "*particular* agenda" (7) to actually function as an argument, Healy contends, Hauerwas needs to be able to point to an *empirical* church that embodies what he claims. "According to the terms of Hauerwas's account," Healy summarizes, "for the empirical church to be a contrast community, a sufficient number of its members must have contrast identities. This [empirical reality] is logically necessary if those members' congregations are to be identifiably contrast communities" (80–81). But this is precisely where Healy says "Hauerwas's social theory" runs into an "empirical problem": "The identity-formation of most Christians is generally insufficient for them to be recognizably Christian in their everyday lives" (82). And so we arrive once again at something like our Godfather problem: "To what extent are such people actually

Ethnographic attention to the dynamics of cultural formation is not only a strategy to diagnose *de*formation; it also becomes a way to (1) affirm positive interplay between "public" and "ecclesial" liturgies, attuned to listen and look for the work of the Spirit beyond the church,[58] and (2) help distill and highlight those effects of formation that can be more specifically attributed to congregational life and immersion in worship. If we are going to be able to see the effects of virtue formation, we need to consider a multiplicity of formative factors in the lives of congregations and Christians. "If the church is a community 'shaped by Jesus' as Stanley Hauerwas claims, or constituted as 'the other city' as Milbank claims, then what constitutes such an identity? Since the members not only worship God together in particular churches but also are involved in many other spheres of social life, such claims beg for a context in order to make sense. And it will not do simply to roll out church-world distinctions; in so many ways the church is 'worldly' *even* in so far as it serves as a counter society."[59]

What I find refreshing and promising about this conversation is its refusal of reductionism without floating off into aspirational idealism. As Luke Bretherton summarizes it, "The broader point to draw for the relationship between ethnography, ecclesiology, and political theory is that the church cannot be read as simply a microcosm of broader political processes and structural forces: it has its own integrity. Yet neither can an analysis of the church be separated from how it is in a relationship of codetermination (and at times

---

formed by the liturgy and other Christian practices? How different are they from others who are not Christian?" (87). These are fair questions, ones we are taking seriously in this chapter. But Healy's alternatives, insofar as he suggests any, fall flat. He seems to work with a stunted philosophy of action that is prone to an intellectualism and decisionism—a model I criticized in *Imagining the Kingdom*—that is both inadequate and ungrounded (91–92). In the end, Healy offers only hand-wavey responses that, when pressed, say almost nothing. "Going to church does not, of itself, make us more Christian," Healy argues. A lot hinges on the "of itself" and whether Hauerwas would ever claim such (he wouldn't), in which case the view Healy rejects here is not Hauerwas's. Nonetheless, Healy then continues: "As most people admit, most Christians are much the same as everyone else in their daily behavior. The only way to become really different is to work hard at it, both inside the church, and especially outside, in all our daily situations, by making cognitive as well as behavioral changes" (94). Really? That's the prescription for discipleship? "Work hard at it"? What that even means is left vague. More significantly, the claim is left without any justification or argument except the seeming justification that it is *not* what Hauerwas thinks.

58. This is more pronounced in Scharen's more recent book *Fieldwork in Theology*, where he seeks to complicate overly confident and simplistic distinctions between "the church" and "the world." In this sense, theologically primed ethnography can also be a means to recognize "what God is up to in the world" (30). For a Kuyperian, pneumatological underpinning of such attention, see Vincent Bacote, *The Spirit in Public Theology: Appropriating the Legacy of Abraham Kuyper* (Grand Rapids: Baker Academic, 2005).

59. Scharen, "'Judicious Narratives,'" 131–32.

co-construction) with its political environment."[60] That seems just right to me: an antireductionism vis-à-vis sociology, an antignosticism vis-à-vis theology.

Ultimately, ecclesiology *as* ethnography is a set of disciplines for paying attention to the lived reality of our congregations, diagnosing our between-ness, our hybridity, but also our complicity and compromise. This is crucial in addressing "the Godfather problem" because it is the only way we will be able to identify the *functional* theologies that trump the official theologies of our churches and congregations.[61] In other words, sociologists might be able to detect (performative) heresies that theologians would miss.

Picturing Conflictedness: Identity in the Colonies

While the church is—and is called to be—distinct, peculiar, called-out (*ek-klēsia*), it is not called to retreat, withdraw, or huddle into an enclave. The New Testament epistles are addressed to a "peculiar people" who are in the midst of the world, embedded in the contested territory of creation that in the meantime we call the *saeculum*. The call to follow Christ, the call to desire his kingdom, does not simplify our lives by segregating us in some "pure" space; to the contrary, the call to bear Christ's image complicates our lives because it comes to us in the midst of our environments without releasing us from them. The call to discipleship complicates our lives precisely because it introduces a tension that will only be resolved eschatologically.

Daniel Mendelsohn's memoir, *The Elusive Embrace*, provides insight into what this sort of tension *feels* like.[62] Actually, to describe the book as a memoir is already too simplifying. The essay is part memoir, part intellectual history, and part literary criticism in which Mendelsohn draws on his classical scholarship to illuminate his experience as a Jewish gay man with a passion for the Greeks and classical culture, emerging into a self-understanding of this identity and then figuring out how to navigate what that means. It can be read as an analogy, even an allegory, of what it means to embrace one's *Christian* identity.

60. Luke Bretherton, "Generating Christian Political Theory and the Uses of Ethnography," in Ward, *Ecclesiology and Ethnography*, 161.
61. Elizabeth Phillips gets at this at the end of her very helpful essay in *Perspectives on Ecclesiology and Ethnography*, which is a case study of Christian Zionist congregations. She concludes that "the deeply problematic eschatology of Christian Zionism so alters their Christology and ecclesiology as to disconnect them from the Christological and ecclesiological resources that are necessary for well-formed Christian social ethics" ("Charting the 'Ethnographic Turn': Theologians and the Study of Christian Congregations," in Ward, *Ecclesiology and Ethnography*, 104). But not all of our "theologies" are articulated, of course. They are often *practiced* more than they are stated.
62. Daniel Mendelsohn, *The Elusive Embrace: Desire and the Riddle of Identity* (New York: Vintage, 2000).

Most germane in this context is his reflection on two tiny particles in Greek: *men* and *de*. Grammatically these particles function in a couplet to signal "on the one hand" and "on the other hand." "What is interesting about this peculiarity of Greek, though, is that the *men . . . de* sequence is not always necessarily oppositional. Sometimes— often—it can merely link two notions or quantities or names, connecting rather than separating, multiplying rather than dividing. . . . Inherent in this language, then, is an acknowledgement of the rich conflictedness of things."[63] It is this *conflictedness* that should interest us here as we think about the realities of (de)formation and the church's embeddedness in the world.

Mendelsohn sees this kind of *men . . . de* conflictedness in his own experience but also where he lives. Chelsea is often described as a gay "ghetto" in New York City, but Mendelsohn resists that description. Unlike, say, the Castro in San Francisco, which, like the shtetls of Poland, was a ghetto made necessary by oppression and exclusion, Chelsea, he points out, has a very different history. "Chelsea came into being in the mid-1980s not as a safe haven in which gay men might take shelter" but instead as a neighborhood renewed and gentrified by an influx of citizens with the freedom to live according to their identity. And so, Mendelsohn emphasizes, the analogy for Chelsea isn't medieval Jewish ghettos but rather the colonies of the Greek city-states. "'Colony' is a word that was to acquire its own evil history, of course; but it began fairly innocuously. The restless body-loving Greeks solved their own perennial overpopulation problems by sending out their more vigorous citizens to settle hitherto unknown outposts of the map. They called these places *apoikiai*, 'away-from-homes.' The colony is a place to be associated with expansion and, hence, success—as opposed to the ghetto, which we associate with oppression and compression and, eventually, death."[64]

But, of course, Chelsea is not a colony across the Mediterranean/Hudson in some distant land—it is a "colony" in the thick of Manhattan (and now prone to be gobbled up by innumerable bobos). And yet it is on the edge; its center is on the edge of the dominant city's makeup and habits and expectations. It is a *men . . . de* sort of place. And so this *topos* is also a paradox: "*para*, against, *doxa*, expectation." "What else do you call a place," Mendelsohn asks, "that must somehow be both an edge and a center, somewhere you could simultaneously feel utterly different, as you knew you were, yet wholly normal, as you wanted to be?"[65] But it also means such a place is unstable, conflicted, a place where one lives but perhaps without ever feeling settled ("the place hovers between identities"). "To me," he admits, "wandering as I do between the two geographies of my own life, the most interesting and yet always suspect topos in the ongoing debate about gay culture and identity is that there is such a thing as

63. Ibid., 26–27.
64. Ibid., 29.
65. Ibid., 30.

'gay identity' at all."[66] If there is an "identity" here—and Mendelsohn is skeptical—it is bound up with a *men . . . de* conflictedness, a hybridity and betweenness that doesn't mean one *lacks* identity but, in fact, has assumed it. ("All Americans," Mendelsohn remarks, "are, in the end, inauthentic, something else, something multiple and hybrid.")[67]

And yet: "This is the place where I decided to live," Mendelsohn concludes, "the place of paradox and hybrids. The place that, in the moment of choosing it, taught me that wherever I am is the wrong place for half of me."[68]

The engagement between ecclesiology and ethnography is nothing if not a call for the church to be honest about its conflictedness, its hybridity, its contested formation and identities. The church is not unlike Chelsea, both an edge and a center, and to be "in Christ" in the *saeculum* is to inhabit a paradoxical place.

The Pastor as Ethnographer: Cultural Exegesis of the Rites of Empire

When we appreciate the significance of ethnography for critical, even prophetic service to the body of Christ, perhaps in the context of a congregation's worship we might imagine the pastor as a political theologian.[69] And the first task of the pastor as political theologian is to serve a congregation by being an ethnographer of the rites of the empire that surround it, teaching it to read the rituals of late modern democracy through a biblical, theological lens.

As we discussed in chapter 1, the "political" is not just the administration of law—as if political life boiled down to trash-removal service, keeping the

66. Ibid., 31.
67. Ibid., 32.
68. Ibid., 35.
69. In suggesting a role for the pastor as political theologian, I will also be focusing on a role the pastor plays as *local* theologian, to use Hiestand and Wilson's term. See Gerald Hiestand and Todd Wilson, *The Pastor Theologian: Resurrecting an Ancient Vision* (Grand Rapids: Zondervan, 2015), 81–83. However, I'm not sure I share their implicit "ranking" of the pastor-theologian's role (local, popular, ecclesial), so I don't see this priority of local theology as diminishing. In particular, I'm not sure I buy their claim that "evangelicalism will never reclaim the emerging generation of theologians for the pastorate if our only conception of the pastor theologian is that of a local or popular theologian" (85). I think there are pastors who find the unique challenges of local theology to be exactly the intellectual challenge they've been looking for. And I think the particularly local, contextualized challenges of political theology pose a challenge worth tackling.

Furthermore, I think this task of theologically inflected ethnography is really a task for the priesthood of all believers and that, in fact, pastors will have to learn from a host of laypeople. But in this context, I am simply focusing on the role that the pastor's preaching and teaching can play as a moment in gathered congregational worship.

traffic lights operational, and policing legal obligations. The "political" is not merely procedural; it is formative. The *polis* is a *koinōnia* that is animated by a vision of the good. And while Aristotle couldn't imagine competing visions of the good within the walled city's territory, this reality of competing *poleis* and rival goods was something early Christians appreciated from the beginning. There are rival *poleis* within the confines of the nation-state. The formative power of the *polis* is not embodied in its sword but in its rituals. In this respect, the *polis*'s vision of the good life is carried in all kinds of nonstate rhythms and routines that reinforce, say, the *libido dominandi* of the earthly city, or the ultimate mythology of independence and autonomy that is not only articulated in a constitution but enshrined in a million microliturgies that reinforce our egoism.

So part of the role of the pastor as political theologian is apocalyptic: to unveil and unmask the idolatrous pretensions of the *polis* that can be all too easily missed since they constitute the status quo wallpaper of our everyday environment.[70] It requires thoughtful, rigorous, theological work to pierce through the everyday rituals we go through on autopilot and see them for what they are: ways we are lulled into paying homage to rival kings. This requires what Richard Bauckham calls a "purging of the Christian imagination."[71] At stake here is nothing less than true versus false *worship*.[72]

So part of the pastor-theologian's *political* work is to enable the people of God to "read" the practices of the regnant *polis*, to exegete the liturgies of the earthly city in which we are immersed. This is an essentially *local*, contextualized task, both in time and in space: the political idolatries that tempt us and threaten to deform us are localized. The political hubris of today is not the same as the political hubris of even eighty years ago, let alone of fifth-century Africa or sixteenth-century New England. Such cultural exegesis has to be local and contextual, but it also has to be theological (and, as I've argued, theologically *sociological*). If you want to deepen the theological capacity of the church, try offering a theological ethnography of Independence Day (which, admittedly, might also be a good way to *shrink* a church).

We can see ancient exemplars of this. A standout is a sermon Augustine preached on New Year's Day in 404 (likely in Carthage), in which he offers a theological and cultural exegesis of the pagan festivals that would dominate

70. For work by a pastor-theologian that does this, see T. Scott Daniels, *Seven Deadly Spirits: The Message of Revelation's Letters for Today's Church* (Grand Rapids: Baker Academic, 2009). See also my discussion of an "apocalyptic" theology of culture in *Desiring the Kingdom*, 90–93.

71. Richard Bauckham, *The Theology of the Book of Revelation* (Cambridge: Cambridge University Press, 1993), 17.

72. Ibid., 35.

the city that day.[73] (This might also explain why his sermon was three hours long, a kind of filibuster to keep his parishioners away from the temptations as long as he could.)[74] He takes as his text a line they've just sung from Psalm 106: "Save us, Lord our God, and gather us from among the nations, that we may confess your holy name" (v. 47). How do you know if you're "gathered from among the nations"? Augustine asks. "If the festival of the nations which is taking place today in the joys of the world and the flesh, with the din of silly and disgraceful songs, with the celebration of this false feast day—if the things the Gentiles are doing today do not meet with your approval" (198.1) . . . well, *then* you're gathered from the nations.

But this isn't just pietistic moralizing. Augustine launches into a theological and philosophical analysis of the rites of pagan feasts. At stake, he argues, are faith, hope, and love:

> If you believe, hope, and love, it doesn't mean that you are immediately declared safe and sound and saved. It makes a difference, you see, what you believe, what you hope for, what you love. Nobody in fact can live any style of life without those three sentiments of the soul, of believing, hoping, loving. If you don't believe what the nations believe, and don't hope for what the nations hope for, and don't love what the nations love, then you are gathered from among the nations. And don't let your being physically mixed up with them alarm you, when there is such a wide separation of minds. What after all could be so widely separated as that they believe demons are gods, you on the other hand believe in the God who is the true God? . . . So if you believe something different from them, hope for something different, love something different, you should prove it by your life, demonstrate it by your actions. (198.2)

The remainder of Augustine's sermon is a sustained cultural exegesis that aims to make explicit the (pagan) faith, hope, and love that is "carried" in the city's feasts and rituals, which too many of his parishioners merely considered "things to do" rather than rites that do something *to* them. The burden of Augustine's theological analysis is to highlight the incoherence of both singing the psalm and participating in the festivals.

This is an ongoing task. One of the responsibilities of the pastor as political theologian, then, is to help the people of God "read" the festivals of their own *polis*, whether the annual militarized Thanksgiving festivals that feature gladiators from Dallas or the rituals of mutual display and haughty purity

73. Augustine, Sermon 198 (Mainz 62), in *Sermons*, trans. Edmund Hill, ed. John E. Rotelle, *The Works of Saint Augustine* III/11 (Hyde Park, NY: New City Press, 1997), hereafter cited in text.
74. Suffice it to say that Augustine wouldn't be hosting Super Bowl parties in the cathedral.

that suffuse online regions of "social justice." Our politics is never merely electoral. The *polis* doesn't just rear to life on the first Tuesday of November. Elections are not liturgies; they are events. The *politics* of the earthly city is carried in a web of rituals strung between one occasional ballot box and the next. Good political theology pierces through this, unveils it—not to help the people of God *withdraw* but to *equip* them to be sent into the thick of it. When we are centered in the formative rites of the city of God, Augustine reminds his hearers, "even if you go out and mix with them in general social intercourse . . . you will remain gathered from among the Gentiles, wherever you may actually be" (198.7).

This points to the second, constructive function of the pastor as political theologian. It is not sufficient to unmask the rites of earthly city politics. We also need to help the people of God *cultivate* their heavenly citizenship. Citizenship is not just a status or a property that one holds; it is a calling and a vocation. I can hold a Canadian passport and a Canadian birth certificate and yet fail to be a *good* Canadian citizen. Citizenship is not only a right; it is also a virtue to be cultivated. The pastor as political theologian plays a role in shepherding civic virtue in citizens of the city of God (cf. Phil. 3:20).[75]

If Christian worship constitutes the civics of the city of God, then liturgical catechesis is the theological exercise by which we come to understand our heavenly citizenship. In other words, a key *theological* work that is charged with political significance is to help the people of God understand why we do what we do when we worship. Liturgical theology *is* political theology. Cultural exegesis of Christian worship makes explicit the political vision that is "carried" in our liturgy. The pastor-theologian has responsibility to unpack the *telos*, the substantive, biblical vision of the good, that is implicit in Christian worship.[76]

Picturing Political Discipleship: Epistles to a Governor

The pastor as political theologian—actually, every pastor—is a pastor not only of the *gathered* church but also of the *sent* church. In Abraham Kuyper's terms, the pastor is called to shepherd not only the church as institute but also the church as organism. The pastor-theologian shepherds the work of citizens of the city of God who answer the call to enter the messy *permixtum* of the *saeculum*.

75. Since I endorse Presbyterian forms of church government, I would not want to limit this role to the *teaching* pastor. Indeed, I do worry that the picture of the pastor-theologian in Hiestand and Wilson, *Pastor Theologian*, seems to assume either a Baptistic or an Episcopal model.
76. See my exegesis of this in *Desiring the Kingdom*, chap. 5.

We can see a case study of this role in Augustine's ongoing relationship with Boniface. Boniface was a Roman general and African governor. In their ongoing correspondence we see a spiritual friendship in which Augustine the pastor-theologian is not afraid to challenge and exhort the imperial soldier. But we also see a political practitioner who is hungry for theological wisdom, and not merely blessing or permission. In fact, Boniface was the recipient of a long, intricate theological letter about the Donatists (letter 185) that Augustine later, in his *Retractationes*, described as a book (*The Correction of the Donatists*). After this lengthy letter, Augustine sent Boniface a short, simple note: "It is highly pleasing to me that amid your civic duties you do not neglect also to show concern for religion and desire that people found in separation and division be called back to the path of salvation and peace."[77]

In Letter 189, Augustine dashes off an eloquent articulation of the faith fused with theological counsel in response to a pressing request from Boniface for help (189.1). Augustine begins where he always does: with love. "This, then, I can say briefly: *Love the Lord your God with your whole heart and with your whole soul and with your whole strength, and Love your neighbor as yourself*. For this is the word that the Lord has shortened upon the earth [alluding to Rom. 9:28]." He exhorts Boniface to "make progress" in this love by prayer and good works, bringing to fullness the love that has been shed abroad in our hearts (189.2). For it is "by this love," Augustine reminds him, that "all our holy forefathers, the patriarchs, prophets, and apostles pleased God. By this love all true martyrs fought against the devil to the point of shedding their blood, and because this love neither grew cold nor gave out in them, they conquered." And it is the same love that is at work in Boniface, Augustine points out: "By this love all good believers daily make progress, desiring not to come to a kingdom of mortal beings but to the kingdom of heaven" (189.3).

Augustine then speaks directly to some of Boniface's doubts and questions: "Do not suppose that no one can please God who as a soldier carries the weapons of war" (189.4). Look at the examples: "Holy David," the centurion who displayed great faith, the prayerful Cornelius who welcomed Peter, and others. These are exemplars for Boniface to emulate. But Augustine also offers vocational wisdom that is rooted in some fine points of eschatology. While some are called to lives of chastity and perfect continence and cloistered devotion, "*each person*, as the apostle says, *has his own gift from God, one this gift, another that* (1 Cor. 7:7). Hence others fight invisible enemies by praying for you; you struggle against visible barbarians by fighting for them." While we might long for the day when neither sort of battle is necessary—neither prayer warriors nor weaponized soldiers—we need a more nuanced eschatology, Augustine counsels. "Because in this world it is necessary that the citizens of the kingdom of

---

77. Augustine, *Letters 156–210*, trans. Roland Teske, SJ, ed. Boniface Ramsey, *The Works of Saint Augustine* II/3 (Hyde Park, NY: New City Press, 2004), 185A (hereafter cited in text).

heaven suffer temptation among those who are in error and are wicked so that they may be exercised and put to the test like gold in a furnace," Augustine says, "we ought not to want to live ahead of time with only the saints and the righteous" (189.5). Don't think we can "live ahead of time" is Augustine's way of saying: don't fall for the temptation of a realized eschatology.

So answer your call, Boniface, but take up your vocation in ways that are faithful, in a way that longs for kingdom come without thinking *you* can make it arrive. "Be, therefore, a peacemaker even in war in order that by conquering you might bring to the benefit of peace those whom you fight" (189.6). As he begins to draw the letter to a close, Augustine seems attentive to the unique temptations the soldier faces, attuned to the cultural liturgies of military life: "Let marital chastity adorn your conduct; let sobriety and frugality adorn it as well. For it is very shameful that lust conquer a man who is not conquered by another man and that he who is not conquered by the sword is overcome by wine" (189.7). He closes with an exercise in liturgical catechesis. Appealing to the Preface of the Mass ("Lift up your hearts" / "We lift them up to the Lord"), Augustine encourages Boniface to find in that a posture *for life*, for his work and vocation: "And, of course, when we hear that we should lift up our heart, we ought to respond truthfully what you know that we respond" (189.7). In other words, don't just *say* "we lift up our hearts"—*lift up your heart* in your work.

Augustine's affection for Boniface did not preclude admonishment. Letter 220 is an intriguing case. After the death of his wife, Boniface seems to be lost. He seems to be wavering in his sense of calling as a soldier and imperial servant, but he also seems wayward in his grief, making bad decisions. When they had last seen each other in Hippo, Augustine was so depleted by exhaustion he could barely speak. And so he follows up with a letter, by which he intends, he says, "to do with you what I ought to do with a man I love greatly in Christ."[78]

After the death of his wife, Boniface wanted to abandon his public life and retreat to a monastery to devote himself to "holy leisure." But when he expressed this to Augustine and Alypius in private, they counseled otherwise. "What held you back from doing this," Augustine reminds him, "except that you considered, when we pointed it out, how much what you were doing was benefitting the churches of Christ? You were acting with this intention alone, namely, that they might lead *a quiet and tranquil life*, as the apostle says, *in all piety and chastity* (1 Tim. 2:2), defended from the attacks of the barbarians" (220.3). These pastor-theologians exhorted him to remain steadfast in his public life; indeed, in some ways *their* pastoral/theological work depended on his public work as governor and defender.

---

78. Augustine, *Letters 211–270, 1*–29**, trans. Roland Teske, SJ, ed. Boniface Ramsey, *The Works of Saint Augustine* II/4 (Hyde Park, NY: New City Press, 2005), 220.2 (hereafter cited in text).

Though Boniface continued to answer the call to public office, the weakness of grief seemed to compromise his moral judgment, and thus Augustine confronts him for abandoning continence, for being "conquered by concupiscence" (220.4), and for becoming embroiled in webs of intrigue. Augustine forthrightly reminds him of the need for repentance and penance. And then Augustine the pastor-theologian presses Boniface *theologically* to be more resolute in the execution of his public duties. "What am I to say about the plundering of Africa that the African barbarians carry out with no opposition, while you are tied up in your difficulties and make no arrangement by which this disaster might be averted?" (220.7). While Boniface is trying to secure his status in a contested imperial court, he is in fact shirking his duties to the common good (see: election season). "Who would have believed," Augustine asks,

> who would have feared, that with Boniface as head of the imperial bodyguards and stationed in Africa as count of Africa with so great an army and such great power, who as a tribune pacified all those peoples by battling them and terrifying them with a few allies, the barbarians would now have become so venturesome, would have made such advances, would have ravaged, robbed, and devastated such large areas full of people? Who did not say, when you assumed power as count, that the barbarians of Africa would not only be subdued but would even be tributaries of the Roman state? (220.7)

Augustine the pastor-theologian is mounting a theological case for the Roman general to man his station, do his job, be faithfully present as count and governor. Behind his counsel is a crucial theological distinction between the earthly city and the city of God. There is not a hint of the "Holy Roman Empire"-ism for which Augustine is often mistakenly blamed. To the contrary, Augustine relativizes Rome without demonizing it. So whatever disputes or frustrations Boniface might have with Rome, he still owes a debt: "If the Roman empire has given you good things," Augustine says, "albeit earthly and transitory ones, because it is earthly, not heavenly, and cannot give save what it has in its control—if, then, it has conferred good things upon you, do not repay evil with evil" (220.8).

In these letters we hear something of Augustine's hopes for Boniface and those like him: the hope for faithful agents of the coming kingdom who answer the call to public life, who administer the common good in this *saeculum* of our waiting. Such public servants bear heavy burdens on our behalf and find themselves pressed on every side. Many, like Boniface, are honestly hungry for theological counsel and scriptural wisdom for a messy world. The pastor-theologian not only needs the theological chops to answer their questions with a robust theology of public life. Above all, the pastor-theologian needs to love. Thus Augustine closes his letter to Boniface: "Love commanded me to write these things to you, my most beloved son; by that love I love you by God's standards, not by those of the world" (220.12). If Augustine enjoins Boniface to love not the world, it's because Augustine loves him, and loves him enough to equip him with a rich political theology.

Accounting for Disordered Loves

So, in the end, how can we answer our opening question: Why doesn't Christian worship seem to create the "peculiar people" we sometimes claim? Don't the Michael Corleones of the world prove our fundamental thesis false since their participation in the liturgies of the church doesn't seem to prevent their persistent participation in the litanies of the devil and the rites of injustice? The only adequate response is complex and nuanced; there is no "silver bullet" answer to this question, even if there is, I will argue, a defense to be made. We need to attend to multiple factors to make sense of the Godfather problem.

The Liturgies of Vice

First, we should recall that the anthropology and cultural theory that undergirds my Cultural Liturgies project is *not* sequestered or compartmentalized to Christian or "religious" rituals. In other words, my claim about the liturgical formation of desire (and hence identity and action) is not a claim *only* made about how Christian worship creates an "alternative *polis*" or "contrast society." To the contrary, our liturgical anthropology is equally offered as a way to diagnose and make sense of our cultural assimilation to the disordered loves of consumerism, militarism, nationalism, and other performative idolatries that bend our hearts and actions toward rival "kingdoms." It is important to remember that our liturgical model is an account not just of virtue but equally of vice.[79]

So if the Godfather problem poses a challenge for claims about the counter-formative power of Christian worship, rejecting a liturgical anthropology creates the same problem on the other side of the ledger: If our loves and longing (and hence actions) are not shaped by the rituals and practices we give ourselves over to, then how does a Michael Corleone come to embrace "the family business"? Is he *argued* into it? Does he carry out assassinations because he reached a logical conclusion and hence made a

79. See discussion of a "phenomenology of temptation" in Smith, *Imagining the Kingdom*, 140–42.

"rational" decision? Does Michael Corleone take on the role of the Godfather because he *thinks* about it? Is this a way of life he adopts as the conclusion of some syllogism?

I don't think so. Indeed, this is signaled in the very opening line of *The Godfather*: "I believe in America." Is this "belief" in America the outcome of some apologetic argument that *convinced* Bonasera? Is this a devotion that is the outcome of didactic teaching? Or is it rather the kind of belief and devotion that has been caught by swimming in the water of America's rituals?[80] If the critic of our liturgical anthropology wants to point out the limits of liturgical formation's "success," she or he will then have to provide an account of just how and why so many Americans—including American Christians—are assimilated to ways of life that consist of consumerism and nationalism. To imagine that this happens by means of some didactic, intellectual conversion, as if people *think* their way into consumerism, would, I expect, be almost laughable. If the antiformative critic thinks a liturgical account is inadequate, the burden of proof is on them to sketch the alternative. And what would that be? Is their point that, in fact, we *think* our way to Christlikeness and hence that our assimilation is the result of bad ideas or inadequate theology or faulty logic? Is it because we're not *thinking* "hard enough"? Was it a failure to think well that led Christians to endorse slavery? Would a better ethical theory have made a difference? Isn't it rather the case that our disordered hearts are prone to generate theories ex post facto that will give comfort to our disordered desires?

So, in fact, only a liturgical account can make sense of our *de*formation. This is why the Cultural Liturgies project has had an ethnographic impulse from the beginning (and why Bourdieu figures so prominently in *Imagining the Kingdom*). The only adequate way to make sense of our *de*formation is to recognize the formative power of practices in shaping the nerve center of human action and being-in-the-world, which is less the deliberative intellect and more the affective heart (even though there is no dichotomy between these).[81] In short, it would seem that only a liturgical anthropology and theory of culture can adequately make sense of our deformation or assimilation, which then also undergirds claims made about the counter-formative nature of Christian worship. The critic who keeps invoking the Michael Corleones of the world can't decry a liturgical/formation account on the one hand and then employ it on the other.

80. *The Godfather* is nothing if not a meditation on the dynamics of immigrant assimilation. This is perhaps even more true of *The Godfather: Part II.*
81. See Smith, *Imagining the Kingdom*, 41–73.

Worship as a Way of Life

That said, we also need to be honest about the realities of duplicity. It does this project no favors to ignore the Michael Corleones of the world. In that sense, it is important to appreciate that a recognition of these realities does not put the liturgical account itself in jeopardy; to the contrary, the recognition of such conflictedness is internal to the practices of Christian worship. Part of the narrative arc of the liturgy is the practice of confession, which is nothing if not a discipline of honesty about our divided hearts. This is well captured in a classic confession from the Book of Common Prayer:

> Almighty and most merciful Father; We have erred, and strayed from thy ways like lost sheep. We have followed too much the devices and desires of our own hearts. We have offended against thy holy laws. We have left undone those things which we ought to have done; And we have done those things which we ought not to have done; And there is no health in us. But thou O Lord have mercy upon us, miserable offenders. Spare thou those, O God, who confess their faults. Restore thou those who are penitent; According to thy promises declared unto mankind in Christ Jesus our Lord. And grant, O most merciful Father, for his sake; That we may hereafter live a godly, righteous, and sober life, To the glory of thy holy Name. Amen.[82]

In this respect we might fairly ask, does Michael Corleone ever go to confession? Or is his participation in the rites of the church more ad hoc, on his own terms? While Coppola obviously wants to frame the tension—yea, contradiction—between Corleone's religious participation and his "business" transactions, we have no indication that Corleone actually gives himself over to the cogency of a *way of life* governed by the rhythms and habits of the church's worship. Instead we see selective participation in certain "public" religious rites that are easily confused with merely "ethnic" identities: weddings, baptisms, funerals. So it's not at all clear that in Michael Corleone we see someone who is at once participating in the practices of the body of Christ and at the same time wantonly carrying out the devil's work. More than likely we see someone who participates in only *some* of the practices of the body of Christ, practices that for him function as a means of acquiring and securing social capital in an (ethnic) enclave.[83] In this way, Michael Cor-

---

82. "Daily Morning Prayer: Rite One," *The Book of Common Prayer . . . according to the Use of the Episcopal Church* (New York: Church Hymnal Corporation, 1979).

83. In an important essay, "Love and Liturgy," philosopher Terence Cuneo asks how worship relates to love of neighbor (in *Ritualized Faith: Essays on the Philosophy of Liturgy* [New York: Oxford University Press, 2016], 20–36). Does liturgical participation really help us better conform to the commandment to love our neighbors? Focusing on prayers of petition, Cuneo

leone is not really a "practitioner" of the practices, because he participates in only some of them, some of the time, as a kind of baroque ritual decoration on a way of life that finds its center in other practices. Wedding and funeral observance, Christmas and Easter participation—this is not really *practicing* the faith that is, as Craig Dykstra has said, "the practice of many practices."[84] To call Corleone's sporadic participation in these life events and occasional rites a "Christian liturgical way of life" would be like describing someone as a Christian because they attend annual performances of Handel's *Messiah* and Bach's *Mass in B Minor* at the performance hall downtown. And so to say that his immersion in Christian worship obviously hasn't (re)formed his heart and life isn't really a fair or accurate claim, because, in fact, he *hasn't* been immersed in "Christian worship"—he has shown up for selective *events*. And no one—not me, not Hauerwas, not MacIntyre, not Milbank—would ever claim that such sporadic, selective participation should be confused with proper *habituation*.

However, we should immediately restate two key points that we have emphasized already in the Cultural Liturgies project. First, as pointed out in *Desiring the Kingdom*, our formative claims about Christian worship are never staked on some supposed adequacy of "Sunday only" participation.[85] Even if we grant a significant, central place to gathered, sacramental[86] worship around Word and Table, this is understood to be the center of a web of Christian disciplines and practices that make up a Christian way of life seven days a week.[87] The Michael Corleones of the world generally don't give

argues that "a central function of the cycle of petitions is to help break the grip that an ethic of proximity can have" (28). However, he is also well aware of the failures of formation in this respect and makes an important distinction between the "motives" we bring to worship and the "stance" we take in worship. The "liturgical script," as he calls it, "might be more or less non-committal with regard to the motives from which the petitions and blessings should be offered. But it is not neutral with regard to the *stance* from which those assembled offer their petitions and blessings. They are to issue from a stance in which those who offer these petitions actively repent of their own shortcomings and, insofar as these petitions are offered as a community, for the failures of their community" (35). What's missing from Michael Corleone, we might suggest, is this stance.

84. Dykstra, *Growing in the Life of Faith*, 56.
85. See the section "Worship, Discipleship, and Discipline: Practices beyond Sunday" in Smith, *Desiring the Kingdom*, 207–14.
86. The assumption that worship is *sacramental* is a key, fundamental conviction that cannot be ignored or underestimated. See ibid., 139–44.
87. This is why I've suggested in *You Are What You Love: The Spiritual Power of Habit* (Grand Rapids: Brazos, 2016) that my project should be seen as an ecclesial complement (and corrective) to the "spiritual disciplines" projects of Dallas Willard, Richard Foster, and others. The "Christian practices" project of Dorothy Bass and Craig Dykstra does a better job of emphasizing both communal/ecclesial practices and individual disciplines.

themselves over to the Divine Office the rest of the week. Hence it shouldn't be a surprise that the liturgies of consumerism, nationalism, militarism, and egoism effectively *trump* the limited, token-ish participation in merely one facet of Christian discipleship—that is, Sunday gathered worship. Second, nothing in the liturgical account of formation precludes recognizing the importance of catechesis. To the contrary, we have emphasized that liturgical catechesis is integral to such an account, and therefore a failure of catechesis contributes to a failure of formation.[88] In particular, the failure of catechesis often contributes to a compartmentalization that effectively nullifies the liturgical practices of worship, undercutting their counter-formative power. When we are never invited to understand why we do what we do when we worship, then the repertoire of practices is no longer worship but something else—an ethnic identifier, a superstitious hedge, a way to consolidate social capital, or whatever. Liturgical catechesis is an integral aspect of formative worship.

Liturgical Capture

Ethnographically, we need to attend to the dynamics by which the litanies of Christian worship can become co-opted by rival Stories. This often seems to be a dynamic of domestication whereby the ultimacy of the Christian vision is demoted to a penultimate or subultimate ritual serving some other ultimate good—The Nation or The Market or Our People or even The Family.[89] This seems especially true given the vagaries and contingencies of history whereby the rituals of Christian worship came to be closely identified with an ethnic "people" (and perhaps particularly in immigrant situations)—whether Scottish Presbyterians or Irish and Italian Catholics or Dutch Reformed immigrants. In this case, the same rites would seem to function as something other than Christian worship; in Wittgensteinian terms, we could say the performance looks the same but in fact the *use* is different.[90]

Eschatological Expectations

It is equally important that we retain an appropriate, eschatologically disciplined expectation on these matters. While the call to image Jesus is a call to

88. See the section "Redeeming Reflection: On Liturgical Catechesis and Christian Education" in Smith, *Imagining the Kingdom*, 186–89.

89. This seems to be the cautionary tale woven by Jennings's chilling analysis of the church's role in Portuguese slavery. See my discussion of "liturgical capture" above in "Picturing Liturgical Capture in *The Mission*."

90. See my discussion of George Lindbeck's famous example of the crusader who cries, "Jesus is Lord!" in *Who's Afraid of Relativism? Community, Contingency, and Creaturehood* (Grand Rapids: Baker Academic, 2014), chap. 5.

holiness that doesn't let us off the hook, neither should we expect perfection. The adventure of sanctification is temporal and ongoing and stretches as long as the *saeculum* itself. There is no graduation from the school of charity that is the church; there is no preeschatological attainment of perfection. Every disciple's life is a video, not a snapshot. While the snapshot at any particular moment might freeze a way of life that fails to exhibit the way of the cross, a video of a person's or congregation's life might tell a story of formative progress of sorts. "You should see who I *used* to be." This is a common trope in Paul's epistles—you once *were* but now *are*: "You used to walk in these ways, in the life you once lived," Paul reminds the Colossians. "But now you must also rid yourselves of all such things as these: anger, rage, malice, slander . . ." (Col. 3:7–8). "You were dead in your transgressions and sins, in which you used to live when you followed the ways of this world and of the ruler of the kingdom of the air," he reminds the Ephesians. "But because of his great love for us, God, who is rich in mercy, made us alive with Christ" (Eph. 2:1–2, 4–5). But it's not as if Paul's proclamation of these positional realities leads him to imagine that these Christians have achieved perfection. To the contrary, the positional reality "in Christ" engenders ongoing commands and exhortations, with Paul constantly encountering the failure of the "saints" to live out who they are.[91] What sometimes gets described as "Augustinian realism"[92] is actually Pauline. And that realism is rooted in an eschatology.

Or, to put it crassly: even Michael Corleone could be worse. This brings to mind the curmudgeonly, some might say dastardly, Catholic, Evelyn Waugh. A woman once challenged the callous, dismissive Waugh: "Mr. Waugh, you say such horrible things to people, I cannot believe you are really religious. How can you behave as you do, and still remain a Christian?" To which Waugh replied: "Madam, I may be all the things you say. But believe me, were it not for

---

91. Paul's communication with the Corinthian Christians is another good example. On the one hand, Paul reminds them of a remarkable reality *in Christ*: "And that is what some of you were. But you were washed, you were sanctified, you were justified in the name of the Lord Jesus Christ and by the Spirit of our God" (1 Cor. 6:11). But the remainder of his correspondence with the Corinthians hardly suggests a perfect community.

92. In his magisterial biography of Augustine, Peter Brown notes that Augustine's realism was the fruit of a decade of spiritual wrestling after his conversion and signals his abandonment of naïve Neoplatonic hopes of achieving perfection. By the time Augustine turns to write his *Confessions*, "a new tone has come to suffuse his life. He is a man who has realized that he was doomed to remain incomplete in his present existence, that what he wished for most ardently would never be more than a hope, postponed to a final resolution of all tensions, far beyond this life" (*Augustine of Hippo: A Biography* [Berkeley: University of California Press, 1969], 156). Brown also notes that this eschatological tempering was a lesson learned in ministry: "Five years of sad experience in battling with the hardened wills of his congregation have flowed into [the *Confessions*]," yielding a new appreciation for the power of habit (173).

my religion, I would scarcely be a human being."[93] Sanctification, you might say, is relative. While the failures of formation might be glaring and obvious, we might also have to imagine how much worse we would be without even the minimal mitigating effects of liturgical participation.

Worship Is Not Instrumental

Finally, the argument about the centrality of worship and the importance of historic Christian liturgy is not, ultimately or only, a claim about effectiveness. In other words, Christian liturgy is not just a strategy of discipleship or an instrument of formation. While we believe that it engenders formation, it is a normative good apart from its effectiveness precisely because it is the way we meet God, the practice by which the Spirit invites us into the triune life of the Godhead. It is the lived performance of the catholic faith that draws us into the story of God in Christ reconciling the world to himself. And thus it is an enactment of solidarity with the body of Christ across time and around the globe, a performative way to anchor our faith outside the vagaries of the contemporary. Worship is ultimately and fundamentally a theocentric act, commanded and invited by the King.

In sum, the pastoral response to our assimilation needs to be as complex as its cause. We are liturgically deformed; and by the grace of the Spirit, we are liturgically reformed, albeit inadequately, in fits and starts, in need of the Spirit's counter-formation throughout our lives. Internal to the logic of Christian worship itself is a habitual recognition of both our failure and our aspiration. Christian worship is never accomplished; it is not the repertoire of a people who have arrived but precisely the rhythms of a people all too aware that they remain on the way. To show up for worship is tantamount to an admission of failure. Commenting on how we undertake participatory prayer in the context of worship, Terence Cuneo observes:

> The dynamics that move us to express concern for the other in petitionary prayer are often malformed: we care too little, we go through the motions, our minds are elsewhere. Often, moreover, we are unaware of the degree to which our motives are deficient. Indeed, rather deep in the Christian tradition is the conviction that, given how opaque we are to ourselves, we are often unable to genuinely appreciate the extent to which our motives are deficient. To repent

93. Christopher Sykes, *Evelyn Waugh: A Biography* (Harmondsworth, UK: Penguin, 1977), 448–49.

while offering these prayers is in effect to acknowledge, to help one see, and
to distance oneself from these deficiencies; it is to strive for something better
while we pray.[94]

But that is why, as Cuneo points out, the final word here is *kyrie eleison*.
Repentance, he says (citing Alexander Schmemann in *The Great Lent*), "is,
above all else, a desperate call for . . . divine help."[95] "Lord, have mercy" is
not a way to throw up our hands in despair; it is not a quietist way of saying
"Nothing's ever going to change." "Lord, have mercy" is a *cri de coeur* to the
only One who can ultimately transform us and hence undo the injustice we've
wrought. We cannot deliver ourselves from our own complicity.

94. Cuneo, *Ritualized Faith*, 36.
95. Ibid.

Conclusion

The City of God and the City We're In:
Augustinian Principles for Public Participation

Two Cheers for Heaven: A Report from a Century
of "Transforming Culture"

In his landmark tome *A Secular Age*, Canadian philosopher Charles Taylor gives us a genealogy of our present, trying to make sense of how the Christian West ended up in a "secular age." How did we move from the almost magical enchantment of the Christian Middle Ages to the rabid disenchantment of the world in modernity? How did we go from a sacramental understanding of the world suffused with the presence of God (and other spirits) to the flattened, immanent enclosure of the universe as a wholly natural (and self-sufficient) reality? When and why did we abandon our pilgrimage to the city of God and become so comfortable in the earthly city?

An important part of Taylor's genealogy will make Protestants skittish: on Taylor's persuasive account, the disenchantment of the world that eventually yields our "secular age" was, in some significant sense, an unintended by-product of the Reformation. More and more concerned to emphasize *this*-worldly realities, the Protestant valorization of domestic, economic, and political life was susceptible to Frankensteinish trajectories in which *this* world of creational life was valorized *instead* of a transcendent "heavenly" end (Taylor describes this as the "eclipse of heaven"). Who needs the beatific vision when there's so much work to be done "down here"? Indeed, Protestantism would come to be marked by a deep anti-Platonism, as Platonism would come to be construed as an incipient gnosticism. It's not so far from this story to those veritable Kuyperian hymnbooks that seem to relish singing, "Heaven is *not* my home." But is something lost in our tenacious emphasis on the goodness of creation? Do we perhaps protest just a bit too much? If we lose heaven, do we also lose creation, left only with "nature"? Does our eagerness to affirm the good of the so-called earthly city come at the expense of longing for the heavenly city? With our vigorous abandonment of fundamentalist "otherworldliness," can we muster any sympathy for St. Augustine when he reminds us that "it is, strictly speaking, for the sake of eternal life alone that we are Christians"?[1] I think we get a bit squeamish when people talk like that.

Why raise this question in connection with political theology? Because I think a newfound evangelical valorization of "this world" is already showing signs of overemphasis, as if the Kuyperian antignosticism project was a little too successful and has begun to generate an "immanentized" evangelicalism, an evangelicalism tempted not only to try to instantiate heaven on earth but also to reduce heaven *to* earth. We can end up naturalizing shalom. More specifically, newly earnest in our concern with justice, it seems to me that evangelical overidentification with the political (or the reduction of Christian concern *to* the political) is part of what has fragmented the church's proper political witness in a North American context. It is when we immanentize Christian political concern that we are most prone to succumb to regnant ideologies and hence ideological conflict—sometimes even in the name of being "nonpartisan" or "postpolitical." Here I can't help but recall Graham Greene's cautionary commentary on political involvement in *The Quiet American*.

Picturing Engagement in Graham Greene's *Quiet American*

In Greene's charming naïf, Pyle, we see something of an allegory for earnest evangelicals newly committed to justice, social activism, and political hopes (whether on the Right or on the Left). Pyle, you might remember, is the transplanted Bostonian who has arrived in Indo-China (Vietnam) with something more dangerous than weapons: he has arrived with an ideal and is devoted to instantiating it. At once boyish and dangerous, Pyle's newfound activism is the worst kind: it is the vision of philosopher-kings, of "theorists" who have dreamed up the very Form of justice and democracy, now looking for experimental territories to function as laboratories for their visions of the kingdom. In this case, Pyle has arrived with the works of York Harding on his shelves, dog-eared and annotated, a blueprint for building democracy in the region. "What the

---

1. Augustine, *City of God*, trans. Henry Bettenson (London: Penguin, 1984), 6.9, hereafter cited in text.

East needed," according to this Harding, "was a Third Force"; and Pyle was here to mobilize it.[2] An intellectual disciple with activist fervor, Pyle "was absorbed already in the dilemmas of Democracy and the responsibilities of the West; he was determined . . . to do good, not to any individual person but to a country, a continent, a world. . . . He was in his element now with the whole universe to improve" (*QA*, 18).

On top of all that, Pyle is there with illusions of purity—with the ammunition of good intentions and the dangerous cover of a "good conscience."[3] He is a liberal, says Greene's narrator, Thomas Fowler, in the sense that we are all liberals: "I've been in India, Pyle, and I know the harm liberals do. We haven't a liberal party any more—liberalism's infected all the other parties. We are all either liberal conservatives or liberal socialists: we all have a good conscience. I'd rather be an exploiter who fights for what he exploits, and dies with it" (*QA*, 96). The "best of intentions" coupled with a robust "theory" becomes a blank check for not *Realpolitik* but *Idealpolitik*, with disastrous repercussions. As Fowler will later remark, "I never knew a man who had better motives for all the trouble he caused" (*QA*, 60).[4]

If Pyle's character can be read as a cautionary allegory, we need to also recognize that he's something of a cartoon. Indeed, all we know of him we learn through the jaded voice of Fowler, a foreign correspondent who has taken up with a local woman named Phuong but remains tethered to his English Catholic wife (who refuses to grant him a divorce). If Pyle is the picture of earnest (evangelical) activism, I sometimes wonder if Fowler isn't a portrait of a reluctant Augustinian.[5] While we might be tempted to read him as simply cynical, Fowler explicitly refuses such cynicism.[6] Rather, he is skeptical of political ideologies that pretend to be salvific. He is not given to revolutionary impulses, because he has seen just enough to conclude that the new regime is usually just bad in different ways. As he usually puts it, Fowler is not *engagé*: he is not committed to a cause, not identified with a movement.[7] He is aloof from such machinations.

2. Graham Greene, *The Quiet American* (New York: Penguin, 1975), 25 (hereafter cited in text as *QA*).

3. Hence "that look of pain and disappointment" that would "touch his eyes and mouth when reality didn't match the romantic ideas he cherished" (*QA*, 74).

4. "That was my first instinct—to protect him. It never occurred to me that there was greater need to protect myself. Innocence always calls mutely for protection when we would be so much wiser to guard ourselves against it: innocence is like a dumb leper who has lost his bell, wandering the world, meaning no harm" (*QA*, 37).

5. Phuong, of course, *is* Vietnam, treated by both Pyle and Fowler as something of a pawn or instrument. Pyle arrogates himself to a high road, claiming that he is really concerned with her "interests." Fowler is more crassly honest: "You can have her interests. I only want her body" (*QA*, 59). This comes with the decidedly cynical confidence that it is Fowler who truly loves Phuong, while Pyle's supposed concern for her "interests" is actually not concerned with the concrete Phuong at all, but rather treats her as only a vessel to be filled with his ideal(s).

6. Early on, Fowler appreciates the earnestness of Pyle as a refreshing "change from the denigrations of the Pressmen and their immature cynicism" (*QA*, 24).

7. Note that *engagé* is from the old French *engagier*, "to pledge."

Here is merely a "reporter," an "observer" of the "facts."[8] "I am not involved. Not involved," he repeats as "an article of [his] creed" (*QA*, 28).

But this distance and disengagement is an unsustainable ruse. First, in the ruins of
a shelled watchtower, with cries from the wounded, Fowler discovers that he's already
engagé, that he is implicated and responsible for what surrounds him. While Pyle is denied the purity of a good conscience, Fowler is denied the purity of aloofness: "I was responsible for that voice crying in the dark: I had prided myself on detachment, on not
belonging to this war, but those wounds had been inflicted by me just as though I had
used the sten [gun]" (*QA*, 113).[9] Like Pascal's epistemic gambler, one is always already
embarked: "You must wager. It is not optional" (*QA*, 138).[10] And then Fowler becomes
quite intentionally "involved," bent on thwarting Pyle's misguided efforts. "He's got to
be stopped," Fowler impresses upon Monsieur Heng, who rightly reminds him: "Sooner
or later . . . one has to take sides. If one is to remain human" (*QA*, 174).[11]

Reading this as a parable, you'll forgive me if I suggest a backhanded moral
of the story: if Pyle's well-intentioned activism is dangerous, Fowler's sense
of disengaged neutrality is illusory. And so we are constrained (or free?) to
inhabit the space of culture with a certain calculated ambivalence and cultivated circumspection. I wonder if there isn't here a lesson for us as we think
about Christian engagement with the political, which seems tempted either
by a this-worldly activism or a quasi-Benedictine withdrawal into the church
as an "alternative" society.[12]

In his masterful book *Heavenly Participation*, Hans Boersma seems to
be motivated by a similar worry: as Protestantism valorizes the goodness of
creation and "immanent" life, it risks disenchanting the world—unhooking
it from its subsistence in the Son (Col. 1:17). While such Protestant affirma-

8. "Isms and ocracies. Give me the facts. A rubber planter beats his laborer—all right, I'm
against him. He hasn't been instructed to do it by the Minister of the Colonies. In France I'd
expect he'd beat his wife. I've seen a priest, so poor he hasn't a change of trousers, working
fifteen hours a day from hut to hut in a cholera epidemic, eating nothing but rice and salt fish,
saying his Mass with an old cup—a wooden platter. I don't believe in God and yet I'm for that
priest" (*QA*, 95–96).

9. Cf. this introspective soliloquy: "How much you pride yourself on being *dégagé*, the reporter, not the leader-writer, and what a mess you make behind the scenes" (*QA*, 119). Perhaps
he's not so different from Pyle after all.

10. Pascal has been hovering over the book since the opening scene, the *Pensées* sitting on
Inspector Vigot's desk at the initial interrogation.

11. And, of course, Fowler was never willing to be a disinterested party when it came to
Phuong.

12. See Rod Dreher, *The Benedict Option: A Strategy for Christians in a Post-Christian
Nation* (New York: Sentinel, 2017).

tions of the goodness of creation might be rightly rejecting what they see as a functional gnosticism in evangelical piety, Boersma (and Taylor) would emphasize that there's more than one way to reject gnosticism. If one ends up with an ontological framework that grants autonomy to the created order, what we're left with is not creation but rather a flattened "nature." A significant part of Boersma's worry is that evangelical Protestants have unwittingly bought into just such an ontological paradigm. And I would suggest there is a political correlate of this that finds expression in a new sort of evangelical activism—whether Right or Left—that, in Pylesque fashion, seems bent on instantiating the kingdom of God and thus is more prone to being hooked (or hoodwinked) by ideologies whose provenance is the earthly city. We're more Pelagian than we realize.[13]

Thus Boersma is concerned that younger evangelicals, overreacting to the "other-worldly" piety of their heritage, have swung the pendulum in the other direction. This is why he counters such a surprising sparring partner in this book: what he calls "antiheaven" evangelicalism.[14] I imagine some of us being puzzled that such a creature exists. Indeed, many of us in the Kuyperian stream of the Reformed tradition have spent entire careers trying to get otherworldly evangelicals to value the goodness of creation. Boersma, on the other hand, is worried that the pendulum has already swung the other way: that heaven has been eclipsed. If that's the case, I'm going to suggest, then the heavenly city has also been abandoned. And yet it is precisely our citizenship in the heavenly city that guides our commingling with the earthly city; it is our pilgrimage *toward* the heavenly city that helps us navigate the terrain of a fallen-but-redeemed creation. The politics of the city of God finds its center in an ecclesiology that becomes the space for cultivating what we might call a holy ambivalence or engaged distance, leaning into the hard work of loving our neighbors in the *saeculum* while remaining anchored to kingdom come. This is why we have much to learn from two central themes in Augustine's *City of God* that we have explored above: (1) a liturgical or ritual analysis of politics as a mode of *worship* and (2) an ecclesiocentric understanding of Christian political engagement that centers political identity in the liturgical practices of the body of Christ but then spills over into concern for the common good. In closing, then, I want to consider the implications of this for an ecclesial posture toward our calling as political animals.

13. For a discussion of "cultural Pelagianism," see James K. A. Smith, *How (Not) to Be Secular: Reading Charles Taylor* (Grand Rapids: Eerdmans, 2014), 55–57.
14. Hans Boersma, *Heavenly Participation: The Weaving of a Sacramental Tapestry* (Grand Rapids: Eerdmans, 2011), 187.

Cultivating Circumspection: Building an Ecclesial Center of Gravity

Evangelical Protestants are some of the most eager participants in political life—and cultural engagement more generally—precisely because they are eager to leave behind the otherworldly, acultural, antipolitical Christianity of their fundamentalist past. Both the Religious Right and the Christian Left are evidence that evangelical Protestants have shed their otherworldly quietism. Now what we get are evangelical (and often "Kuyperian") affirmations of "the political" in the name of "the goodness of creation." Politics is affirmed as one of the "spheres" of creation over which Christ resolutely says, "Mine!" So let us enter the political sphere with a sense of divine vocation, remaking the world in the shape of the kingdom, preparing heaven on earth.

I share this affirmation of the goodness of creation and the good of politics.[15] But one of the dangers of eagerly diving in to the political sphere is that it tends to underestimate the strength of the currents already swirling around in that "sphere." In other words, such Pylesque eagerness tends to think of politics just as a matter of strategy (and hence getting the *right* strategy in place), as something that we *do*, and underestimates the *formative* impact of political practices, that they do something *to* us.[16] It is here that I think Augustine's more nuanced analysis of the politics of the empire has something to teach us in the twenty-first century. Because he defines the political in terms of *love*, and because the formation of our loves is bound up with *worship*, Augustine is primed to recognize what we might call the "liturgical" power of political practices, which engenders critical nuance.

As we noted in Augustine's definition of a "people" (*City of God* 19.24), the earthly city's different political configurations qualify as "commonwealths," but they fail to be just because they are aimed at the wrong objects of love (that is, they wrongly constitute objects of love). So Augustine's revised account of the empire yields a fundamentally critical evaluation, nothing like the rather rosy affirmation of the "earthly city" we tend to hear from those who (mistakenly) invoke Augustine as if he fathered the Holy Roman Empire.[17]

15. I have unpacked this positive account in detail in James K. A. Smith, "The Reformed (Transformationist) View," in *Five Views on the Church and Politics*, ed. Amy E. Black (Grand Rapids: Zondervan, 2015), 139–62.

16. As we emphasized in chap. 1, this is true of the *polis* beyond the narrow constraints of "government."

17. Cf. Oliver O'Donovan, *The Desire of the Nations: Rediscovering the Roots of Political Theology* (Cambridge: Cambridge University Press, 1996): it is precisely when the church thinks it no longer needs to judge rulers—that the kingdom has arrived—that we slide from the missional project of Christendom to Antichrist. This was the temptation to which Eusebius of Caesarea fell: "The temptation was precisely to see the conversion of the rules as achieved and complete, and to abandon mission" (197). Eusebius confused Constantine's victory with the

In this respect, Augustine's "liturgical" analysis of the political enables him to be attentive to an antithesis that evangelical (Pylesque) enthusiasm for political activism seems to not recognize: that at stake in participation in the political configurations of the earthly city are matters of *worship* and *religious identity*. The public practices of the empire are not "merely political" or "merely temporal"; they are "loaded," formative practices aimed at a *telos* that is ultimately antithetical to the city of God. In other words, the public practices of the empire are *idolatrous* practices because embedded in them is a very different *telos*, a rival version of the kingdom. The political refuses to remain penultimate.

However, Augustine's still radical critique of the empire and political configurations of the earthly city does *not* entail a simplistic, wholesale rejection of Rome or other political configurations of the earthly city. So an antithetical Augustinianism does not entail a "total" critique of modernity or liberal democracy, even if it involves a radical and substantial critique. Rather, Augustine's antithetical assessment still permits a nuanced account of the earthly city's love that retains a kind of affirmation. This will not be an affirmation that neatly translates into a sanguine confidence in the ability of the citizens of God to blithely participate in the machinations of the empire, but it is one that grants and even encourages a Boniface to take up his imperial role in a way disciplined by his allegiance to Christ.

One might suggest that this comes down to something like trying to locate the "center of gravity" of political activity for citizens of the city of God.[18] If citizens of the heavenly city occupy the contested territory of creation in the *saeculum*, living amidst citizens of the earthly city as "pilgrims," exiles, and a "society of aliens" (*City of God* 19.17), then it becomes a question of locating the core energy of their political life. Too many readings of Augustine simply equate "the earthly city" with "the political"; as a result, any case made for more limited and suspicious participation in the earthly city is taken to be

---

parousia (198); in other words, he eliminated the eschatological remainder. In short, Eusebius abandoned the Christendom project *because* he abandoned mission (rather than the standard line that Christendom just *is* the abandonment of mission). "The ambiguities of Christendom . . . arose from a loss of focus on its missionary context. . . . The peril of the Christendom idea—precisely the same peril that attends upon the post-Christendom idea of the religiously neutral state—was that of negative collusion; the pretence that there was now no further challenge to be issued to rulers in the name of the ruling Christ" (212–13). But, following the lead of Ambrose (and not Jerome), this is precisely the mistake Augustine did *not* make (199–202).

18. Or, if we go with a slightly different "tether" metaphor as suggested above, we could say that Christians inhabit the contested territory of creation, alongside citizens of the earthly city, but are suspended in their work in that city by their tether to the heavenly city and the coming kingdom of God, like a window washer on a skyscraper who is suspended from an anchor on the top of the building.

advocating an *a*political stance. But the earthly city and the political should not be so equated. The city of God is also political, in the sense that it is a mode of social organization that functions beyond networks of kin. So the question of whether, or to what extent, the "society of aliens" can participate in the earthly city is *not* a question of whether these aliens can be "political," and if so, to what extent, but rather a question of to what extent they can participate in *earthly city modes* of politics.[19] Augustine never says we hold dual citizenship. The citizen of the city of God will always already find herself thrown into a situation of being a resident alien. The question isn't *whether* to "be political"; the question is *how*.

Calculated Ambivalence: Four Principles of Ad Hoc Collaboration

While Augustine suggests the center of gravity for heavenly citizens' political energy is *ecclesial*, and while his ultimate evaluation of the politics of the earthly city is critical, this doesn't translate into a Manichaean, absolutist rejection of participation in the politics of the earthly city. Rather, Augustine's political phenomenology advocates selective, intentional collaboration based on four factors, which I see as distilled implications of the argument I've undertaken in this book.

1. *Even disordered loves attest to creational desires.* On a formal level, even the structure of disordered love continues to attest to an ineradicable creational desire. Here Augustine's account of the politics of the earthly city might be said to mirror his account of idolatry. Idolatry is a persistent witness to the ineradicable religious impulsion to worship that is constitutive of human be-ing. Thus idolatry is a testimony to a perduring *structure* of the creature that is mis*directed* by the fall. While Augustine will remain critical of the perverted direction of idolatrous worship, the desire itself is evidence of a creational structure. So too with respect to the politics of the earthly city: while the political desire or love of the earthly city is ultimately perverted and misdirected, nonetheless its directional perversion indicates a creational structure. In this sense even the earthly city, he says, is a "sign" of the heavenly city (*City of God* 15.2). Thus one can make sense of Augustine's tempered evaluation of the "peace" of Rome. The desire for peace is structural: even a beast like Cacus, Augustine notes, desired a kind of peace. "For no creature's perversion is so contrary to nature as to destroy the very last vestiges of its nature." If this was true of Cacus, then certainly it was true of the empire. But

---

19. Thus I will regularly refer below to "the politics of the earthly city" in order to avoid collapsing the two.

note Augustine's ambivalence at this point: affirming the *structure* of peace does not preclude him from articulating a radical critique of this peace: "The peace of the unjust, compared with the peace of the just, is not worthy even of the name of peace" (19.12).

But this is followed by an important "yet": "Yet even what is perverted must of necessity be in, or derived from, or associated with—that is, in a sense, at peace with—some part of the order of things among which it has its being or of which it consists" (19.12). This, however, is an *ontological* claim, not a moral evaluation. It is paralleled by Augustine's ensuing account of the devil's misdirection: "Not even the nature of the Devil himself is evil, in so far as it is a nature" (19.13). The earthly city is an analogue of the devil: both, despite their perversions and misdirections, testify to an enduring structure that participates in the Creator.

2. *Every critique is ad hoc; no (Christian) critique can be total or absolute.* So Augustine's critique of the earthly city can never be a "total" or "absolute" critique, precisely because his participatory ontology precludes it. So we have a second aspect of his nuanced account of the earthly city: Augustine's attention to the *intentionality* of love also makes him attentive to the teleological nature of virtue. This permits an ad hoc recognition that the semblance of virtue is to be preferred to vice. This nuanced description—which is not quite an affirmation—can be seen once again in Augustine's account of the "peace" of Rome. As already noted, even the band of robbers maintains a "semblance" or a "shadow" of peace (19.12). And semblances are to be preferred to absence, shadows to pure darkness. This is why "even *that* [earthly] city is better, in its own human way, by their possession" (15.4, emphasis added). The desire for an earthly peace—which is only a semblance of peace—is nonetheless preferred to its absence, so even the citizen of the city of God can rejoice when the just*er* triumphs over the (even) *less* just. Crucially, Augustine encourages us to recognize elements of *degree*.[20] But Augustine's account of

20. One can hear a similar nuance in Bavinck:

As Christians, as Protestants, as Reformed Christians, there is therefore no need at all to confront the modern age antithetically, for it is governed by the same will of the heavenly Father who has assigned us a place to live and work. If we were Rousseau-like naturalists, we might easily revert to stark conservatism if we did not have a standard from above and beyond reality, or if we would borrow such a standard from the realm of imagination, we might easily seek our well-being in an unhistorical radicalism. However, when we believe in a higher order of things, the holy and gracious will of God, which comes to us not only through the facts of history, but also through the testimony of his Word, then we have found a norm with which to measure the present and change it. And then we overcome the danger to condemn reality unconditionally or to justify it, at least in principle. (Herman Bavinck, "On Inequality," in *Essays on Science, Religion,*

degrees ("just*er*") should not be understood in terms of degrees of attainment, like a cup of "justice" being more or less full, or a matter of how far
the earthly city gets on the "road" to true justice. The degree-of-attainment
model diminishes the fundamental antithesis that Augustine asserts. Instead,
the evaluation of degree is an evaluation of *direction*, and the degree to which
the semblance is more or less pointed in the right direction. The tool for mea-
surement here is a protractor, not a yardstick. To affirm the preference of the
semblance of peace over its absence does not translate into an affirmation of
semblance per se; rather, the very accounting of earthly peace and justice as
a semblance has embedded in it a fundamental critique of its essential failure.
Too many readers regularly overestimate Augustine's affirmation here and
seem to regularly ignore his persistent affirmation that "justice is found where
God, the one supreme God, rules an obedient City according to his grace,
forbidding sacrifice to any being save himself alone" (19.23). Because this is
de facto ruled out as a possibility in the earthly city (whose very origin is the
*mis*direction of the fall), the earthly city can never be home to "true justice"
(19.24). Nonetheless, because Augustine's account can recognize degrees of
disorder, he avoids the "pox-on-all-your-houses" demonization and dismissal
that usually precedes a retreat into the church as enclave.

3. *Recognize penultimate convergence even where there is ultimate divergence*. This nuance—which allows Augustine to recognize that some cultural
configurations are closer to being properly directed than others—also permits
an ad hoc recognition that there can be aspects of congruence in the *saeculum*
even if there is ultimate, teleological divergence. In other words, Augustine's
attention to the fact that loves can be ordered more and less badly (more and
less oriented toward the *telos* of shalom) provides the criteria and platform
for a kind of cultural critique that eschews the all-or-nothing*ism* that tends
to characterize some contemporary screeds about "empire." I am suggesting
that it is Augustine's "intentional" account of love (as opposed to the static
dissection of the issue in terms of "spheres") that allows him to articulate
cautious affirmations of social configurations that are *less* misdirected than
others, while retaining a trenchant sense that what's at stake in participating
in the cultural practices of the earthly city comes down to *worship*, and thus
idolatry.

But it is also this emphasis on the dynamics of love that leads him to envision the political "fallout" of the heavenly city as reparative for the earthly
city. We can see this in Augustine's response to a query from Volusian, a pagan

and Society, ed. John Bolt, trans. Harry Boonstra and Gerrit Sheeres [Grand Rapids:
Baker Academic, 2008], 161–62)

inquirer, who has questions about the incompatibility of Christian faith and the interests of the state. "The preaching and teaching of Christ is in no way compatible with the practices of the state, since, as many say, it is clear that it is his commandment that we should repay no one with evil for evil."[21] To the contrary, Augustine responds. In fact, in Jesus's great commandments—"Love the Lord your God with all your heart and with all your soul and with all your mind" and "Love your neighbor as yourself" (Matt. 22:37, 39)—is "found the praiseworthy safety of the state, for the best city is established and protected only by the foundation and bond of faith and solid harmony when the common good is loved, namely, God, who is the highest and truest good, and when human beings love one another in complete sincerity in him by loving one another on account of him from whom they cannot hide the disposition with which they love."[22] It is the call to love our neighbor that both propels us into the shared territory our neighbors inhabit and compels us to affirm those goods that resonate with what God desires for our fellow citizens. While Augustine couldn't quite imagine how widely shared responsibility for the state would be, the realities of liberal democracy only heighten this call and responsibility.

4. *Don't lose your eschatology: cultivate a teleological sensibility.* Augustine can offer a limited, ad hoc affirmation of aspects of even *dis*ordered communal love and provide an account of how citizens of the city of God can "use" such love. Consider just one instance: Augustine clearly states that the immanent peace of the earthly city "is not to be rejected" (19.26) even as he points out its ultimate emptiness and unsustainability (its nihilism?). Nevertheless, he admonishes the citizens of the city of God to "make use of the peace of Babylon." Since the two cities are "intermingled" in this time between times (the *saeculum*), it is in the interest of the "pilgrims" of the city of God to seek the welfare of the earthly city, just as the Israelites in exile were admonished to seek the welfare of Babylon—for "in its welfare you will find your welfare" (Jer. 29:7 ESV).

What does it mean to "make use" of the earthly city's "peace," and *for what ends*? There are two key components to notice here. First, "making use" of the earthly city's peace does not indicate a program for the "Christianization" of the empire; Augustine is not Eusebius. The purpose of seeking some modicum of political peace in the earthly city is *ecclesial*: "that we may lead a quiet and peaceful life with all devotion and love" (19.26, citing 1 Tim. 2:2).

---

21. Augustine, *Letters 100–155*, trans. Roland Teske, SJ, ed. Boniface Ramsey, *The Works of Saint Augustine* II/2 (Hyde Park, NY: New City Press, 2003), 136.2.
22. Ibid., 137.17.

This does not sound like a project for "transforming" the empire. To recall O'Donovan's formulation, "The most truly Christian state understands itself most thoroughly as 'secular.'"[23] It knows what time it is, is awaiting a coming King, and has expectations disciplined by this eschatology.

Nonetheless, second, that does not excuse us from the creaturely calling to respond to creation's own call for political realization. In other words, the cultural work of creating *polities* is something that is demanded by the very nature of creation. The cross, resurrection, and new creation do not displace that calling; they renew it. In particular, they reframe it as equally a calling to love our neighbors, to create polities and policies, systems and institutions that protect the vulnerable, caring for the widows, orphans, and strangers among us while also making room for us to pursue an array of creaturely callings in commerce, education, the arts, and even our play. As Bernd Wannenwetsch argues, "Even though Christians have continually been tempted to view politics as a necessary evil, Christian worship, rightly understood, actually permits only a fundamentally positive attitude. As a worldly affair which is, when all is said and done, necessary, politics are not to be despised but, like private life as well, represent the necessary space in which faith proves itself, where the purpose is solicitude for human beings in their bodily, social needs as a joint attempt to alleviate their lot."[24] So we participate and collaborate in the *permixtum*, the contested but good space of our life in common, and do so in ways that hope to bend, if ever so slightly, the earthly city toward the city of God.

It is in this context that Augustine introduces the importance of patience. Responding again to Volusian, Augustine argues that in fact Jesus's command to forgo vengeance ("If anyone slaps you on the right cheek, turn to them the other cheek also" [Matt. 5:39]) is actually a gift to the state. "Otherwise, in pursuit of vengeance rather than of patience, you might value eternal goods less than temporal ones." Indeed, he continues, "we must beware that out of a desire for vengeance we do not lose, to mention nothing else, patience itself, which we should value more than everything that an enemy can take, even against our will."[25] This is ultimately an eschatological tempering of our political expectations. The kingdom is something we await, not create.

Finally, there are limits to our political participation: "Thus even the Heavenly City in her pilgrimage here on earth makes use of the earthly peace and defends and seeks the compromise of human wills in respect of the provisions relevant to the mortal nature of man, *so far as* may be permitted without

---

23. O'Donovan, *Desire of the Nations*, 219.

24. Bernd Wannenwetsch, *Political Worship: Ethics for Christian Citizens*, trans. Margaret Kohl (Oxford: Oxford University Press, 2004), 175–76.

25. Augustine, *Letters 100–155*, 138.11.

detriment to true religion and piety" (*City of God* 19.17, emphasis added). The issue is discerning this "so far as": At what point, and in what way, are the practices of the earthly city's political configuration *detrimental* to true religion? And here, once again, Augustine's intuitions are more liturgical than doctrinal: In what ways and to what extent do these political practices—these secular liturgies—deform and deflect the people of God from their longing for the heavenly city?

Conversely, we can see the church's worship as the political centering of the people of God. We gather to be sent, and we are sent to do—to undertake Christian action that participates in the *missio Dei.* "Mission," then, is just shorthand to describe what it is for Christians to pursue their vocations to the glory of God and in ways that are oriented to the shalom of the kingdom. But any Christian emphasis on mission and vocation and culture-making has to be rooted in a more fundamental concern with "dispositional deflection." If the church is a centrifuge, sending out image-bearers to take up their commission in God's good-but-broken world, it must also be a community of practice that centripetally gathers for dispositional reformation. In this way, Christian worship constitutes the "civics" of the city of God, forming a people who are sent out for the sake of the common good, sent to love not only their neighbors but even their enemies.

In Praise of the Quixotic

There will always be something quixotic about the church's politics of hope amidst the grim realism and calculating rationality of earthly city politics.[26] After all, doesn't political theology invite us to imagine the kingdom and await a King who never seems to arrive? Isn't Don Quixote laughable precisely because he has let his perception of the world be framed by his imagination, which has been fueled and filled by books of chivalry and romance? Isn't Don Quixote almost the poster child of the reality-denying Christian whose imagination is captive to a Book and thus sees what isn't there?

Do we want to deny the analogy or save Don Quixote?

Isn't there something beautiful in Don Quixote that we are loath to deny?[27] Indeed, there is something deeply gospel-ed about the knight-errant's fanciful

26. See Adam Y. Stern, "Political Quixoticism," *Journal of Religion* 95 (2015): 213–41, for a fascinating study of Don Quixote's adventures in German philosophy from Kant and Hegel up through Carl Schmitt and Walter Benjamin.

27. This hit home for me, I must confess, in seeing a performance of *Man of La Mancha* at the Stratford Festival.

perception. Consider, for example, this moving passage of what he sees in the scrub woman at the inn:

> As soon as she walked through the door, Don Quixote heard her, and sitting up in his bed, despite poultices and the pain in his ribs, he extended his arms to welcome his fair damsel. The Asturian, who, tentatively and quietly, was holding her hands out in front of her and looking for her beloved, collided with Don Quixote's arms; he seized her by the wrist and, pulling her to him, while she did not dare to say a word, forced her to sit on the bed. Then he touched her chemise, and though it was made of burlap, to him it seemed the finest and sheerest silk. On her wrists she wore glass beads, but he imagined them to be precious pearls of the Orient. Her tresses, which were rather like a horse's mane, he deemed strands of shining Arabian gold whose brilliance made the sun seem dim. And her breath, which undoubtedly smelled of yesterday's stale salad, seemed to him a soft, aromatic scent wafting from her mouth; in short, he depicted her in his imagination as having the form and appearance of another princess he had read about in his books who, overcome by love and endowed with all the charms stated here, came to see the badly wounded knight. And the blind illusions of the poor gentleman were so great that neither her touch, nor her breath, nor any other of the good maiden's attributes could discourage him, though they were enough to make any man who was not a muledriver vomit; on the contrary, it seemed to him that he clasped in his arms the goddess of beauty.[28]

This scene could be set to the tune of Hosea and Gomer, which is also why it evokes Christ and his bride. And in other ways it signals what the bride is called to, the political vocation of the body of Christ: to see in our neighbors and enemies what others can't see or refuse to see, even if it means enduring their laughter and scorn for holding out hope that the world is—and can be—otherwise.

Don Quixote is laughable, and Sancho is the empirical reality check who keeps us laughing. Sancho is the straight man who soberly tells it like it is, never cracking a smile, making Don Quixote all the more laughable. He is the voice of the shrewd purveyors of *Realpolitik* who dryly remind us of "the way things are" when we Christ-inspired politicians of hope dare to imagine the world could be otherwise. To work for justice—laboring to build humane economies and life-giving cities and empowering systems of education—must sometimes look like tilting at windmills in an age of will-to-power political

28. Miguel de Cervantes, *Don Quixote*, trans. Edith Grossman (New York: Ecco, 2005), 113. One of the differences between the novel and the musical, *Man of La Mancha*, is that in the musical the force of Don Quixote's imagination is such that even the maiden begins to see herself anew in fits and starts.

self-interest and cynical power grabs. To imagine that forgiveness and mercy and compassion could make a dent on political systems is the sort of posture that political operatives dismiss with a snicker as naive and benighted. "Here comes a tribe of Don Quixotes," they chortle, "foolish enough to imagine that faith, hope, and love belong in the *polis*!"

Such dismissive, mocking laughter depends on the same thing that the humor of Cervantes's novel depends on: a narrator who believes he sees without a slant, who presumes to give us a God's-eye view of "objective" reality. We're all in on the joke because he's showing us the way things *really* are. The political "realists" among us believe they have such an unfiltered take on the world; and those Christian postures that despair for the future unwittingly concede reality to these secularized takes.

But we still read *Don Quixote* because the world Cervantes shows us is a world we want, and his construal of the world haunts us enough to make us wonder whether the narrator has missed something, has dismissed something, or is hiding something. So too with the politics of fear and retrenchment that claims to be facing up to "reality": there is no "take" on the world that isn't informed by some *faith* in what's ultimate. What parades itself as political realism is somebody's ultimate take on the world—rooted in some *faith* (even when it mostly breeds suspicion), oriented to some *hope* (even when it takes the form of despair), animated by some *love* (even though, as Augustine taught us, that default love is love of self and the *libido dominandi*).

This also means that every take that parades itself as "realist" is contestable and that a biblical vision for a flourishing *polis* is not precluded because it is "religious." There is no politics that isn't ultimately religious. And so the opportunity and opening is for the proclamation of the gospel to be offered as a radically different way to imagine politics—a rival version of faith, hope, and love that doesn't paper over reality but *discloses* it. It all depends on who you think narrates the world. What if it's a King who loves us, laid down his life for us, and rose from the dead?

Granted, any "verification" of these competing takes on the world can only be eschatological. That's why central to a Christian political posture is *waiting*. We don't bring about the kingdom; we await the King. This is not the timid waiting of quietism or the resigned waiting of indifference. In *The Justice Calling*, Bethany Hanke Hoang and Kristen Deede Johnson look back to Habakkuk as an exemplar. Lamenting injustice, confronting God, Habakkuk stations himself on a rampart as he awaits God's response to his complaint (Hab. 2:1). "What could it mean for us to 'station' ourselves?" they ask. "What could a rampart represent in our own lives, and what would be the point of getting up on top of it? What is the role of waiting when

everything around us begs for action? Can waiting itself be an act?"[29] Active
waiting is a distinguishing trait of citizens of the heavenly city, resisting both
a quietism that concedes the world to the powers-that-be and an activism that
imagines amelioration apart from grace. If, as Hoang and Johnson suggest, "a
'rampart' can be any place that we go to see reality more clearly,"[30] then I've
been arguing that the *ekklēsia* is our most important rampart. Its formative
disciplines and practices are how God sanctifies our perception[31] so that we
can see reality more clearly—that is, in light of revelation and the hope of
the world. In the *ekklēsia* our loves are recalibrated, indexed to the King, so
that we are then sent into the *permixtum* to bear witness to how the world
could be otherwise.

Our most revolutionary political act is to *hope*. As the novelist Marilynne
Robinson succinctly observes: "Fear is not a Christian habit of mind."[32] To
be a Christian is to be a person who engages in politics but does so *without
fear*. Fear drives us to panic, and no one makes good decisions when they're
panicked. We overestimate some threats and ignore others. We can't see clearly,
and we're prone to being manipulated by those who would foment our panic.
But we ought not to be a panicked people. Our King has told us over and over
again, "Be not afraid." You have already heard good news that brings great joy.
The King is alive and seated on his throne, and he reigns. And not only that:
he is also interceding for us at the right hand of his Father. "Be not afraid."

29. Bethany Hanke Hoang and Kristen Deede Johnson, *The Justice Calling: Where Passion Meets Perseverance* (Grand Rapids: Brazos, 2016), 102.
30. Ibid.
31. See James K. A. Smith, *Imagining the Kingdom: How Worship Works*, Cultural Liturgies 2 (Grand Rapids: Baker Academic, 2013), 151–64.
32. Marilynne Robinson, *The Givenness of Things: Essays* (New York: Farrar, Straus and Giroux, 2015), 125.

Name Index

225

Subject Index

Antichrist, 96, 101, 111–12, 116, 160–61n12, 214n17

Antigone, 101n18

ascension, 65, 77–81, 89, 110, 117, 159

authority, 67, 71–79, 103, 107–8, 120–21, 151, 157
  divine, 71, 102
  political, 70, 72–73, 100–101
  of Scripture, 61
  secular, 159–61

autonomy, 6, 33, 44, 103, 105n25, 150, 195

Babylon, 35, 47, 50, 79, 115n41, 219

baptism, 2, 7–8, 25n20, 53, 115, 166–67, 178, 186–88

benediction, 2, 61, 167

black theology, 18. *See also* race

Book of Common Prayer, 57, 61, 203

calendar, liturgical, 80–81

Canada, 117

Carthage, 195

Chelsea, 193

Christendom, xiii, 17, 39n68, 92, 100–102, 109–10, 115–21, 131, 151–64, 214n17

citizenship, 3, 24, 46, 58, 145–48, 197
  dual, 19, 45–46, 216
  heavenly, xiv, 15, 58, 105, 197, 213
  market, 35

civil religion, xiii, 5, 28, 119

civil rights movement, xiii, 17, 163–64

civil society, 13, 27, 32, 87–89, 91–92, 114, 116, 119, 125–30, 135–40, 145

colonialism, 173–76
  as imaginary, 174

common grace, xi–xii, 35n51, 67, 86, 88, 95n8, 97n13, 122–24, 142

conquest, 97, 171, 173, 176n20

Constantinianism, 114, 115n41, 160, 173n12

Constantinople, 114

Constitution, US, 42n78, 102n19, 161–62n13

constitutionalism, 108, 115, 118

constitutional law, 101, 146

democracy, 14, 17, 23, 35–43, 51–52, 70–72, 92–125, 139, 146n51, 148n58, 151, 157, 194, 210, 215, 219

discernment, 16–17, 58–59, 95–98, 105, 112, 116, 120, 122, 124

divorce, 156

earthly city, xiii–xiv, 6, 12n29, 14–15, 17–18, 19, 27, 35, 37, 43–52, 53, 55, 79, 82, 92, 103, 115n41, 122, 133, 149, 153, 181, 195–97, 200, 209–21

ecclesiology, xii–xiii, 36, 37n56, 86, 116, 119, 124, 164n18, 188–92, 213

enkapsis, 138n25

Enlightenment, the, 93, 171n8

eschatology, 11, 31, 80–81, 135, 148, 176n21, 192n61, 198–99, 206, 219–20

Eucharist, 61, 81, 82, 148, 190

exclusive humanism, 31, 107

faithful presence, 55n5, 125

First Amendment, 102n19, 161n13

231